Ever-Changing Sky

01 02 03 04 05 16 15 14 13 12

Caitlin Press Inc.
8100 Alderwood Road,
Halfmoon Bay, BC V0N 1Y1
www.caitlin-press.com

Text and cover design by Vici Johnstone.
Printed in Canada

Caitlin Press Inc. acknowledges financial support from the Government of Canada through the Canada Book Fund and the Canada Council for the Arts, and from the Province of British Columbia through the British Columbia Arts Council and the Book Publisher's Tax Credit.

Canada Council for the Arts Conseil des Arts du Canada
BRITISH COLUMBIA ARTS COUNCIL
An agency of the Province of British Columbia

Library and Archives Canada Cataloguing in Publication

Lee, Doris (Doris Colleen)
Ever-changing sky : Journey from schoolteacher to Cariboo rancher / Doris Lee.

ISBN 978-1-894759-89-2

1. Lee, Doris (Doris Colleen). 2. Women ranchers—British Columbia—Cariboo Region—Biography. 3. Ranch life—British Columbia—Cariboo Region. 4. Cariboo Region (B.C.)—Biography. I. Title.

Ever-Changing Sky

Journey from Schoolteacher to Cariboo Rancher

Doris C. Lee

Caitlin Press

Dedicated in memory of my husband,
who, with much love, patience and understanding,
gave me the opportunity to enjoy the great outdoors.

Contents

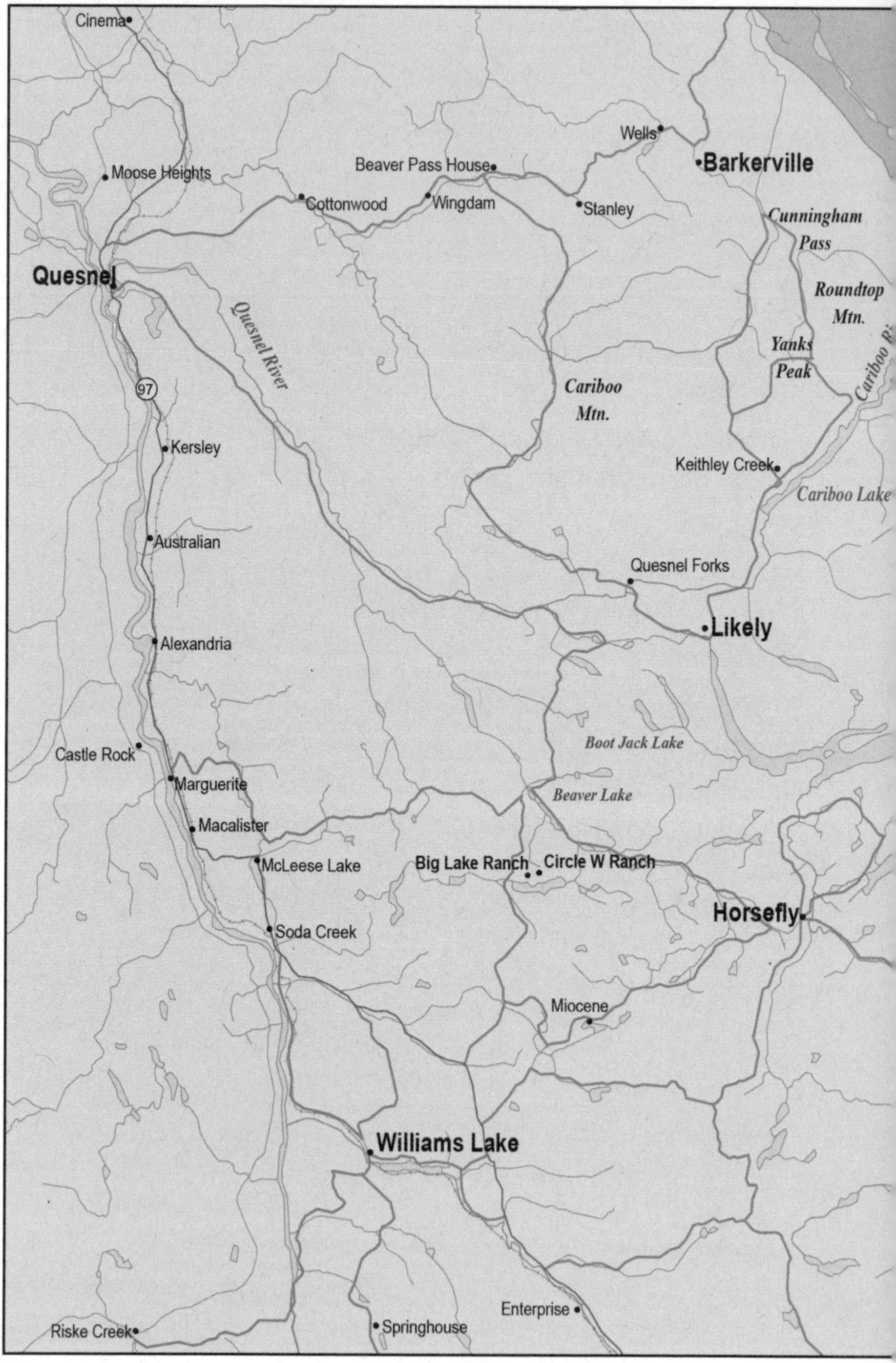
Cinema
Moose Heights
Quesnel
Cottonwood
Wingdam
Beaver Pass House
Wells
Barkerville
Stanley
Cunningham Pass
Roundtop Mtn.
Yanks Peak
Quesnel River
97
Cariboo Mtn.
Kersley
Keithley Creek
Cariboo Lake
Australian
Quesnel Forks
Likely
Alexandria
Boot Jack Lake
Castle Rock
Marguerite
Beaver Lake
Macalister
McLeese Lake
Big Lake Ranch
Circle W Ranch
Horsefly
Soda Creek
Miocene
Williams Lake
Enterprise
Riske Creek
Springhouse

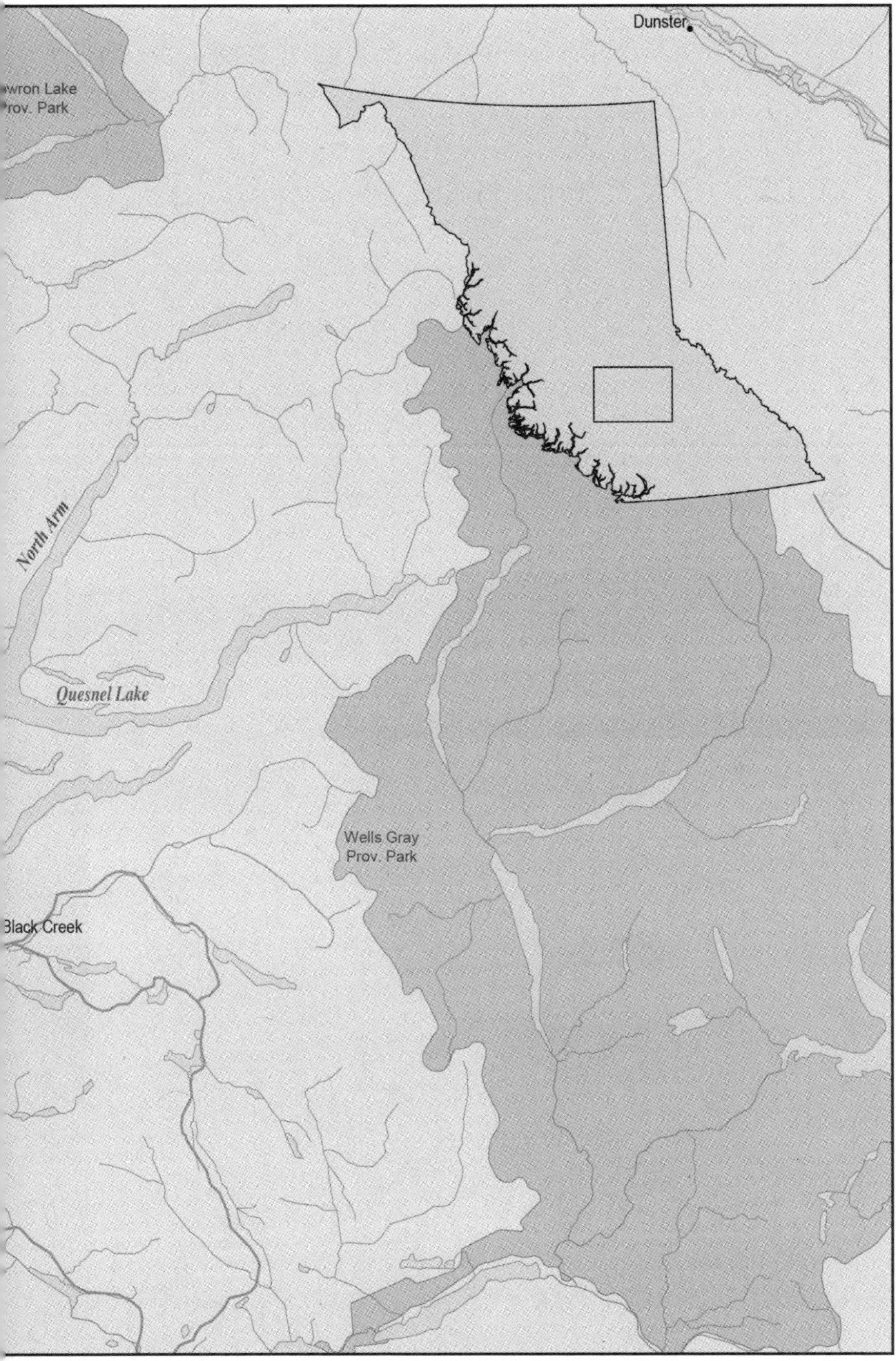

Dunster
wron Lake
rov. Park
North Arm
Quesnel Lake
Wells Gray
Prov. Park
Black Creek

A Dream of Ranching

If someone had told me I would ever be living in the remote wilderness of British Columbia, far from the modern conveniences I was accustomed to, I would have laughed. Me! A schoolteacher, a real greenhorn, who if asked to saddle and bridle a horse would not have known which end to start with.

Fortunately, one does not always know what the future holds. After teaching for only two years in my home state of California, I chose my lifetime partner, John, a rugged, even-tempered, always pleasant man. He was born and raised in McArthur, California, a ranching area eighty miles northeast of Redding. There his family had one of the largest cattle ranches in the fertile Fall River Valley, but when they decided to form a corporation, John set out to establish a ranch of his own.

For about a year we spent considerable time and money searching for a ranch. The ranches we liked we just could not afford, and after a while we began to feel a little insecure and very frustrated.

One evening after a hard day's work, while John was relaxing in his easy chair reading the *National Livestock Weekly* and I was finishing the dinner dishes, "Listen to this!" came from behind the paper. "A cattle ranch near Williams Lake, British Columbia, the Cow Capital of British Columbia."

British Columbia is sure a long way from California, but I knew how much he wanted us to find a ranch and settle down on our own.

As a schoolteacher in Redding, California, ranching was the furthest thing from my mind.

"Let me read the rest of the description they have here," John smiled. "Might even sound interesting to you."

We spent the rest of the evening discussing the pros and cons of moving so far away, should this be the ranch we were looking for. To leave the state where we were born and raised was bad enough, but to another country—that would require careful thought.

About a year earlier, in the summer of 1949, we had taken a two-week car trip through the Pacific Northwest and into BC as far north as Burns Lake, on our delayed honeymoon. We took the Cariboo Highway, which bypassed the small village of Williams Lake, then turned at 150 Mile House, went north to 158 Mile House (known as the Mountain House) and returned to the Deep Creek Reserve, fifteen miles north of Williams Lake. We were quite surprised by the surrounding country but never thought it would someday be our home.

Sleep did not come easily for me that night. I tossed and turned. John, who never put the cart before the horse, showed no apprehension. I always worried about things, although the imagined almost never happened anyway. I thought about my only brother, Harlan, a US marine who would soon be leaving for Korea; and my parents, so worried as they had already lost one son by drowning. What if they needed me and I was so far away? I thought about my life-long friends, and my students, and my teaching career, which had been my ambition since childhood.

Finally, mentally exhausted, I drifted into a deep sleep.

Early the next morning I awoke to the aroma of hot coffee and John shaking me. "Ready to go to British Columbia and have a look at that ranch?"

Groggily I raised my head. "It seems like I only just fell asleep."

"Have you been worrying again?" he said. "Let's not get upset, maybe we won't even like it. You know these real estate listings, they make every place sound great. We must look at every ranch that we can. I'd sure like to get something soon."

It was early August 1950. My school trustees were holding my teaching contract open, but I would have to make up my mind very shortly. If we wanted to visit this ranch, we would have to leave immediately.

We decided we would head north the following morning. I had one day to get packed and ready to go, with almost no time to think or plan.

Three days later we reached 150 Mile House, where we stopped at Zirnhelt's General Store to ask directions. A hatless man with slightly greying hair stepped from the store and John asked him the way to Big Lake.

"Keep on this main road until you come to the Mountain House," the man said, "then take the Likely road to the right. You'll know when you get to Big Lake. The road goes right along the west end."

The two men talked for a while about the pleasant weather, and a grin broke over the stranger's stubbled face. "You folks sound like you might be from the States somewhere, eh?"

"Yes, sir," replied John, as the man strode to the front of our car and looked at the licence plate.

"California," he said. "That's a long ways from here. I don't want to be nosy, but what in the hell are you doing up here?"

"We are going to look at a ranch listed for sale at Big Lake," said John.

"I was there once. Pretty country out that way," the man replied. "Better not hold you folks up any longer. Might see you again someday," and he crawled into his mud-splattered pickup truck.

As we drove away from 150 Mile House and passed the Mountain House Ranch at 158 Mile, the corked and narrow dirt road seemed endless. We were eager to reach our destination and to see the ranch after travelling so many miles. Would the ranch be all that the listing led us to expect? We wound our way along the snake-like road with dense forest hovering over on each side, until at last we reached the top of a ridge. There below us, nestled between rolling hills, lay Big Lake, nearly five miles long, with open fertile fields bordering its north shore. A beautiful setting indeed.

Late in the afternoon we arrived at the gate of the Weber Ranch. A yellow collie (whose name, we later found out, was Cap) announced our arrival as Al Weber emerged from the well-built board-and-batten ranch house just a hundred feet from the shore of Big Lake. He was a jovial, rather heavy-set man, and he promptly extended a warm, friendly hand. "Hello, you must be the Lees. The moccasin telegraph told us you might be arriving today."

The Weber house, soon to be ours, was board and batten with a cedar shingle roof. To the left was the log root cellar, which had a sod roof.

John introduced us.

"What kind of trip did you have?" Al inquired. Without waiting for an answer, he continued, "How many days did it take you to come up?"

"It was a great trip and took us three days, as we didn't want to push too hard," said John. "Nice to see all the country between here and California."

"Come in and meet Lil, she's been busy canning blueberries," said Al. He opened the door to the neat, homey ranch house and called to his wife.

Jimmy Weber with the family's pet dog, a yellow collie named Cap.

A dark-haired, large-boned, attractive woman came into the room. After the introductions, she crammed more wood into the hot cookstove. "How about a cup of tea?" she said as she worked. "We've been expecting you since noon. The real estate agent phoned Al's brother in Bend, Oregon, and he called our neighbours at the end of the road telling us you were on the way."

I now knew what was meant by the "moccasin telegraph."

The kettle soon boiled and we gathered around the table to enjoy piping hot cups of tea spiked with thick, rich cream, and a heaping plate of Lil's homemade cookies.

"Guess you would like to get out and look around a little," Al said, pushing back his chair. "You didn't drive all this way just to set here and shoot the breeze. We haven't much time left in this day."

John laughed. "Yes, Doris is anxious to see if she is going to like it here. I think I might have quite a time persuading her to move so far away from home."

Lil decided to stay home and put up a few more quarts of blueberries. "Be sure to be back by six," she called after us. "Dinner will be ready then."

With the little daylight we had left, we could not look over the whole ranch, for that would take several days. So we observed the surrounding buildings, then walked down to the lakeshore and out onto the boat dock. Big Lake shimmered as the sun went its way west, truly a magnificent lake.

We headed back for dinner just before six o'clock. From the distance, breaking the tranquil silence, approached an old black "cut down" Model T Ford, affectionately known, as we soon learned, as "Farting Fannie." The car was used for general ranch duties and other purposes, but most important were the functions it participated in after working hours. It was just a few miles around the end of Big Lake to the Silver Horn Lodge, a guest ranch owned by Ken and Irene McKenzie and their small son, Neil. They catered mostly to people who were raised in cities ("dudes") who liked to vacation in the wide-open spaces. Many dudes were attractive young women, seeking

Our new home was just a hundred feet from the shore of Big Lake, which stretched on for nearly five miles.

the romance and excitement of country living for a summer holiday far from the hustle and bustle of city life.

"Here comes Farting Fannie," said Al. "Do hope the boys have finished haying the big field."

The dust belched out as Fannie came to a halt. Out jumped Jim and Gene Weber, both handsome, husky young men. Jim, with a big, broad smile on his tanned face, reached out and hurriedly shook hands. "You must be the Lees. I'm very glad to meet you." Gene, tall and slender, also offered a warm Cariboo handshake as Roy Mars, a family friend, slid to the ground from Farting Fannie's flat deck. A pleasant but shy young man, Roy worked as a high rigger on Vancouver Island and had come to help his friends with the summer's ranch work.

Jim was tall and broad-shouldered, extremely good-looking with a tremendous personality. He was a real comedian, also the more enthusiastic of the two young Webers about ranching. Horses, white-face Hereford cows and farming held Jim's interest.

Gene was quiet and reserved, not as interested in the livestock but somewhat of a genius when it came to mechanics. He could fix anything, often improvising when he lacked the right parts or tools. He was an avid gardener, did the milking of the family dairy cows and kept the outbuildings neat and tidy, often helping with the cattle when required. It was a good working arrangement.

Dinner that night was very enjoyable as we related the events of the day. We felt as though we had known these people for years. Like most people in the Cariboo they were extremely friendly and helpful. I will never forget the dinner Lil had prepared on her old-fashioned wood stove. No aroma can compare to homemade bread, just out of the oven, spread lavishly with fresh hand-churned butter. It also was our first experience to taste moose meat so expertly prepared, accompanied by flavourful vegetables from the weed-free garden just outside the living room window. On the kitchen counter sat two golden brown, luscious-looking blueberry pies waiting to finish a meal fit for a king. It all came from the ranch, not from the supermarkets that I was used to.

After we had eaten gluttonously of the fine food and coffee, Gene pushed his chair back from the table. "Let's all go into the living room. These chairs are getting as hard as the seat on that old hay rake."

The living room overlooked the placid waters of Big Lake, a most relaxing and comfortable atmosphere. The sun cast its last rays as it disappeared beyond the horizon, a brilliant crimson reflecting from the mirror-like lake. The trees of the dense, wild forest along the lake stood like sentinels awaiting the new day.

Jim, Gene and Roy brought out their musical instruments and the rest of the evening was filled with song and laughter. I could see why Farting Fannie made so many trips to the Silver Horn Lodge Guest Ranch. These young men had a flair for entertaining and could easily turn the heads of any maiden with their handsome faces. They all could sing and yodel, and Jim was an excellent mimic.

Cowboys are a breed of their own. No one holds as much fascination for city dwellers as the cowboy with his Stetson hat, tall boots and jingling spurs. These are men of endurance, skill, courage and integrity, with no place for the weak or the timid. They are the epitome of the working man of the West, leading an adventurous and seemingly romantic life.

It was getting very late when John looked at his watch and said that we had better get back to the hotel at 150 Mile House and get a good night's sleep before looking over the ranch the next day.

"No need to drive all the way back," Al said. "We have lots of room here. It's twenty-five Cariboo miles back to 150 Mile House." Nothing else would do. We just had to spend the night with our new-found friends.

Next morning I awoke to the resounding crow of a rooster, broadcast from the neat log chicken house just across the driveway from the ranch house. John's side of the bed was vacant; he must have slipped out early to join the Webers for breakfast. The rooster was still crowing as I hurriedly dressed, wondering why such a nice building was used for a chicken house. I had never seen a log building until now, and did not know that they were common in Canada. I was really impressed with those homey buildings with their roofs made of hand-hewn shakes, or covered with sod.

As I hurried toward the bathroom to wash, I was a little embarrassed. Breakfast must be long over and I, a guest, was late. But luck was with me—when I opened the kitchen door everyone was sitting there having coffee while Lil was preparing the morning meal.

"How did you sleep?" she asked, pouring me a cup of coffee from the big enamel pot on the cookstove.

"I must have slept like a log. I didn't even hear John get up," I replied rather sheepishly.

"If you hurry with that cup of coffee," Gene said in his quiet manner, "I will take you with me while I do the barn chores. By that time Mom should have breakfast ready."

We emerged into a bright, sunny morning with not a cloud in the sky. Undisturbed reflections of the rolling timbered hills gave Big Lake the appearance of flat, smooth, dark glass. The air seemed so fresh and clean; I was in another world, far from my polluted, over-populated California home.

The log outbuilding called the "cow barn" was about twenty-five feet from the lakeshore, convenient for the cows to go for a drink. The log "horse barn" was about fifty yards from the lake, and both barns were small but meticulously clean.

I waited outside while Gene milked the two Jersey cows, after he told me that sometimes strangers upset the cows and caused them not to give down their milk. I had no idea what he meant, but in the years to come I was to learn that and many other things about cows. After the barn door closed, the silence was broken only by the sound of fresh milk squirting on the sides of the shiny galvanized bucket.

The horse barn is on the left, and just past the garden behind the fence you can see the top of the cow barn.

I walked over to the horse barn, which had a two-part door. In warm weather the top half was left open for ventilation, and in winter both the top and bottom doors were closed. Inside the log barn were Chub and Dan, a team of work-horses. They briefly lifted their heads from the manger filled with hay as they ate, fuelling up for the day's work in the field.

When Gene had completed his chores we returned to the ranch house to find everyone seated at the table. After a hearty breakfast of flapjacks and bacon and eggs, chased down by numerous cups of coffee, we decided how we would spend the next few days. John wanted to see as much of the ranch as possible, look at the summer range and take a closer look at the equipment, for the only power machinery was a Model N Ford tractor, plus a plow and a disc, which operated from the power takeoff. All the other equipment—plows, hay rakes, mowers, overshot stackers—was drawn by horses. The obsolete grain binder, originally horse-drawn, had recently been converted by installing a snub tongue so that it could be pulled by the small Ford tractor. The machinery held no interest for me.

Al discussed the tasks for the day with Gene, Jim and Roy. Haying was such an important part of ranching, and there was no time to waste. They gathered their belongings and got things underway.

"First place I'll take you folks this morning is to the summer range," said Al, "and then we'll swing by and see Annie's. Lil, don't worry about lunch as we don't know when we'll be back. See ya later."

I had heard the name "Annie's" many times since I had arrived at Big Lake and my curiosity could no longer be contained. "What is Annie's?"

Al looked at John and winked. "Doris, it's a real swanky place," he chuckled. "Just wait until we get there."

We climbed into the Chevy pickup and drove up the narrow dirt road. Now and then, views of Big Lake flashed through the trees to the left of us as Al pointed out locations of interest. On a high rolling hill just before we reached the main road was the grave of William Parker, a previous owner of the ranch at Big Lake and a freighter in the early gold rush days. What a nice place to be buried, I thought, overlooking his kingdom. On the main road where we had turned to go down to the Weber ranch, I recognized the two-storey house with a large veranda. Later, underneath the white siding, we would find the well-constructed log stopping house of yesteryear.

"This was a popular stopping place in the area during the gold rush, known as Big Lake Ranch," Al continued as he brought the pickup to an abrupt halt. "Just have to stop here. I want you to meet the best neighbours and friends in the Cariboo."

Harold and Paddy Cripps' house "Big Lake Ranch" was a popular stopping house during the gold rush.

As we approached the back door, a voice from within called, "Come in, come in!" Al pushed the door open. "Paddy and Harold Cripps," he said, "I want you to meet Doris and John Lee. They might be your new neighbours soon."

"Let me fix you folks some coffee," said Paddy, a tall woman dressed in jeans. "Guess you are in a hurry—I suppose you are on your way to see the range and Annie's." There was that name again. Annie's. I had a funny feeling there was something strange about the place.

Harold, a big man, reached for a can sitting on the sideboard and began to roll a cigarette. All the cigarettes I had seen before were factory-made, in neat packages. I had never seen anyone roll a cigarette from a can, except in cowboy movies. I tried not to stare but was fascinated as the tobacco wiggled and twisted in the small, thin paper he manoeuvred in his large hands, seemingly with no problem. After a quick lap of the tongue, he was lighting his skinny cigarette. He placed the tobacco can back on the sideboard and, in a booming voice, asked me, "How do you like the country around here?"

"Well, I am not sure yet," I said. "It is very pretty here, and Big Lake is one of the most beautiful bodies of water I have ever seen." I was glad our conversation was interrupted when Paddy set down coffee mugs on the large, round oak table and filled each with a steaming stream of coffee.

"You are from California, aren't you?" she asked.

I told her that we were from Redding, in northern California, where our families lived. "Both of us still have our mother and father, and John has eight brothers and sisters. I have only one brother, a marine awaiting his call to Korea."

John said that he wasn't sure I would like to live and work on a ranch. "It is so far from her friends and family," he said. "Doris is a schoolteacher with no ranching experience. For me, ranching is all I know. I was born and raised on the same ranch and have lived there my entire life."

Harold glanced at me. "Yes, it must be quite a decision to make," he said. "You Americans might live faster, but I will bet you one thing for sure, we'll live longer."

The conversation then turned to local happenings, and for this I was glad. I felt like I was on the hot seat, for I had my doubts. Would I be happy?

"Thanks for the coffee," said John as he put on his cowboy hat. "It has been a pleasure meeting you folks, and perhaps we'll see you again before we leave."

Like a thundering herd, Clint and Wade Cripps came bursting through the door, two cute but mischievous little fellows. Clint was nearly two years old, Wade was approaching four and behind them came Julie, a tall, slender girl of seven. "We've been upstairs playing with the new kittens," said Julie as she leaned shyly against her mother's leg.

"Children," said Paddy, "this is the Lees, they might be our new neighbours. Maybe they will need a kitten." We completed our good-byes and climbed into the pickup once again. Time was flying fast, and one thing for sure—I wanted to see Annie's.

Al drove across the main road and headed west. All was quiet except for the steady hum of the motor. "John, didn't you think those Cripps boys adorable?" I said. Before John could reply, Al chuckled. "Just wait!" he said. "Just wait until you get to know them."

We enjoyed the scenery as we bounced up one road and down another, trying to see as much of the country as we could. Many of the so-called roads were hardly more than cow trails, the tall, lush grasses practically untouched. Abundant feed and water were everywhere, so different from the drier, more scanty California rangeland we knew.

As we rounded a bend in the narrow road, two girls on horseback came riding toward us. "There's Cherie Harris, Paddy's daughter by a previous marriage," said Al. "Cherie is quite a girl! Paddy also has a son, Jimmy, from that marriage." He stopped beside them. "Hello, what are you two doing out riding so early?"

"Can't find those two miserable milk cows," Cherie replied, most indignantly.

"You better meet our new neighbours, or perhaps I should say they might be, if John can convince his wife the Cariboo is the only place to live!"

Cherie Harris was a slender, dark-haired, attractive girl of sixteen, a real tomboy. Later we learned that she had a great sense of humour and loved to play practical jokes on anyone she could. She was well liked by all who knew her. The girl accompanying her was Lena Sellars, a shy, attractive girl from the Deep Creek Indian Reserve, who had been hired by Paddy to help her with the children and housework during the busy haying season.

Al slipped the pickup into gear and we slowly began to move ahead. "Hope you find those cows, Cherie!" Al called. "We will keep our eyes open for them."

As the girls disappeared from sight, Al continued. "Cherie will find those cows. She really knows livestock and is a very capable hand." He pointed to a log house at our left, surrounded by other outbuildings. A collection of poultry and other farm animals scattered as we approached.

"This is where Einar and Edna Jacobson and their three children live—Marie, John and Carol," said Al. "They are old-time ranching people, and our cattle ranges are separated mostly by natural barriers, but as you well know, John, sometimes cattle get mixed."

As we drove on, we could see in the distance a two-storey log house with a long, good-sized hay barn and numerous smaller outbuildings. "This is known as the Keith Place," Al said. "Ian and Gladys Keith and their daughter, Ardell, and two sons, Don and Graham, lived here at one time but went on to greener pastures. No one has lived here for some time now."

Yes, there was another gate—the eleventh since we had left the home ranch, and John, sitting on the passenger side, had the pleasure of opening and shutting them all. Most of them were made from wooden poles and slung open fairly easily, not like barbed-wire gates, which twisted and tangled when they were opened.

The road was almost non-existent from here on. Driving through the gate John had opened, Al turned to me and said, "Doris, this is Annie's."

Annie's. I don't know what I expected, but all I could see was the same type of country we had just come through—small open glades with stands of cottonwood, willow, forests of evergreens and more grass.

"I think Doris is a little disappointed," Al said to John, "but the best part is yet to come." In a picturesque spot, nestled between tall cottonwood and spruce trees overlooking a good-sized hayfield, was Annie's house. It was a small log building with a shake roof, and like others we had seen, it was not occupied. A fleeting question passed through my mind: Why are all these places vacant? Then more questions. Don't women like to live in this country? Do they find life is too hard for them? Do they find it too lonely, so far away from their home and family and friends?

Al shut the engine off and pointed to a creek at the edge of the hayfield. "This small creek comes from nearby Camille Lake and joins the creek running from Marguerite Lake through the south side of Annie's property, continuing on to Big Lake. Nice to have a creek running through your own property with excellent trout fishing earlier in the season!" He explained that there was a chain of lakes. The water of Big Lake flowed down over the hill as Big Lake Creek, emptying into the creek coming from Lake George in the peaceful Beaver Valley.

"I am curious," I said excitedly. "Where is Annie?"

"Well, it's rather a sad story," Al replied. "Annie DeBryant and her daughter, whose name was also Annie, lived here for some time. Mr. DeBryant died from an incurable disease, and these two women worked from daylight to dark carving a ranch out of the wilderness.

Then at last they decided to sell. We had always been interested in this property, although it had some drawbacks, but when gathering the cattle from the range in the fall it was a real asset. It produces quite a bit of hay—something one always needs in the Cariboo. At long last we had the opportunity to purchase it."

With a gentleman's gesture he opened the door to the cabin and said to this city slicker, "Doris, you better come in and see this swanky place. We batch here when we are haying and when we are gathering our cattle in the fall. It is quite comfortable after a hot day in the hayfield or long day's ride."

I could not imagine myself staying in this cabin. There were basic utensils plus an old wood cookstove, a generous stack of neatly piled firewood, a few supplies in case one had to stay overnight unexpectedly, a table, a couple of benches, a place to lay out your bed roll and a partition separating the living area from the bedroom. I still could not imagine myself staying here.

"Look here, Doris, you will have a cellar to put your expensive wine in!" said Al jovially, as he pulled up a trap door in the middle of the rough board floor.

The cabin was certainly neat, but it did not meet my standards. I was brought up by a mother who was exceptionally clean and tidy—a mouse in her home was a near-disaster. Here I could see evidence of many mice, and rats, and that was enough for me!

The rest of the day, punctuated with much teasing by both Al and John, was spent looking over the range, in which I did not see the values that John did. One could say I just went along for the ride, for I knew nothing about the cow business. I did see the awe-inspiring beauty of the land, the timbered rolling hills, the vast natural Marguerite and Tyee lakes, and the bubbling creeks rushing along on their journey to somewhere. The air smelled clean.

John saw acres and acres of great grass everywhere, money in the pocket of the cowman! We saw stirrup-high peavine vetch, with its climbing tendrils and purple flowers, growing in abundance along with white clover and other nutritious native grasses. John saw the high-quality white-face Hereford cows, so heavy with flesh, contentedly lying in the open cottonwood glades. Water was always close by. When it came to water and summer feed, the Cariboo was a cattleman's paradise.

To drive to the summer range we had to double back to the Keith Place, turning left and crossing a glistening, gurgling creek on a small, low bridge made of split jack pine logs. "This is the creek coming from Marguerite Lake that runs down through Annie's," Al told us. "The creek is pretty low at this time of year, but see those deep holes down below the bridge? They are always good for a few fat trout."

The pickup crawled up a small incline to yet another gate leading to the summer range. It was slow going. What road existed was in poor condition, and the sun beat down through a cloudless sky, making it very warm in the pickup. This was a different type of heat than what I was accustomed to in California. Here in the Cariboo, the evenings and nights were cool, and getting a good night's sleep was no problem. In California, in summer, the mercury often stayed between 100 and 125°F right through the night. An air conditioner was a must.

As we travelled along, Al told us more about this vast area, where a person could go for days and not see anyone else. "You are really back in the bush here," he said. It was the first time I had heard the term "bush," one of many new words we had learned since our arrival.

Just outside the gate, on Crown land on both sides of the road, were many lodgepole pine trees. Under normal conditions they are tall, slender trees holding their girth nearly all the way to the top, with thin limbs on the top third of the tree. This straight-grained, easy-to-split tree was highly valued, abundant and easily accessible. It was used mostly for railroad ties and for fencing gates, firewood and various other purposes on ranches.

We passed from the thick forest into a large, open glade, to our left a trampled salt ground in need of replenishing, and to our right the lower portion of Marguerite Lake, much smaller than Big Lake but nevertheless beautiful. The surface of the water rippled in the slight breeze.

Al stopped the pickup. "Be just a minute. I'll throw out a couple blocks of salt here." As he stepped out, a doe mule deer appeared from nowhere, bounding high and gracefully to the edge of a cottonwood stand, wide-eyed, then pausing in curiosity. Such a sleek animal! She vanished as quickly as she had appeared.

We left the salt ground and followed the road over the top of a small timbered hill, a rocky point jutting out into Marguerite Lake. Here we could see the entire lake, as it reflected the rays of the late summer sun. Near the far end of this point was a huge, well-weathered old Douglas fir, overlooking all that surrounded it. This aged fir had seen the coming and going of many seasons. It had seen the beautiful, peaceful lake hidden by a shield of ice and turned wicked by wind and storm. This fir had long since reached maturity, indicated by the partly dead top that supported a large nest of a family of American bald eagles, which gave the area its name, Eagle Point.

I had never been this close to such a majestic bird or to its habitat. The adults make their nest of branches, lined with grass and leaves, and add new sticks and lining each spring. The nest can reach eight feet wide and thirteen feet deep. As we invaded their wilderness sanctuary, a harsh screaming note pierced the stillness, and both male and female swooped and soared closer and closer, warning us away. We went on our way, following the trail-like road along Marguerite Lake. Everywhere was grass, many types of wildflowers and shrubs of all descriptions—almost like an enormous park.

As we rounded a bend in the road, there before us stood an old cabin, quite small, in such a peaceful setting. A greying log barn with a shake roof sat amid the tall Timothy and redtop grass, near a meandering creek that Al told us originated at Tyee Lake and made its way to Marguerite Lake, hidden just behind the willows below the barn.

The log cabin had a sod roof with vegetation growing on top, like others we had seen since arriving in BC. I asked Al about the sod roof, and he said that sod was great insulation. "The heat cannot escape through the ceiling," he said, "and believe it or not, a sod roof will last for many, many years. This is one of the warmest cabins in the country. A little stove in there with a few sticks of wood will warm the place up in nothing flat. Today it would be nice and cool in there." The cabin belonged to the Cripps family and was known as Cripps Cabin. "They use it like we do Annie's place, during haying season, hunting or fishing, and we all stay here when we are gathering the last few cattle in the late fall because it is pretty central. The 'cow camp' cabins are never locked, in case someone gets caught out here in bad weather. There is always firewood and a few basics stashed away. Sort of an unwritten agreement between us—just leave it as you found it and replace the wood you have used. Pretty miserable to come in half froze with no wood split to start a fire."

The expression on Al's face began to change, and turning to me he said, "Doris, you know when that wind is blowing from the north and the thermometer is hovering below the freezing mark, this cabin looks like a castle."

John joined Al in the laughter. "I know all about cow camps," he said, "but Doris here, she has led an entirely different life. Better not tell her any more or I will never convince her to move to this country."

The water in the willow-lined creek was shallow, and as the pickup eased across it, we could see fish darting to their hiding places. On the other side of the creek on an open nearby hillside lay numerous cows and calves, some grazing, others contentedly chewing their cuds, all showing the positive effects of the feed and water this country had to offer.

A few more miles up the road, as we came to a large, open area, Al announced, "Here is Prairie Chicken. I will take you up on that high knoll, where you can get a good view of Cripps meadow."

This large area was dotted sparsely with cottonwood trees, so we could drive almost anywhere we wanted to go; wheeling out across the open ground to the top of the bare point. Below us lay a natural hay meadow. It was all very picturesque with the tall meadow grass waving in the summer breeze and a thick fir and spruce forest growing to the edge of the meadow on the far side.

"Notice the creek running down through the meadow?" Al pointed. "That creek is coming from Tyee Lake, the same creek we just crossed at Cripps cabin. The meadow is fenced on the north and east sides and the remaining two sides have natural barriers. We always have to watch this meadow so cattle don't get inside. There is a bad bog hole, a natural death trap for cattle. Sometimes Old Mother Nature can be pretty cruel. The creek washing back under the sod weakens the banks and when the cows walk out on the overhang, the sod breaks off and the cattle drop into a quagmire, unable to get solid footing, and there they stay. You are never lucky enough to find them before they die. Luckily the cattle don't bother this meadow too much. They prefer other, more nutritious grasses than meadow grass." As we continued on our way, we could see many of the cows, all in excellent condition.

Not far from where we had dropped the salt, we came to a small body of water called Jefferson Lake, named after an old-time settler.

At one point this cabin on the Cripps' property had a sod roof, which was excellent insulation and would have kept the cabin warm and dry.

The lake was situated in a small valley, between two rolling hills that were heavily timbered with fir, much of it very large. Far out into the lake were yellowish-green, cup-like pond lilies, floating on the water with green fleshy leaves that grew as large as twelve inches in diameter.

"Look," said Al. "Across the other side of the lake toward the far end. There's a big bull moose! This is their natural habitat. The moose relish water lilies and the roots of aquatic plants, and they swim out to deep water when it's hot like this. Helps keep the flies away, too."

Neither of us had ever seen a moose. I looked everywhere in excitement, trying to spot the animal. It took several seconds to make out the huge, ungainly-looking moose with large humped shoulders. Its massive head, with a pendulous muzzle, was surmounted with large

The old barn on the Cripps' property.

antlers, still in the velvet. Despite its size, the moose blended into its surroundings so well that it was difficult to see. It remained motionless as we went on toward Tyee Lake.

It was getting late and we would have to hurry to get back in time for dinner, but Al wanted us to see Tyee Lake where it bordered on his range. "It's very beautiful there," he said. Now the road truly became only a cow trail; we crossed the small creek coming out of Tyee Lake and soon came to a good-sized open field. This land had been owned by Ernie Lang and had once been cultivated and farmed, but now was reverting to nature. All that remained was a couple of log buildings whose hand-hewn shake roofs were deteriorating with age.

How hard the early settlers must have worked before our time! Would John and I have to work like that, only to have our efforts end in abandonment? Why had these places been deserted?

The clear, sky-blue waters of Tyee Lake were even more beautiful in colour than Big Lake. Here lay an immense natural body of water largely untouched by mankind—no summer homes, no campgrounds, no boats. Only the haunting call of a loon pierced the silence. The air smelled clean, nature at its very best. "If this was California," John remarked, "there would be hundreds of boats, camps and cabins. If you wanted to fish, you would have to bring along your own rock to stand on. Some day the property around this lake will be taken up with summer homes and command a big price, seen it happen in California."

"Wish we could take longer here but Lil will be waiting dinner," Al said. "You know how these womenfolk are, John. Can't keep them waiting, they might throw it out." Soon we were on our way back to the home ranch.

Jouncing all day over rough roads had left me totally exhausted. Shortly after dinner, when darkness fell, I excused myself and crawled into the cool, crisp white sheets and awaited sleep. I could hear Al and John in the next room talking about fence lines, how much hay the ranch put up and how to make the ranch more productive.

The time was fast approaching when I must let John know whether I wanted to make this ranch my home, but my thoughts were so mixed up. The location of the ranch was ideal, and nowhere could there be a lake as beautiful as Big Lake, but there was no electric power. My father had worked at a generating plant for many years, providing us with all the power we needed—for free. No telephone! What if someone was hurt or seriously ill? There was the big wood stove and what seemed an endless job sticking fuel in that wood eater all day. And no refrigeration during the warm summer months? I thought about my California home and the double-oven electric range, refrigerator, upright deep-freeze and even the electric dishwasher. The cons far outweighed the pros. How could I give up all those conveniences?

John was up and gone when I awoke with bright sunlight streaming in the window and heavenly aromas coming from the kitchen. I got dressed and went to breakfast—golden brown hotcakes with homemade syrup and jelly made from wild berries that were yours just for the picking, and fresh eggs from the farm flock.

Today we would be leaving, and John would have to indicate his intentions. What was I going to say? I liked it here, but to live here was another thing. While I was helping Lil with the dishes, John came to the door and asked me to go outside with him. I could not stall any longer. I dried my hands on the towel hanging near the wood stove as my eyes filled with tears. I stepped outside, swallowing hard so John would not see that I was about to cry. Men don't like crying women, and John was no exception.

"Let's go down to the lake," John said. "Sure is a nice day."

Big Lake was like glass with only the odd wisp of wind catching the water. "Doris, do you like it here?" John asked. "How would you like this ranch to be our home?" Before I could answer, he went on. "I like this ranch better than any place we have looked at. It has unlimited potential and is priced more in line with what we can afford."

Finally he paused.

"I like the ranch all right," I said, "but I don't know what I'll do without power. We would have to sell all our electrical appliances and they are only a year old."

John suggested that we could buy a lighting plant and bring it with us. "You know they make lighting systems that can run everything we own, including our electric welder."

Tears welled up in my eyes again. "I think I can adjust, but let's not make a deal today. Can't we stall them for a while? You know it is a real big decision to make."

John smiled and put his arm around my waist. "I knew that I could count on you," he said.

When we got back to the house, Al had just returned from the shop. "Next time I go to town I will have to buy a new battery for the tractor. Doesn't seem to take a charge anymore. Can't complain, I guess, been a good battery—I ordered it from Simpson's catalog better than two years ago. Let's go in and see if the coffee pot is on."

After we had consumed several cups of Lil's delicious coffee, John set his cup down and turned in his chair. "Soon as Doris is ready we are going to head back to California," he said. "She is anxious to get home, as she must let her school trustees know her plans. They are holding her teaching contract open hoping she will return. The parents and the children really like her." He said that we wanted to drive in and take a look at Williams Lake, perhaps stay overnight and get an early start the next morning. "I am really interested in the ranch," he said, "and if we decide to buy it, I will be back in about two weeks to spend more time looking it over. If you have an extra horse I can use, I will bring along my saddle. I can see more on horseback and was never much for walking when I could ride." John looked across the table at me with a smile coming over his face. "It will take me at least two weeks to sell Doris on the idea of moving north."

Before long we were extending our thanks to our new-found friends and heading south in the Chrysler. "So long for now," called John. "I hope to be seeing you again soon." The road back to the 150

Mile House did not seem half as long as the trip in.

John was enthusiastic as he spoke of the many possibilities and challenges we would have if we purchased the ranch. I knew he could meet these challenges. Hard work was what it would take to make it a success, and he was a very hard worker.

"Look at the gas gauge; must be running on the fumes," said John as he drove up in front of the 153 Mile House store. Like the other buildings of the 153 Mile Ranch, it was built of logs. "Good thing I noticed, or we would soon be walking. Not many gas pumps in this part of the country."

A middle-aged, dark-haired woman of Italian descent came out of the general store. "Good morning," she said pleasantly, working the handle of the gas pump to and fro. "Guess you need some gas, eh?"

We all introduced ourselves and then discussed the weather, which was always a topic for conversation in the Cariboo, and the current problems of the world.

I had never seen a store like that. It had everything somewhere. One could get a harness for a horse or some sewing notions, outfit the family from head to toe, and find every kind of food, including fresh meat and vegetables. The store did a large business, serving almost everyone in the Likely, Big Lake and Horsefly areas. Lil Crosina, a single woman, owned and very capably operated this store, which was left to her by her father, Louis Crosina. When traffic in the store became hectic, Lil could always call on Peggy, Joe or Bryceson Patenaude to give her a hand. A customer could phone or send in an order and it would be loaded on the freight and mail truck when it made its weekly run, or Lil would send it along with the first neighbour to come along. Everyone here was always eager to help everyone else. Living so remotely, people needed each other and thought about the well-being of their neighbours.

The late summer sun beat down on us as we left the 153 Mile general store and wound our way west along the gravelled road, until the six-mile-long Williams Lake lay before our eyes.

Looking down Oliver Street in the '50s. Mackenzie's General Store is on the left and across the street is the Famous Restaurant where we had our first cup of coffee in WIlliams Lake. Photo: Museum of the Cariboo Chilcotin.

To the left lay the hewn logs of the Sugarcane Indian Reserve, established in 1884 and named for a common reed, resembling sugar cane, that grows in the area. About two hundred people lived on the reserve, under the tall white spire of the local Catholic church.

On the west end of the lake was the small village of Williams Lake. Both the lake and the village were named after Chief Willyum of the Sugarcane Reserve, whose grave now lies on the outskirts of town. The village boasted a population of about five hundred and a "Wild West" appearance, with its unpaved streets and board sidewalks. Cattle raising was the prime industry, and the cowboy, with his wide-brimmed hat and his dusty leather cowboy boots, was still king.

The sleepy village of Williams Lake, peaceful and quiet in the heart of the Cariboo, lay basking in the afternoon sun. There were no logging trucks, no sawmills, no tourists, just a small village of people descended from Native Indians, fur traders, gold seekers and, more recently, farmers and ranchers. The dwellings and business establishments were of wood-frame construction and supplied with power from a diesel lighting system in the village.

The home of the *Tribune* in 1950. Photo: Museum of the Cariboo Chilcotin.

The village was nearly deserted when we arrived. All the ranching people were haying, except for the odd rancher who had come to the village for supplies or a part for his haying equipment. Weather was a controlling factor—when it was time to hay, these people made hay.

Williams Lake was quiet and quaint, but I must say I was not impressed. As if he had sensed my thoughts, John said, "Seems like there is a place to buy everything a person might want. There's the Famous Restaurant. Let's go have a cup of coffee."

Yes, I guess he was right. There was Lockwood's Law Office, Alf Eagle's Barber Shop, Smedley's Hardware Store, the *Tribune* newspaper, one doctor—Dr. Avery, a single-storey wooden hospital (where the Town Hall is now located), an Overwaitea grocery store and Western, Rife and Pigeon, a smaller grocery store. And Cariboo Home Furnishings, which we later learned was owned by Bill Sharpe, an ex-police officer and avid boxer, and his lovely wife, Marie, who was a schoolteacher, and Mackenzie's, a general store, owned

The Wiliams Lake Pharmacy on Oliver Street. Photo: Museum of the Cariboo Chilcotin.

by Roderick Mackenzie and later turned over to his daughter and son-in-law, Ann and Doug Stevenson. Doug was a mining engineer who had worked in the mines of Ontario and Quebec. He was an extremely helpful and accommodating man who was interested in community affairs and was a great collector of historical artifacts. Doug managed the store while his wife, Annie, taught school.

"Looks like someone must be making money," said John, continuing the sales pitch. "There's the Canadian Imperial Bank of Commerce and the Bank of Montreal!"

We decided to spend the night at the Maple Leaf Hotel, centrally located and just around the corner from the Famous Restaurant. The hotel was a two-storey frame building owned by Benny Abbott, a tall, slender, distinguished greying man with a tremendous personality.

We were a bit of an oddity with our foreign licence plates, and the people of the Cariboo were curious but extremely friendly and helpful everywhere we went. It wasn't long before Benny Abbott found out we were Americans and extended to us true Cariboo hospitality.

We were escorted to the adjoining "Licensed Premises," another unfamiliar term, where only beer was served. These licensed premises, better known as beer parlours, were strictly regulated. Hard liquor was only available through the government Liquor Control Board store. This was a new experience for us, coming from California, where alcohol of all types could be purchased anywhere from a drug store to a supermarket by anyone who was twenty-one years old.

Outside hung two signs, "Men" and "Ladies," as if they were restrooms. Benny explained the regulations in his quick-witted way, sending us into peals of laughter. The beer parlours were split in half by a wall; on one side men were served, and the other side was for "ladies and escorts." At no time were women allowed to enter the side for men, but men could enter the women's side as long as they were escorting women.

"John, you are safe," said Benny. "You can always get away from your wife here in Canada, but you can always go and see what Doris is doing over on her side."

It was strange not to have any music or dancing, but this was against all regulations. Eventually we stopped noticing, for soon the place seemed like one happy family. Apparently our American "drawl" was quite pronounced, because Benny Abbott, all in fun and laughter, insisted we Americans slaughtered the English language. The Canadians easily detected our accent and likewise we noticed their vocabulary. Expressions like our "huh" and the Canadian "eh" were always a topic of conversation.

Here we heard the names of the very early European explorers of the Cariboo—Alexander Mackenzie, David Thompson, Simon Fraser. Then came Ogden, Pinchbeck, Borland, Lyne, Meldrum, Eagle and Bates. Those people had contributed much to the economic growth of this vast land. In the following years we were lucky enough to meet them or some of their descendants, including the Pigeons, Paxtons, Crosinas, Patenaudes, Hamiltons, Jeffersons, Westwicks, Zirnhelts, Twans and Armes, as well as the distinguished gentleman Antoine Boitanio, his wife, Mae, and many, many others.

The evening passed far too quickly. At 11:00 p.m., closing time for the Maple Leaf beer parlour according to the strict laws of British Columbia, we said goodnight. Amid tables laden with empty beer glasses we had made many new acquaintances and truly experienced the amicable and hospitable Cariboo.

Big Lake

John was very impressed with the ranch and had seen many possibilities for further development. He had the equipment and knowledge that were required, along with the ability to work hard. All he needed now was for me to make the decision. There could be nothing worse than to bring along a dissatisfied woman, he claimed. I was brought up with the idea that a woman went wherever her husband could make a living—one of her contributions to a successful marriage. We tossed the idea around for a couple of weeks and finally, with mixed emotions, I told John I was ready to make the move.

On September 27, 1950, which also happened to be John's birthday, we officially purchased the Weber ranch. Over the next few months we told family and friends our plans, and many of them thought we were crazy to move to Canada. They predicted that we would soon be back, that we were moving to a still uncivilized land of Eskimos and Indians, that we would starve or freeze to death. Little was known about British Columbia in our part of the country. It was just too far north.

Once we had made the decision there were many things to do. The first thing for me was to cancel my teaching contract. For John it was to return to BC and go over the whole ranch from one end to the other, having only briefly seen the two outlying parcels on Peavine Ridge, known as Kirbys and McCades. The Webers had purchased these small ranches to add to the property they already held, to supply additional hay and pasture.

The Kirby place consisted of 360 acres, with considerable open land and a small lake plus a lovely but weary-looking barn with a badly worn shake roof and a small two-room cabin. Kirbys, as it was known, had been pre-empted by Frank Kirby in 1914 when he travelled to the Cariboo from Chicago. Peter Hamilton of Lac La Hache, BC, the eldest son of the Hudson's Bay Company factor Gavin Hamilton, had brought Kirby into the area as a trapper.

The McCade property was 180 acres in size and bordered Kirbys on one corner. McCade came from Portland, Oregon. He first worked at Beaver Lake, for Gavin Hamilton (who had the same name as his famous father). McCade later pre-empted his choice piece of property. The only building remaining there now was a fallen-down barn slowly slipping back into Mother Nature's domain.

McCade and Kirby were enemies. Kirby, reported to have a violent temper and a foul tongue, was disliked by all who knew him. The two men became involved in a fight over the attentions of a local widow, Mrs. McNutt, who lived at Big Lake. At one point McCade went to confront Kirby. Kirby stabbed McCade with a knife and a bitter battle ensued, during which Kirby split McCade's face open with an axe. Somehow McCade dragged himself several miles to the Harper place, where the police were summoned. McCade lost an eye, and Kirby was placed in an institution, where he later died. When we bought the ranch, we could still see large bloodstains on the logs of Kirby's small cabin, left by this legendary fight.

Such a long move, from northern California to central BC, presented many problems. We had to ship our heavy equipment by rail. John had a diesel truck and trailer—the first in the Williams Lake area—which he would use to haul our smaller equipment and household furnishings. Several trips would have to be made to get everything moved. John's brother and his wife, Elbert and Claudia, brought two of John's favourite quarter horses to British Columbia in the early fall so they would become acclimatized before the extreme winter cold. Although seventeen head of average Cariboo ranch horses had been included in the sale, they were not the high-quality horses John was accustomed to working with, so he decided to bring along the quarter horses, Banjo and Nugget.

There was government paperwork to be done at the border before our entry as landed immigrants. We were lucky—most Canadians were eager to have Americans move here. Many descendants of Americans had settled here, and this vast country of Canada had little more population than our home state of California. A growing country needs people.

After dark on February 2, 1951, we arrived at Big Lake. I was towing an army Jeep behind the Chrysler sedan and John drove our small Chevrolet truck, pulling a horse trailer loaded with the remainder of our belongings. We were now in permanent residence at our new home! The sides of the main road were piled high with snow, but the mile-long side road to our house was drifted with a heavy, thigh-deep blanket of white. We could go no farther. John trudged down to

When we arrived in Big Lake in February 1951, we were greeted by a deep blanket of snow. It was a stark difference from the ranch we had seen only a few months before.

Later I grew to love the beauty of the Cariboo winter, but that first year I was not at all impressed by the endless and relentless cold.

the ranch to get Chip Kerr, whom he had hired to look after the ranch and feed the stock during the transition period, to harness the team and come out and get me. We had pulled our vehicles into Paddy and Harold Cripps's plowed driveway, later to become my home away from home, where I awaited John's return. After quite some time, John and Chip finally arrived. After a short visit and a quick cup of coffee, we continued to our destination.

Doubts flooded into my mind. This cold, empty-looking land was not the place I had seen a few months back, and I felt lonely already. We packed some things, such as anything that might freeze in the extreme cold, onto the sleigh and left the vehicles at Cripps'. This was my first experience on a horse-drawn bobsleigh. The air was bitterly cold and the moon played hide and seek behind white clouds as we slid along with the runners of the sleigh creaking and groaning. The team of horses, Chub and Dan, pranced and snorted, eager to get back to their warm log barn and manger full of hay. The summertime rippling waters of Big Lake were now a vast sea of white, covered in a blanket of crystal ice. Smoke from the chimney spiralled lazily into the bright, cold night sky, and from inside the batten-board ranch house the soft glow of a kerosene lamp beckoned.

The house lacked all signs of a woman's touch, as the Webers were long gone and Chip had been batching to keep the water system from freezing. The stark interior bore little resemblance to the warm, homey décor I had enjoyed on our first visit. I was exhausted, and the next few days found me very ill with a bad cold, although I almost never got sick. Perhaps it had been brought on by the extreme change of climate.

The next few months were the worst of my life. The days seemed to go on endlessly and the place was depressing as the snow drove viciously against the windowpanes. When would spring come, I wondered? Everything was so unfamiliar. I could not go outside, never having experienced such bitter cold, and I had all I could cope with just trying to get unpacked and learning about the inconveniences of remote ranch living. My temper was getting very short, and I often found myself in tears of frustration without the least provocation. More and more each day, I began to wonder why I had given up so much to come here.

I was homesick for my family and friends, and I missed my students and my collegial friendships with the school and fellow teachers. It was a very isolated life compared to the one I had left behind. I was lucky to have such a wonderful husband, who understood my mixed emotions, but I knew that John could not stand a whining woman. I had to quit feeling sorry for myself. John had made every attempt to make things as easy for me as possible, and unlike most individuals, he always took life in stride, never getting upset when his day did not go exactly as planned.

I looked forward to the mail, for every bit of news from home was most welcome. Mail day once a week was a big day, provided the roads were not snowed in or we could get an automobile going for the sixteen-mile trip to the post office. If the oil was cold, John would have to put a small amount of diesel in a can, light it and place it under the vehicle to warm up the motor and the oil in the pan—without setting anything on fire. Sometimes it would take all day to get a vehicle or tractor going, and by then it was too late to go anywhere.

Feeding the stock with a team and sleigh was an advantage, for one could always get the animals fed, plus John preferred working with horses. Temperatures of 30, 40 or 50 below zero Fahrenheit were not uncommon. On one occasion the thermometer reached 64 below. The cold was hard on both man and beast, but the extremely cold periods were short-lived, usually lasting three or four days. That first year the winter months dragged by so slowly as I longingly waited for spring. Everything seemed to be inconvenient and difficult, and I wondered over and over whether I would ever adapt.

Early on we found that the ranch house was not wired for electricity, making it impossible to use the army surplus lighting plant we had brought with us. When the roads and the weather improved, John would hire an electrician to come out from Williams Lake to install the plant and wire the ranch buildings. Meanwhile, we would have to get along with various lanterns and lamps until spring. At some time during each day it was necessary to fill all the lanterns and lamps with fuel, an unpleasant task. Regardless of how careful we were, the repulsive odour of kerosene and gas filled the house, not to mention lingering on our clothing and skin.

I especially detested the gas lanterns—everything from the hissing noise of the temperamental fuel burners to the flimsy, easily damaged mantle, which I often touched accidentally in my nervousness. If the fuel regulating knob was turned too far, a startling flame burst upwards, and if I added too little fuel, the lamp would not ignite. I

We were unpleasantly surprised to find that the house was not wired for electricity. It would be months before an electrician could come out to wire up the house and out-buildings. In the meantime we lived with the stench of kerosene from the lanterns.

always hoped John would be home before darkness fell so he could light the lanterns.

Searching for a light source that might compare to incandescent lamps, we purchased two Aladdin lamps, which fell far short of living up to their magical name. With their tall, slender chimneys, these lamps gave a bright light, but they needed careful watching so the flame did not burn too high and blacken the mantle and chimney. The most trouble-free light of all was the common kerosene lamp, which absorbed its fuel through a tape-like wick, producing a small, steady, warm, soft light.

Water was another problem, at least for me. I was accustomed to turning on the faucet and having all the hot or cold water I could use, thanks to electricity, which I had once taken for granted. Here in our isolated ranch house, instead of an electric pump that conveniently came on automatically when the pressure dropped to a certain point, we had a tank controlled by the amount of water used, and we always seemed to be out of water.

However, we were much more fortunate than many of our neighbours. Some of them had no running water of any type. We had a water storage tank holding 150 gallons. When the level in the tank reached its lowest point, we had to start the engine that ran the pump to fill the tank. In the wintertime this was a job in itself. We had to dress warmly against the bitter cold, then shovel any snow from the doorway to the pumphouse, and possibly get fuel for the stubborn gas motor.

The pumphouse, located near the shore of Big Lake, had three-foot thick double walls, constructed of logs from the nearby forest, filled in between with dirt and covered with a sod roof. Any gaps between the logs were chinked with moss. All of these features helped to protect the water system from the severe penetrating cold. But even so, the water did occasionally freeze during a prolonged and extreme cold period.

The pump that filled the storage tank was operated by a small Briggs & Stratton gasoline engine. Like most gas engines, they were touchy and needed a great deal of persistence to start. It seemed as if everything around this place was temperamental, including myself! This small engine taxed my patience beyond all limits. Should I run out of water while John was away I would make an attempt to start it, but only sometimes would succeed. It seemed that when I desperately needed water, the engine was always out of gas, or the spark plug was fouled up, or I choked it too much or not enough. In this country, no one took water for granted.

Getting the water storage tank was one thing; getting hot water was another. Behind the large stove was a thirty-gallon galvanized water tank, connected to a water jacket inside the firebox. To get hot water, one had to keep a fire going. First, the cookstove and the large wood heater in the living room had to be fed. We had to get up during the night and rise early in order to keep the house warm and prevent the water system from freezing. When the water was hot in the water tank (certainly not a wintertime problem), the water pressure tank filled, the sensitive gas engine of the washing machine started and the washing could finally be done. My patience was exhausted and more often than not I was in tears.

Next came the drying and ironing of the clothes. I hung the clothes on a wooden rack that I placed indoors, then turned and shifted them until dry. If hung outside they would freeze stiff immediately and remain frozen for weeks and weeks.

Then came my introduction to the "sad iron," a two-part contraption that was heated by placing it on top of the hot wood stove. I would either forget to snap off the wooden handle, which would then burn on the stove, or I would forget to set the iron back on the stove and it would burn the ironing board cover. I would either let the fire in the cookstove get too low, or I would have it so hot that we could hardly stay in the house. Temperature was crucial; an iron too cool produced no results, an iron too hot could leave a scorch mark, the size and shape of a sad iron, in the most conspicuous spot. This iron was not designed to stand upright like the electric iron I had received for a wedding present. It seemed I could never win, but after my first few experiences I fully knew the reason for the iron's name—it certainly made me sad.

For every hardship there is compensation if one takes time to look for it. Slowly I began to look around at the beauty that surrounded me, and I could not imagine a place as beautiful as the Cariboo. Our country is spectacular—even a quick glimpse unveils the great beauty of the many lakes and the rolling hills covered with vast forests. A deeper beauty is evident to those who look and listen in silence. For these people, the land holds treasures of peace and serenity. The drifted snow curved over the landscape, the wind-sculpted caverns and hollows—everything was utterly silent, the air crisp and clean, the snow gleaming under the moon and the stars.

To the north we could often see the aurora borealis, or northern lights, long quivering streamers of light in the night sky. These luminous bands are usually white, sometimes intermingled with varying shades of red, green and yellow. They may be almost straight or they may wind back and forth in serpentine formation. Watching the rays move up and down, I was reminded of immense curtains being drawn just before a great show.

No human artist can equal the infinite skill of Jack Frost in working out his delicate artistry, creating masterpieces of which no two are alike. The windowpanes were often covered with wonderful landscapes, flowers or fairy lace as steam from the tea kettle added to these intricate patterns.

The outdoor winter scenes were even more beautiful than Christmas cards, for no one can create like Mother Nature. Sometimes, after a warm evening and a clear, cold, still night, we would wake to find the world blanketed with glittering white hoarfrost. Occasionally it was several inches thick with inch-long crystals, leaving a brilliant diamond-like coating on the branches of barren deciduous trees and shrubs.

We enjoyed countless impressive sunsets on Big Lake, in both summer and winter. One evening during our first winter, the light remaining above the horizon was a turmoil of brilliant reds and pallid pink, silhouetting the leafless cottonwood trees and the wind-shaped firs and spruce trees reaching for the sky, all accentuated by the white of the snow.

"Looks like a nice day today," John said at the breakfast table the next morning. "How about putting on your shearling-lined coat and come feeding with me? Chip hasn't been to Williams Lake for better than two months and he needs a break."

I shivered. "Looks too cold out there for me."

"You must have almost everything unpacked and pretty well settled now. You will be getting cabin fever if you stay in here all the time," John said as he poured another steaming cup of coffee. "We will get a load of hay from the alfalfa field beside the main road, and if you get too cold I promise I will bring you home right away."

I put so many clothes on I could hardly move. The sky was a brilliant blue and the air was invigorating—about -20°F—carrying a fresh smell of the forest. I stood against the front rack of the bobsleigh, the extreme cold biting my cheeks and nose as John snapped the lines on Dan and Chub's backs.

Everything was buried under shimmering snowdrifts, so delicately white and clean, as we slid over the snow to the stackyard. Old Mother Nature had all but concealed the effects of the human race upon the earth. John pitched from the loose haystack the Webers had made with the overshot stacker. Pitching hay required a certain amount of skill, and John made every forkful count. "It's easy—nothing to it," he said, smiling and rolling huge forkfuls onto the sleigh. I tried my hand and got only small amounts of hay on my fork, but the effort kept me warm.

Before long the sleigh was heaped with the sweet-smelling hay, ready for the cows waiting hungrily on the feeding grounds. I burrowed deeply into the hay as John closed the stackyard and climbed onto the sleigh for the drive home. A slight wind stirred the frozen branches of the nearby forest as we rode along. The white-face Hereford cows came running, bawling and pulling huge mouthfuls of hay from the sleigh.

"How about driving the team while I pitch the hay off?" John's eyes twinkled, well aware I knew nothing about horses of any kind. "Let me give you a lesson," and he proceeded to do so. I had to admit I enjoyed myself, and it was not nearly as cold out as I thought it was going to be. Secretly I hoped he would soon ask me to go again.

John led Dan and Chub into their stalls in the small log barn to feed them. Then he reached for the ice-coated axe leaning against the side of the barn. "Have to cut the water hole open in case the cattle come to drink before I get back from lunch," he said, adding that cutting water holes in the ice was one job he really disliked.

I soon saw why. He sank the axe into the ice with terrific blows, sending ice chips flying in every direction. As with everything else, there was a knack to this job. If you were not extremely careful, a misplaced blow would send icy cold water into your already frozen face. The water hole must not be too wide, or a cow could slip into it and die on the spot, but the hole had to be long enough for several cows to drink at one time—it seemed if one cow wanted to drink, they all wanted to drink. The hole must be maintained in a small sectioned-off area of lake edge, adjacent to the feeding grounds, with a strong fence of rails or poles to keep the cattle from going onto the lake during the early winter and spring, when the ice was not strong enough to hold them. This fence had to be constructed before freeze-up so that it was ready when cold weather struck.

The days had lengthened, the snow began to settle and then at last we knew spring was on the way. Thunderous noises came from the massive two-foot-thick sheet of ice covering Big Lake as it contracted and expanded with the warm days and cold nights. The burgeoning earth, dormant all winter, was now awakening to the sun's warming touch. Mother Nature would soon roll out her magic carpet of colour.

One late March morning a wedge of geese flew overhead, winging their way north; the honking flock shifted and wavered trying to hold a V formation behind the leader. These geese were a special symbol, a sign of spring. The arrival of the killdeer, robin, bluebird and meadowlark is enjoyable, but to winter-weary ranching people, the sight of geese is full of meaning—it tells us that the backbone of winter is broken. At night we could hear the passing of flock after flock, and we knew the geese had left behind the stubble fields of the San Joaquin Valley in California, where the weather was already hot.

As a rule, the first small bird to return in the spring was the killdeer, its shrill cry known to all. The killdeer make their home in a spot that could hardly be called a nest, amid a few pebbles resembling the large brown and black splotches on their eggs. If an animal or human approaches the nest, the killdeer pretends to have a broken wing. It hobbles along pitifully with its orange-banded tail spread wide, trailing its wings on the ground and seemingly unable to stand on its feet, a decoy to lure the unknowing away from the nest.

More signs of spring arrived as each day passed. We were often awakened by the cheery spring-like song of robins. Then came the bluebirds, such a brilliant blue, a sign of happiness, or so I had always heard. Now I questioned it. The snow had gone at last, leaving the landscape dull, ugly and depressing after the long winter. The new green buds and grass had yet to make their appearance.

A rancher's work was never done, and ranch life was always hectic. John and Chip were busy from daylight to dark. In early spring there were cattle to feed, and when the cows began calving, a near twenty-four hour vigil was needed for the young heifers having their first calves. There was much to learn for a beginner, and I learned a good deal of it the hard way.

John understood the language of the animals. He could just look at a cow or a horse and know whether it was contented or sick, whether it was getting enough to eat without wasting precious hay, or whether it was ready to give birth. He knew what to do should a cow have problems calving. "Never want to upset those critters, especially a first-calf heifer," he told me. It seldom happens that a cow does not claim her calf, but if she is disturbed while calving, the upset can make plenty of extra work. A cow might have to be put in a small corral or even hobbled until the calf takes hold and the inexperienced cow gets used to her newborn. "I have been around cattle all my life and rarely do you find a cow that doesn't want her calf," John said. "Cows have superior maternal instincts, although some people claim animals are dumb, something I strongly disagree with."

It was typical spring weather—rain, snow showers, warm days with cold nights, almost any kind of weather you could imagine. The frost was starting to come out of the ground and John was eager to begin the spring work he had planned. With the short spring and summer of the north country, it seemed that all work had to be done immediately, and one hardly knew where to start.

Among the equipment John had brought with him from California was a HD-7 Allis Chalmers bulldozer with a blade and scraper, the

In the spring the lake would start to sing and chime as the ice melted. It was a beautiful and magical sound.

first of its size in the area. He enjoyed working the equipment and was anxious to get started clearing ground for more hayfields close to the home ranch, beginning with the area east of the ranch buildings. The task would be time-consuming on this land, so dense with cottonwood, birch, willow and conifers that it was hard to ride a horse through, but with dark, rich fertile soil.

John brought his Allis Chalmers bulldozer all the way from Califorina. It was a good decision as it became a crucial tool for clearing our land.

The days were considerably longer now, and the budding trees and plants burst forth. Each day was a new experience. The hills developed a greenish cast, and soon the clear ice on Big Lake turned dark and became honeycombed. The bright yellow dandelion, champion among plants for getting along in this world, was blooming everywhere we looked. It was not only nutritious for the animals but also useful to us, added to salads and spinach and making a very tasty wine. Spring was here!

Dawn had already entered my room when I awoke one morning to the sound of bells. I could smell the smoke from the wood stove, and the morning coffee John had prepared. But what were these mystical, musical bell-like sounds, tinkling like harmonious glass chimes? I jumped out of bed and looked out the bedroom window, wondering if I had lost my sanity. A warm westerly wind carried the scent of spruce and fir trees to my nostrils. Though I could see nothing, softly came the tuneful sounds. I slipped into my dressing gown and opened the kitchen door. "John, come and listen. I hear noises, like bells made of fine glass, beautiful but so eerie."

He finished putting wood into the cookstove, and we went out on the front porch and stood quietly and listened. John suggested we go to the lakeshore, and there before our eyes lay the answer. "I know what is happening," John said. "There was a terrible wind during the night, I don't think you heard it as you were sleeping so soundly." He pointed to the immense bank of ice piled along the shoreline. "Big Lake is opening up."

The wind had shifted the massive sheet of deteriorating ice to the shore, where millions and millions of long ice crystals were constantly moving and shifting, creating the beautiful musical sounds at our feet. With an overwhelming feeling of reverence, we listened to the melodious sounds, like music of the angels, that could only have been produced by God. Within a day or two Big Lake was clear of ice, and the beautiful, icy cold water was rippling clean and clear.

Soon the open water brought the goldeneye and mallard ducks in their colourful breeding plumage. Then came the merganser, the diving, fish-eating duck, then the common loon. This bird can only take off from water and even then has difficulty rising from the surface, but once airborne it is a strong flyer. Atmospheric conditions are a factor as well. Only a newcomer to the Cariboo, or a darn fool, would try to predict weather in the Cariboo, but according to the old-timers, loons flying and calling is a sure sign of an approaching storm.

With the advent of spring, I began to see things with a more positive attitude. In my younger years I had vowed to marry a man with money and not be subjected to the drudgery of housework, but I had obviously forsaken this dream. Now I was determined to find gratification in my role as a rancher's wife. It was my habit to accomplish everything I set out to do, putting all effort into any task I tackled. I certainly did not want to return to California and give our friends and relatives the opportunity to say "I told you so."

My whole life had already started to change, and as the saying goes, in Rome do as the Romans do, in the Cariboo do as the Cariboogians do. I was lucky my mother had taught me to cook and keep house, and I enjoyed preparing meals—a skill perhaps handed down from forebears noted for being excellent cooks. I had to learn to shop not just for a day or two at a time, but for weeks. It was not as if I could run to the nearest supermarket. The small grocery store, Western, Rife and Pigeon, had almost everything a person needed in the basic food line, although one might have to ask for items not displayed. Most of the essential commodities came in bulk, not the fancy showy packages I had grown used to in California supermarkets. The store got its name from the owners, Sid Western, Ken Rife and Les Pigeon, long-time Cariboo residents. Les Pigeon later married Jessie Foster, the first gold commissioner in Williams Lake, and several years later they moved to the Alkali Lake Ranch to manage the company store. The personnel at the store were very helpful, taking an order and having it ready to pick up before we were ready to start home. This gave us the time to pick up the barrels of fuel, grain, salt and other items we needed.

In the first year we shared many laughs at the store, particularly when it came to vocabulary. Once I asked for Purex, a common bleach where I came from, and the clerk, looking bewildered and trying hard not to laugh, would ask, "Do you mean roll?" On further discussion it was revealed that here, Purex was toilet tissue. In the Cariboo there was a sealer instead of a "jar," a tin instead of a "can," a serviette instead of a "napkin," and many other differences.

We found the slower pace of Williams Lake so different from the fast-moving, highly competitive life we had known in California. Every village or town in the Cariboo had a closing day for business, Wednesday being the day for Williams Lake. The beer parlours closed in the evening from six to seven, then locked up at eleven, and never opened on Sunday. At store closing time it seemed to me they even rolled up the board sidewalks, for you could buy absolutely nothing after regular business hours. Americans would never think of closing their stores one day a week as well as Sundays. As time went on, we learned to adjust to the hours and ways of the Cariboo, and sometimes we even managed to enjoy a round or two at the Maple Leaf Hotel beer parlour before returning home.

Big Lake Ranch, owned by Harold and Paddy Cripps, was centrally located and had one of the few telephones in the community, so

This barn on the Cripps' property was originally built by William Parker. Courtesy the Clifford Overton Heritage Collection.

it often became a gathering place for the whole area. Paddy and Harold were always ready to help their neighbours with warm Cariboo hospitality; the coffee pot was always on. During extremely cold weather anyone travelling the road from Williams Lake to the Big Lake area was to telephone Paddy or Harold upon departure, and if they did not arrive within a reasonable time, the Crippses would start looking for them. The roads were usually deserted, and you could easily freeze to death if you had car trouble or got stuck in a snowdrift. There was no radio communication, and very few residents in the entire area.

Just a few years before our arrival, the Big Lake Ranch had a small general store and the original Big Lake Ranch Post Office. The store had closed, and the post office had moved eight miles up the main road toward Likely, taken over by Bill Huxtable, an excellent postmaster. Bill and his wife, Rose, had a daughter named Viola, and in an adjoining building lived Mrs. Vance, Rose's mother. Bill loved to visit, and at any hour of the day or

The general store at Big Lake. Courtesy the Clifford Overton Heritage Collection.

night was very accommodating, fetching mail from the small building near the main road.

The Big Lake Ranch has long been rich in history, especially since the 1860s, when it became a stopping place for miners on their way to the goldfields of Keithley Creek and Barkerville. The famous old Cariboo freighter, William F. Parker, once owned Big Lake Ranch. A great teamster and an expert freighter, also known as "the fighting man of the Cariboo," Parker could break a bottle at twenty feet with the end of his ribbons. He was the freighter in the 1890s, near the 98 Mile post, when one of the biggest gold robberies in the Cariboo occurred—a treasure chest containing $15,000 in gold dust and bars was stolen.

Parker developed the Big Lake Ranch, trading room and board for labour to immigrant Chinese men. He opened up the wilderness for hayfields, supplying feed for teams of horses and shelter for the hardy souls travelling to and from the goldfields; piles of rock cleared from the fields still remain as signs of toil by those

William Parker's Stopping House at Big Lake. Parker is standing second from the left. BC Archives A-03496

early settlers. On a small knob overlooking Big Lake and the ranch he once owned is the grave of William F. Parker, marked with a headstone encircled by a small iron fence.

William Parker's gravestone still stands at Big Lake, overlooking the ranch he developed in the 1860s.

The last fingers of light were disappearing one evening as we finished our dinner, and John suggested we have coffee in the living room. A slow grin crinkled his eyes as I sat down in the reclining rocker Mother Lee had given us as a wedding gift. I knew from his face that there was something in the wind.

"Doris, there is a big day coming up. For you, my dear, I don't know if you will enjoy yourself too much." He hesitated. "I know you like those cows and their small calves, but they must be branded, castrated, dehorned and sometimes doctored. These things just go with ranching. The cows and calves will beller and bawl; there will be blood from the castrating and dehorning, and the smell of smoke, seared hair and hide." His eyes met mine. "Are you going to come out and help us?"

I cringed, thinking of those small calves being hurt, but I knew it was important to have a woman who could help. Other ranchers' wives were so capable, and I felt the determined desire to accept the challenge. I may have been a greenhorn that day, but I would not always be, I promised myself.

"Within the next few days, we will have to go to Williams Lake and get the necessary supplies we need for branding," John continued. "Harold and Paddy, along with their crew, have already offered to help with the cattle. We will need blackleg vaccine, more salt blocks, and it's a tradition to have a beer or two—it's hard and hot work mugging down those little critters. I also have to order a few parts and pick up some fuel. Maybe you could cook up a pot of beans or one of your special dishes. It will take most of the day to get the cattle gathered and worked. I'll tell you, we will be hungry."

There was nothing John enjoyed more than handling cattle and horses. Once he was astride his favourite horse, even with the long hours, exhausting toil, summer heat, chill winter wind and cold blowing snow, he lived the life of a true cowhand.

A few days later, with the trip to Williams Lake and many hours of meal preparation behind us, John rolled out of bed especially early. By the time I got up he had the coffee made and was planning to fix a horseshoe, move some pregnant cows into another corral and go looking for an old cow that had gone missing.

I hurriedly cooked him a man-sized breakfast. I had never experienced this work and knew nothing of what the day would bring, but I felt excited, anticipating a day of work, fun and laughter for those who understood animals and enjoyed competition between their fellow man and beast.

First came Harold, Paddy and Cherie, their spirited horses stepping high as if they too could sense the excitement of the day. "The rest of the crew is on their way. Hope you have the coffee pot on," called Cherie. Shortly the others rode in, dressed in denim jackets and brightly coloured neckerchiefs, leather chaps and jangling spurs, with high-crowned cowboy hats pulled down on their brows and their boots thrust forward in the stirrups.

"Come in, come in," I said, as they tied their horses to the nearby hitching rail. "John and Chip should be back soon." I placed heavy mugs of hot coffee on the kitchen table.

"Look!" exclaimed Paddy as she passed by the kitchen counter. "With all this food you have prepared, looks like you think we might be staying all week. Yum, yum. Chocolate cake, lemon meringue pies and look at those golden brown loaves of homemade bread."

"I don't know how many people will be coming," I said, "and John told me cowboys like to eat!" It was my first attempt at sourdough bread, which I made from a cookbook recipe after John had dropped a few hints. He certainly knew how to get performance.

Harold proceeded to concentrate on rolling a small cigarette with his large, rough hands, a process that still fascinated me. He spoke harshly, trying to get the best of me. "What is this city slicker schoolteacher going to do in all that blood, manure and smoke from the branding fire?"

"Really, Harold, I don't know," I said. "I just hope I won't always be a dude."

Out near the barn the calves to be branded were gathered into a big corral with their mothers. The animals milled around, bellowing and bawling, the cows sniffing each calf until they found their own. Smoke from the branding fire drifted gently into the warm spring air. I wanted to help but I knew nothing about working cattle. Promising myself I would not always be a dude, I decided to pay close attention and see how things were done.

In early spring we had to brand and castrate the cattle. It was critical that all the stock were branded before being moved to the grazing grounds.

"Doris," John called from the far side of the corral, "could you keep the branding irons hot?"

I was so pleased that I could contribute something to the event. Sure! I could keep the fire going. I heaped on the wood, only to find there was much I had to learn about branding fires.

Excessive wood created far too much heat, and no one could pick up the branding irons. Also, an iron too hot would burn through an animal's tender hide, blotching the brand and inflicting a painful wound. If I let the fire get too low, everyone would have to wait longer for the irons, adding more stress for the already struggling calf.

Moving quickly, everyone has a job to do. A roper casts his loop, catches a calf by the two hind feet and takes his dally (secures the rope to the saddle horn), then drags the bawling critter over to the ground crew. Should he miss his calf, there are many comments. "Must have a hole in your rope," someone calls. It was hard work, but great fun for those who enjoy working with stock.

A flanker throws the calf and grabs the head and foreleg, and his

My job was to tend the fire to make sure the branding iron was kept at the correct temperature. Too hot and it would burn the calf, too cold and it would slow down the branding job.

partner grabs the hind leg and removes the rope, holding a leg tight to his body while shoving the other leg out, using his foot as a brace.

One cowhand was dehorning, one earmarking, another inoculating. John was kept especially busy castrating and lacing the Circle W Ranch brand on each animal's left hip. He preferred to do his own castrating and branding whenever possible. He rolled the brand on each bawling red Hereford calf, taking less than a few seconds, smoke from the searing hair floating back into his face. Of all things done to calves, dehorning had to be the most excruciating by far. I felt ill at my stomach and my eyes were heavy with tears. I had to leave, with the excuse that I needed to check on the upcoming meal. No one must know that it was too much for this novice—they would have razzed me unmercifully. In a fleeting but familiar moment of depression, I asked myself whether I would ever make a rancher's wife.

Toward noon, John called to the hands. "It must be nearly chow time, and Doris will soon have lunch ready. I guess we had better have a beer before she's ready for us." They tied their horses to the corral fence and forked a generous helping of hay from the nearby barn to the sweating horses. Some cowboys rested on their haunches, while others sat cross-legged on the ground sipping their beer. Young up-and-coming cowhands, not old enough to consume alcohol, raced around pretending that they too were great cowboys. The women hands, equally as good with the stock, came inside to help me get the meal on the table.

Mealtime was a pleasurable event for all. Conversation ranged from the experiences of the recent calving season, to all the work they had yet to do, the spring range conditions and the weather—always a topic for conversation in the Cariboo. Through it all there was joking back and forth between the ropers and the ground crew.

Once they had eaten, the men seemed to be in no rush to get back to work. Finally John said quietly, "Well, let's go get 'em," and within minutes everyone was on their feet and moving toward the corral. They worked through the rest of the warm afternoon, stopping only a couple of times to enjoy a beer. While they waited for the irons to reheat, the ropers practised casting their loops, and everyone who cared to rope seemed to have an opportunity to try their skills.

There was much laughing and joking, especially when something unusual happened. Apparently nothing was funnier than when a cowboy wrestled with a calf that had diarrhea and was suddenly covered with foul-smelling manure. It seemed to me cowboys got much gratification from seeing their fellow man hurt or humiliated, but John told me this was all in the game and only in fun. "Takes a lot to hurt a cowboy, long ways from their heart," he claimed.

It was getting late when the last calf had been branded and the odd cow with excess milk for her calf had been "milked out." John thanked each volunteer, with a promise that we would help when they were ready to brand. There were still chores waiting at home for everyone.

The lamps were blown out early that night. It had indeed been a big day and we were exhausted. John crawled into bed and immediately fell into a deep, sound sleep. Outside, the bellering and bawling stopped. It was again so peaceful and quiet. The star-studded sky and the silver sickle of the May moon shone down on our batten-board ranch house on the shore of beautiful Big Lake.

Spring had indeed arrived in the Cariboo. Each day brought the awakening of plants and animals, with beauty everywhere. The sky remained cloudy for short periods, but one was conscious of the lurking presence of the sun as the overcast of winter gave way to the brilliant sunlit days of spring and summer.

The creeks stirred as they were released from the hold of winter, filling the air with their song of spring. They burgeoned into torrents as they joined together on their eventual journey to the Fraser River, and onward to the Pacific Ocean.

Spring has a wonderful effect on humankind as well, stimulating the bloodstream, lifting spirits after a long, cold winter and making people glad they had chosen the Cariboo as their home.

A few days after the cattle were safe and rested from the ordeal of branding and castration, it was time to move them to the open range, on land leased from the provincial government. Each ranch acquired a grazing permit at a nominal cost per animal unit, which consisted of a cow and a calf.

When the time came, neighbours were always eager to lend a hand, especially Cherie, who was vitally interested in livestock and ranching. John and Cherie talked about many things that I knew nothing about, especially horses—those that had bucked them off, the ornery ones they had handled, and the funny things that happen in a cowboy's life.

Cherie was born in Vancouver on October 1, 1934, to Paddy and Pack Harris. She spent her first five years among ranching people at the Alkali Lake Ranch, where her parents were employed by her maternal grandparents, Mary Mabel and C. Wynn Johnson. It was here that she learned to ride the gentle horse Coyote, and when asked how long she had been riding, she would reply, "Almost forever!"

In 1939, Paddy and Pack Harris, Cherie and her older brother, Jimmy, moved to Big Lake. There they continued to ranch, and eventually opened a store and the Big Lake Ranch Post Office. The family had purchased the historic Parker's Road House, which during the 1880s had catered to prospectors as they travelled to the goldfields.

Big Lake became "home" to this adventurous girl. There she spent her first three years of schooling, riding her horse to the small log schoolhouse. When low attendance forced the school to close, Cherie went to a private girls' school, Strathcona Lodge, at Shawnigan Lake, Vancouver Island. She was a very lonely child, but strong and determined. During the summer and school holidays, she lived at Big Lake, where she loved the great outdoors and the ranching life. She became a very capable hand with the livestock and the cattle range, and she loved everything about horses.

The cows were always eager to head to the sweet grass and fresh water of the open range.

It was decided that I would drive the pickup, carrying the blocks of salt, lunches for those riding and the odd small calf should it get trail-weary. I felt sure I would be more helpful in this capacity, for I had never driven any cattle and I would not be able to head them off if they decided to start homeward.

John counted the cows on the pole gate just outside our ranch house. They were eager to head to the open range as memories of earlier years stirred within them—the lush new grass, clear streams and peaceful grazing far away from people. A big-boned, smooth-coated, dark red Hereford cow, followed closely by a calf that much resembled her, led the way, knowing exactly where she was headed.

The riders moved along first on one side and then the other, and some followed behind, keeping the cows as close together as possible and making sure no calves bolted. The only thing that would stop these cows on their way to the range was the maternal instinct if a cow went back through the mob searching for her calf. The animals ate greedily, grabbing mouthfuls of tender grass as they ambled along.

In early afternoon, after the twelve-mile drive from the ranch, we arrived at Prairie Chicken, a large, semi-open area of the range with the gentle, fresh green slopes the cattle preferred. The small tassels of a cottonwood were hidden among the bright green leaves, and the slightest breeze caused them to turn and flutter, flashing in the sunlight. The richly forested rolling hills in the distance were a spectacle against the azure of the spring sky.

Here we would eat our lunch and the cattle would be "mothered up," an important part of settling them. The calves were tired and lay down at their first opportunity, and the cows went in search of feed on the slopes. After a short rest, the calves got hungry and tried to start homeward, so the riders had to hold the cattle together, enabling the cow and calf to be mothered up properly in their new setting. Lunch was like a picnic with the food placed on the tailgate of the pickup, and by this time everyone was famished. As they ate, the riders watched closely, and eventually every cow mothered up with her calf and every calf knew what to do. They butted, tugged and pulled, their noses running white with the nourishing milk as their scanty tails wiggled and twitched. No matter what happened from here on, each calf would go back to where it had last nursed. If the mother was not close by, the calf would lie down and wait, confident that she would return.

We had a modest little dock and a modest little rowboat, but we managed to catch some delicious rainbow trout in Big Lake.

Before my eyes was one of the most impressive views I had seen. The cattle were spread out in the warm afternoon sun, and as each cow smelled her calf and each calf nursed, the bawling calmed down and the animals were quiet. Only the creator of the universe could produce such beauty, the cows grazing peacefully on the slopes, drifting in their own world until they would be gathered in the late fall.

Early next morning, John was up and around as usual. Even though there were just a few cattle left at home, there was no time for sleeping late.

"Good morning," I said as I poked my head into the kitchen.

"Good morning," John replied snappishly. "It is amazing how fast the weather can change. Think of the nice day we had yesterday and see what we have for today."

The large raindrops teased each other in fitful frolic as they ran down the windowpane, and the grey sky was filled with heavy clouds, promising more rain. I knew John was disappointed. He had planned to work on clearing more land for hay production, and it was already late in the season. I promised him that I would help by picking the rocks and roots, not knowing that I was offering to do what seemed like a never-ending job. One thing for sure, I had lots of energy, and it was a pleasure to help a man who was always appreciative.

"I have to do some work on the bulldozer this morning," he said, "and if the rain stops we should go fishing. A nice fat rainbow trout would be pretty tasty, and maybe by tomorrow the weather will be better. I guess we have to endure the rain, and at least we don't have to bother with irrigation systems. Suppose I have done enough complaining." He put on his raincoat and closed the kitchen door behind him.

I went about my housework with hopes the rain would soon let up, for I was eager to go fishing. I had gone stream fishing with my father in California when I was a little girl, but fishing in Big Lake would be a new experience. By lunchtime the rain was still splattering on the lake, but to the south the clouds seemed to be breaking away.

John and Chip came in for lunch and John said the wind had changed, which was a good sign. "It is to be hoped by the time we finish lunch and I get a few earthworms dug, and get the boat and fishing tackle ready, it will stop raining."

The last traces of fog and cloud vanished suddenly. The heavy rain had freshened and cleared the air, and we shoved our small green wooden boat into the rippling waters of Big Lake. This was much different from stream fishing—just think, we had the whole lake to ourselves!

As we rowed down the lake from our house and around the first point extending into the water, we heard the loud, clear whistle of the osprey. The splendid bird flew leisurely above the water, keeping a sharp watch for its quarry just beneath the surface. When it spotted a fish, it descended with great speed and force into a prodigious plunge and splash, and emerged with its prey.

John rowed the boat smoothly over the now quiet water, with rainbow trout tantalizing us from all sides. We caught several fat trout, keeping only enough for our evening meal.

Big Lake abounded with a variety of fish. Most important was the rainbow trout, which was excellent eating with its salmon-like flesh. And it is a favourite with anglers, due to its fighting ability and tendency to "break water" with impressive style. In spring and summer, the feisty rainbow virtually exploded from the clear, cold, unpolluted waters and voraciously attacked my hook.

Assembling the bare necessities for a cook-out of freshly caught trout was easy for John, who had packed for the US Forest Service in California. We had brought little more than a frying pan and a billy can, which always made the tastiest coffee. The crispy fried trout, along with something grabbed from the homemade screen cooler just outside our kitchen door, made a wonderful meal.

The shores of Big Lake were also the home of deer, moose and bear coming to have a refreshing drink or to rid themselves of troublesome insects. We also shared the lake with loons, several species of ducks along with their young, and the most beautiful bird of all, the Canada goose.

Once winter set in and the lake was safely frozen, we could fish for the big ones—lake trout and burbot. Lake trout tended to stay at the bottom of the lake during warm weather. The average adult fish weighs seven to fifteen pounds, but before we arrived at Big Lake an individual catch by Frank Stubitch, a long-time resident, weighed in at thirty-two pounds. I have caught the odd twenty-pounder, fully knowing that the big ones always get away. Burbot (ling cod) is an unattractive, snake-like fish with an elongated body and a broad, flat head. The colour is dark olive, marbled with brown or black skin, and the body is covered with tiny embedded scales. I have salted down this fish and stored it without refrigeration. When the excess salt was washed off and the fish was soaked in fresh water overnight, it made excellent creamed cod and other delectable dishes. Ice fishing was one of the highlights of my Cariboo winters, even though it required a great deal of work. Among other things, I had to learn how to chop a hole in ice that was two to three feet thick, without getting a face full of icy water.

John and I started homeward after a very enjoyable afternoon of fishing and relaxation. Most of the clouds had disappeared and the air began to cool quickly as the sun slipped into the horizon. The bright pink and red of the sunset was reflected on the waters of Big Lake as John quietly lifted one paddle, then the other. Looking at the sky in the west, according to the old adage, tomorrow would bring better weather.

"You remember that old saying?" I said, shivering. "Red in the morning, sailors take warning; red at night, sailors delight."

The hours of daylight had now lengthened considerably, and John woke up extra early. I could see the weather was exactly as the brilliant sunset had promised—it was the beginning of another nice day.

Over the next few weeks we continued to prepare the newly broken field for a crop. Picking rocks and roots was a boring job, to say the least. It required no talent at all. One thing, I said to myself silently, at least a dude could pick rocks and roots, and regardless of how boring the job was, I worked hard.

John was busy with the initial clearing, operating the bulldozer and blade. He had found it necessary to purchase a brush-breaking plow, a rugged, single-bottom piece of equipment that could only be used behind the bulldozer. John had brought a five-bottom stubble plow used in farming, but it proved unsuitable for land clearing. Each time the soil was turned, we had to pick more rocks and roots. I loved to make fires, and once the roots were picked and burned they were gone forever. But the rocks, even if dumped in an inconspicuous spot, were always there as a reminder of the many hours of toil.

Nature was constantly changing her floral display. Each day more wildflowers came into bloom—the common yellow buttercup, and violets, be they yellow, white or blue, the shooting star with its pink or purplish petals, and numerous other flowers.

There were edible plants: miner's lettuce used by the Natives, trappers and prospectors as a tasty succulent green, the shaggy mane mushroom, the dandelion, and—most popular with us—lamb's quarters, an excellent green that grew profusely.

There were the sabre-like leaves of the cattail of last year, a strangely solemn member of the bulrush family that grew along Kluigan Creek, which divided the field nearly in half. This creek was a spring-fed watercourse and at some times of the year the small split-log bridge was needed to cross. It was called Kluigan's bridge, after the man before our time who had constructed it, so we named the small body of water Kluigan Creek.

The cattails and willows that grew so profusely there made a rendezvous for redwing blackbirds, which clung to the cattails' surface sending fluted melodies over the small marsh. This was also an ideal spot for the great blue heron, bound by the long vigils awaiting its prey.

Perhaps the most peculiar marsh sounds of all came from the ghost-like American bittern skulking amid the cattails. When an intruder approaches, this bird compresses its buff plumage until it looks like a piece of weathered wood and points its beak skyward to match the tips of the surrounding bulrushes. Its call, the distinct *chunk-a-lunk, chunk-a-lunk*, sounds like an axe driving a stake into the mud, or an old wooden pump.

More days and more days were spent in preparing the fields. It seemed for every rock we picked, two appeared in its place. But picking rocks and roots was not nearly as boring close by the shore of Big Lake. There we could hear the far-carrying yodels and laughs of the common loon, among the most extraordinary sounds of nature. I loved to watch the loons. I began to imitate their calls, and soon, with practice, I had answering calls from all over the lake. One loon talking to another, John joked. I could almost believe it when I thought about my teaching career and looked at all the rocks and roots yet to be removed. Yes, I thought, I do have to be a bit loony!

Perched quietly on a limb twenty feet or more above the unpredictable waters of Big Lake, the belted kingfisher gave its harsh rattling call and waited to dive for its prey.

"Hate to take you from root and rock picking," John said, "but we just have to repair some Russell fence along the bull pasture. The bulls are thinking about spring and perhaps fighting to find out which one will be boss, but one thing for sure, there will be a boss. Time is of the essence." He walked briskly in the direction of the shop to pick up the necessary tools. I must admit it was a glorious change from the rock and root piles.

Lunchtime was fast approaching by the time we arrived at the bull pasture. John had left to check the fence situation while I gathered material for a fire, as the chilly north wind reminded us that summer was yet to come. I could hear sounds that I had heard a few other times since the arrival of spring, almost like a small gas engine being started. Later I found out it was the noisy wooing of the willow or ruffed grouse. During mating season this bird's love calls are dull booming sounds. The male attracts females by standing on a log and drumming the air with his extraordinarily powerful wings, a sound that can be heard a mile away. A relative, the sharp-tailed grouse (sometimes incorrectly called a prairie chicken) has even more elaborate courtship displays. The male bows, stomps his feet, fights with other cocks, struts around with his sac of loose skin inflated and then forces out the air as if playing a bagpipe, making a hollow boom. I once saw this display and I will never forget it—it reminded me of people square dancing.

There was so much to be done. If the proposed grain crop was to reach maturity before winter, we had to get the seed in the ground as soon as possible. I continued to pick rocks and roots whenever time permitted, but in that first year, new to ranch life, I did not always have my priorities straight. After one exhausting day, John said that we would have to finish preparing the field by the first of June, and even if it was not in the condition he wanted, it would provide additional feed.

"Next spring before we plant this field into permanent pasture," said John, "we will work the ground again. The winter frost will cause the ground to heave, uncovering more roots and rocks, and after picking the field once more the ground should be in excellent condition." He told me it was the rocks that were hard on the equipment; the small roots were no problem because they soon deteriorated. He said that the bulls and remaining cows would have to be moved to the range in mid-June and that we could not afford to spend any more time on this one field. He had decided to plant barley, a grain that was good feed and would mature earlier than oats or wheat. After he worked from daylight to dark for a couple of days, the grain was drilled in at last.

He asked if I could prepare another lunch for the day after tomorrow. Harold, Paddy and John all had to take a few cows and bulls to the range, so they would take them all together. "And I meant to mention to you," he said, smiling most affectionately, "after picking all those rocks and roots for the past few weeks, I'll give you a day off."

My housework had been sadly neglected, by my standards, and with the cooking to do and meal preparation for the next day, I had plenty of work on my hands. I spent the whole day doing my household chores while Chip and John worked outside at various ranch duties.

John was up early on the day the cattle were to be taken to the range. When I got up and opened the door to the kitchen, all was quiet except for the crackle of the fire in the wood stove and the simmer of the grey agate coffee pot. John soon emerged from the barn, leading Nugget, the well-reined sorrel quarter horse he had brought from California. I went about preparing a man-sized breakfast, for I knew it would be a long, hard day for all involved.

John and Chip ate their breakfast hurriedly, eager to get the cattle gathered. The Crippses would have their cattle rounded up and be waiting, and John disliked keeping anyone waiting. Chip had loaded the salt and fuelled the pickup, ready to go, and John said I did not need to hurry.

"I will be right behind you, for I fixed most of the lunch yesterday," I said. "Even got the billy can ready so we can have some coffee out there."

The cattle we were now moving to the range had been held back because they had not yet calved, or the calves had not been castrated or branded, or the calves were too small to travel to the range. And we had a few cattle that had been suffering from minor maladies and could now make the trek to the summer range, where the fresh green feed would do wonders after their long winter.

More important now was the addition of bulls, for breeding purposes. This was an annual mid-June event. The bulls had been separated from the cows for several months, and now they would mix with the herd of cattle taken out earlier. The gate opened and the cattle wasted no time heading toward the range. Now and then, one bull would challenge another with his huge horns cracking the air.

When we reached Cripps Ranch and the gate opened, the two herds met defiantly, and the lumbering, previously docile-looking Hereford bulls came to life. They bellowed, pawed the earth and pushed and shoved each other, trying to gore each other with their large horns. One did not want to get in the way of these extremely quick, powerful animals. John had warned me never to trust even the most gentle bull, as they could become very dangerous. Now the most aggressive bulls, having won the fights, took the lead and the other bulls went to the back of the herd. Some bulls remembered other summers on the range and soon lined out with no trouble.

I enjoyed following along behind, being part of the activities and hoping that someday I would become an experienced hand. I watched

John was a natural in the saddle.

closely as the expert riders guided their horses to move in and around the cattle.

The tranquility of the surroundings made the beauty even more captivating, for here I could focus on the wonders of the earth's natural creations. Everywhere I looked there was feed in abundance, and lush plants: green ferns, the freckle-faced tiger lily with its droopy orange blooms, the dainty wild rose with its fragrant perfume and flowers in various shades of pink, the purple Michaelmas daisy and the showy leaf-like bracts of the crimson Indian paintbrush. There were columbines, bleeding hearts and the very common, always showy spikes of the lupine, among many other flora.

Stopping to observe an unfamiliar flower, I caught sight of an overhanging spruce limb, where a spruce grouse peered down from a foot or two above my head. This grouse, also called the "fool hen," views its enemies with curiosity, moving just out of reach.

When the animals and riders reached Prairie Chicken, a couple of riders held the cattle while others gathered cows from the outlying areas. The bulls were divided up and placed with smaller groups of cows, making them available for better coverage when the cows were ready to be serviced. Early calves put more dollars in the pocket of the cowman at the fall livestock auction. The cattle bawled and bellowed as the herd mixed and milled around the open range, searching for their own.

John held the reins of his well-muscled gelding as he climbed into the back of the pickup to get the salt blocks. As the coloured blocks hit the ground, the cattle licked eagerly and steadily, their rough tongues producing a rasping sound.

After lunch, we placed the few leftover odds and ends in the pickup, and John suggested I leave for home as they would be out until after dark. The road was slow and rough, and I took my time driving back home. At the lower end of Marguerite Lake, on the road just in front of me were a long-headed, humpbacked cow moose and her reddish-brown twin calves trotting awkwardly behind, perhaps crossing from one meadow to another. I did not wish to crowd her, as I had heard that a cow moose protecting her young was worse than a grizzly bear, and I certainly didn't care to find out whether it was true. The calves were only a few hours old. Keeping a safe distance, I watched them disappear into the wilderness.

There never seemed to be a day on the ranch when there wasn't more work to be done than one could accomplish in any one year. Soon it would be haying time, and we would need to put the equipment in working condition as well as keeping up with the many other ranch jobs. We had planted our garden between the shore of Big Lake and the ranch house, having been given the rules of thumb by the old-timers. At Big Lake, they told us, one was safe planting out a garden on May 24, and plants that could not stand any frost were safe after June 10. Over the years this proved reasonably accurate. We could not grow tomatoes, cucumbers or corn, but we could grow excellent root crops and cold-weather produce. With the long hours of daylight in the north and the fertile soil, we could nearly see the more

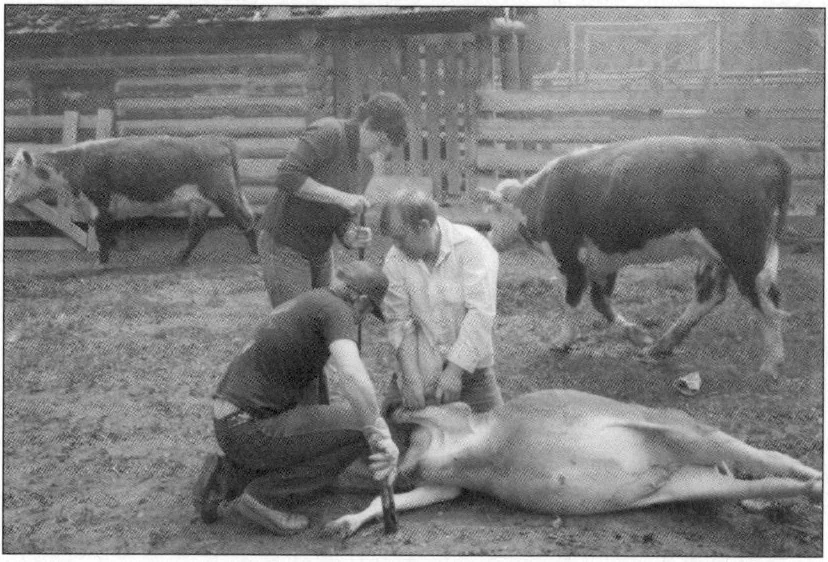

When it was branding season, everyone pitched in. Cherie (standing above the ranch hands) was always there to help.

hardy vegetables growing. When fall came, it was rewarding to see the shelves fill with assorted jars of wild berries, vegetables and meats. I thrived on this part of homemaking, and I loved to see how many different things I could preserve for winter; it was a challenge!

With haying season fast approaching, everyone was getting their equipment repaired, ready to start haying after the Williams Lake Stampede in June. The stampede came at the time of year that would give the ranchers a break after a long winter and the confining hard work of spring. After Stampede, when the arduous task of haying began, there would be no free time, for when good weather prevailed in the Cariboo, haying had top priority.

In preparation for the upcoming haying season, Harold and Paddy Cripps had hired a new man. I was elated when I found out he was a dude, hopefully giving me a break. This newcomer, Bill, was not only a dude but a mouthy one. He had come to the Cariboo from eastern Canada with the ambition, as with many young men, to become a cowboy and live the romantic, exciting cowboy's life as displayed so glamorously in Western movies and novels. Bill arrived at the Big Lake Ranch dressed in the clothes of a cowboy. He had a wide-brimmed black cowboy hat, a red neckerchief tied tightly around his throat and a new pair of shiny cowboy boots with the bottoms of his denim jeans tucked inside. He talked with an arrogant air—equal, in his estimation, to the cowboys in the Hall of Fame. Most real cowboys I had met were shy and modest, and none of them cared for those pretending to be something they were not.

Cherie, with her fondness for playing pranks, thrived with this dude around. Bill thought her incapable of handling stock or knowing about ranching because she was a woman, but he was badly mistaken. She already knew more than Bill would ever know. He would not listen to those who were experienced, as he knew all the answers.

Bill complained that he was not accustomed to smoking tobacco from tins, which was the usual way for people in the Cariboo. "I can only smoke Bull Durham," claimed Bill. "You know, the kind that comes in little white sacks with the drawstring on top. Can't get it out west here!"

Cherie, her eyes dancing, replied, "Bill, I know where I can get you some Bull Durham," and all who knew this young woman knew that Bill would no doubt get his special tobacco.

Somewhere Cherie had obtained a sack of Bull Durham, and a few days before the next Cariboo party, she went to the barn and gathered some dried horse manure from the stall of her stud horse, Bourbon, and mixed it carefully with the small amount of tobacco left in the sack.

The Saturday night party was in full swing when Cherie stepped into the room carrying the Bull Durham tobacco that Bill had been missing since his arrival in the Cariboo. Cherie, hardly able to keep herself from cracking up with laughter, called, "Here, Bill, I brought you some Bull Durham." Bill was pleased. He pulled a brown cigarette paper from the pack pasted on the outside of the bag, and as he began rolling a cigarette, the old hands in the room could tell Bill had little experience with his own rollings. The so-called tobacco went over the sides of the thin paper and onto the floor. Joe Lebanc, a neighbour who was unaware of the prank in progress, took the cigarette and rolled it for him, and as Joe ran his tongue down the cigarette to seal it, he remarked, "This damn stuff tastes like horse shit." Bill took a few puffs but sensed something was not right, and finally Cherie could no longer contain herself and burst into laughter. "It should taste like horse shit, Bill," she said, with tears rolling down her cheeks, "It's Bull Bourbon." Needless to say the dude was embarrassed, and shortly after haying season he moved on to parts unknown, finding life too hard among the real cowboys.

Stampede and Buck Fever

Stampede time came, and John was keen to go. He had participated in rodeos, as they were called in California, since he was a youngster, and Williams Lake would be no exception. I had gone to several large rodeos with John during our courtship but they had never impressed me, because I didn't understand them. I didn't know good stock or good riders and to me it seemed like absolute suicide. But there was something about these competitors, who were usually quite young—they might suffer broken bones and wounded pride, but they didn't give up easily.

The ideal holiday for a ranch cowboy was to attend a rodeo and compete. John and his brother Bill had a string of bucking horses in California and had put on many shows of their own, so when John was asked to look after the calf chute at the Williams Lake Stampede, he jumped at the chance. There were no big names up here as we had seen in the States, but there were strong competitors such as the Bateses, Elkins, Twans, Tommy Desmond, Red Allison, Tom Denny, Lennie Derose and other locals. They had just as much fun as any famous cowboy.

Stampede time was like a big get-together. It was a time for fun, when the ranchers could forget their problems and meet with old friends and new, coming home with memories of good times and laughter. They would then settle down to hard work until it was time for the cattle sale, when once again the serious aspect of ranch life could be turned aside for a day or two of relaxation.

The stampede ground was a natural amphitheatre overlooking Williams Lake. The lake waters rippled away into Williams Creek and onward into deep chasms before reaching the nearby Fraser River. Williams Lake was only a village at this time, and it was crowded with people from all over the Chilcotin, where distance was measured by hours and not miles.

I was overwhelmed when I saw the panorama of around 150 Native camps spread over the gentle rolling hills of the stampede grounds. The people had come by saddle horse, team and wagons with whole families loaded into the back, some travelling from as far as two hundred miles away and travelling for several weeks. There were children by the dozen and dogs by the score. Horses were everywhere, some tied and others hobbled and turned loose to feed. Smoke from the many campfires wafted into the sky, and the children stuffed themselves with the goodies that were only available at Stampede.

Many of the adults were playing a popular gambling game called lahal, accompanied by a sing-song chant and drum-beating that

The Williams Lake Stampede grounds in 1952.

helped keep up morale and perhaps brought good luck. The game is played with two bones one or two inches long, one perfectly plain and one with a mark around the centre. It's a guessing game, and the bone handler's job is to fool the player as to which hand holds the marked bone. It was fascinating to watch them play. They were clever, and a great deal of money changed hands.

Stampedes and racing have always been a natural part of life in the Cariboo and Williams Lake. During the 1860s on the Pinchbeck farm, where the City of Williams Lake now stands, a race was held with a purse of over $100,000. The Native people would bring their horses to match them against the horses of the white man. Spectators would toss money into a hat as a prize for the cowboy who could stay on a wild bronc the longest. Those who were considered experts would come with horses that could not be ridden. As part of the competition, calves were brought from the local ranches to be roped and tied. Soon people started coming around to watch, and a new sport was sprouted.

Kicking off my first Stampede in Williams Lake was the parade. It was small, but it was a great part of the festivities. The local girl who had been chosen as Stampede Queen and her runner-up waved and smiled radiantly at the crowd as the vehicles passed by. Small children dashed from the board sidewalks to pick up the wrapped candies and gum thrown to the dirt road by people walking or riding in the parade.

The ridge behind the Stampede grounds was where the Indians set up camp. One year I counted 150 tents.

The Stampede was the big event of the year. People came from all around to compete, spectate or socialize.

The Stampede announcers were the well-known raconteur hotelman Benny Abbott and Henry Castillou, judge of the Cariboo Court, who was a colourful character. Each of these men had his own distinct style of announcing. Benny Abbott knew everyone and quipped into the microphone, "Coming out of chute number two, one of the Bates boys. Good rider. Poor shot." Judge Castillou had learned the ways of the Cariboo when he worked as a packer in the north as a young man. The bucking horses he announced coming out of the chute could well have been his own.

The bucking horse is a misfit in the horse world, a rebellious cuss who has perhaps soured under the saddle. With a rolling motion, unpredictable as lightning and powerful as dynamite, the defiant animal will pull every trick to dump his rider. The cowboy who enters this eight-second hair-raising twisting, jolting ride must have strength, experience and knowledge to keep aboard.

One event that the Williams Lake Stampede was noted for was the Mountain Race. It took some time for the contestants to wind their way to the selected starting spot up the mountain, but coming down was another story. The horses started high above the stampede grounds, sliding the first few yards on loose gravel and shale. Once they started, there could be no turning back; the riders had to run fast or go end over end down the steep mountainside. The horses would break into a thundering gallop, falling, scrambling to keep their footing, and come out onto the road (Highway 97, which at this time was just a dirt road), down over the next hill and onto a flat stretch of the grounds. Only a few of the riders would reach their destination, and the winning rider would often throw his reins, whooping and hollering, riding

Riding the broncs was a popular event.

tall in the saddle with the horse's body pulsating from the tremendous momentum achieved in the spectacular sport.

Stampede time was for merriment, and I preferred the night life to the stampede events. I had never experienced anything like it. There were people from every walk of life. Ranchers, bankers, dudes, businessmen—you name them and they were here. People were decked out in cowboy paraphernalia, most of which was purchased from Ben Richards's westernwear store, known as the Frontier Shop. Campfires dotted the hillside and sparks drifted up into the quiet heavens. A popular place for both whites and Natives on the stampede grounds was the notorious Squaw Hall. Here loud music penetrated the night air as the noisy celebrants whooped it up, and by morning nearly everyone ended up in the roofless outdoor pavilion surrounded by high board walls. It was one big gala party, and great fun!

Everyone was welcomed to any party throughout Stampede, for there were no strangers. Celebrations went on all night and when the sun rose, there were many celebrants still participating, while others had gone off to catch a few winks in anticipation of the coming day and another wild night. There were more people than there was space at the few beer parlours—as people left, others would come in from the long line-up outside the door.

One evening it was nearly closing time, and I could hardly hear myself think with the noisy celebrants. Our table was covered with beer glasses and in walked a long-time Cariboo resident, Harry Thompson. Harry was good-hearted, friendly and well known for his yarns. "Come on, you two! I want to give you and Mrs. John a ride since you're newcomers to the Cariboo and this is your first Stampede."

Calf roping is a popular event at the Stampede and is an example of the daily work of a cowboy.

John tugged at my arm. He was eager to go, but I was a bit reluctant. "What kind of ride?" I asked as I was pulled out the door, but I received no answer.

Just outside the Maple Leaf beer parlour was a wooden-wheeled farm-type wagon with low sideboards and a high seat across the front, pulled by a big team of horses. "Come on, folks, I'll give you a ride. See Williams Lake at night," barked Harry Thompson. It was almost a carnival-like atmosphere. People clambered aboard from the sidewalks and came rushing out of the beer parlour, and soon the wagon was filled.

The horses pulled into the traces as Harry slapped them on the rump with the ribbons. The wooden wheels crunched in the rock and gravel of the dirt road as the horses plodded around the centre of Williams Lake. It was indeed an enjoyable trip. The singing, whooping and hollering of the participants and the chill of the cool early summer's night were revitalizing. Eventually the rowdy group proceeded back to the Maple Leaf for another round.

Stampede time passed far too quickly, and it was soon time to return home. John drove the narrow, winding road, which only a few short months prior had brought us to our Cariboo home. We were weary but laughing as we bounced along recalling the events of the past three days and four wild nights at our first Williams Lake Stampede. At last we reached our peaceful, batten-board house. Yes, it was indeed great to be home.

The weather is master in the Cariboo, and when good weather prevailed every rancher took advantage of this time for haying. One morning John lingered over his coffee. As a rule he was up and gone early, as there were so many odd jobs to do before going to the hayfield. There were sickles to be sharpened, guards to be replaced and other repairs to be made to the horse-drawn equipment.

"What's keeping you inside this morning?" I asked as he pushed his mug toward me for a refill.

"This haying weather won't last too much longer," he replied. "The wind has changed and according to CBC Radio, a storm is approaching the coast. Doris, I need an extra hand today. Chip has his work cut out for the day and I have so many things to do, I hardly know where to start. Have to cut some poles for the overshot stacker, as the hay is nearly ready to stack." He paused. "I was wondering if after you finished your housework you would do some raking for me. I would like you to take the team and rake the hay by Goose Lake. There is a small area of meadow grass there. It's not bad hay if it's put up properly. Sure beats snowballs at any rate."

I was astounded—I knew nothing about haying. But deep inside I felt a gnawing determination. It would be a challenge.

"Don't worry," John said. "I will take the team and the horse rake up to the hayfield and when you get there I'll start you out. It's easy, and you have handled Chub and Dan a few times now so you won't be too nervous. They're a real gentle team."

"I will try to be there by ten o'clock. I'll have to fix something for our lunches and have our dinner fairly well prepared for tonight," I replied as I finished sweeping the kitchen floor.

John grabbed his well-worn cowboy hat and placed a hurried kiss on my cheek. "Knew I could count on you. I'll see you later."

I whipped around the house with enthusiasm. I might be a dude, but one thing was for sure, I was not afraid of work.

A few minutes before ten o'clock I brought the Chevrolet pickup to a halt at the edge of the hayfield. "Right on time. That's the kind of help I like," said John wiping his brow with a not-too-clean handkerchief. "Just finished working the overshot stacker. Took longer to fix it than I thought." He untied the waiting team, fastening up the neck yoke and hooking the traces to the nearby horse rake.

I felt a twinge of fear as I looked at the ten-foot-wide, iron-wheeled dump rake with the long metal teeth under the precarious-looking hard seat. My thoughts flew back to my school days. I had never excelled in sports, as I was not the athletic type, and now here I was being asked to mount this hulking, hazardous piece of equipment. I felt the tears well up, but luckily I was able to control them. It seemed I had shed more tears in these past few months than I had in my whole lifetime.

John gave me explicit directions and especially warned me always to hang onto the lines. I was quivering as I climbed onto the seat. John showed me how to trip the rake with the foot lever once the long teeth were filled with hay. Approximately every ten feet I was to trip the lever, leaving each pile in a straight, even row, to be picked up later by the buck rake and stacked.

The sky showed little sign of the predicted storm, and with each round I gained more confidence. After hastily eating lunch, I continued dumping the hay in neat windrows until suddenly away went the horses, running faster and faster, kicking, tossing and wildly shaking their heads. I was on the seat of the iron-wheeled monstrosity, going faster and faster. I had never been so frightened! What had happened to this so-called gentle team? Should I jump off? I was remembering the long tines of the hay rake and my poor athletic skills when suddenly a wasp with bright yellow markings attacked me, and then another and another... I soon realized what had caused the disruption. I braced my feet even harder against the iron frame of the rake and the horses slowly came to a stop. Shaking uncontrollably I dismounted, very upset, not so much from the wasp stings but from my wild ride. John came rushing over, but despite his efforts to console me, I went stomping to the pickup in tears. This could only happen to a greenhorn, I thought.

After composing myself and getting a few more words of comfort from John, I started for home. I decided I would stop at Cripps', so I pulled the pickup to a halt beside their welcoming ranch house. I glanced in the mirror to see if anyone could tell I had been crying; I didn't want people to know I'd had another humiliating experience.

Cherie was at home. "Come in, come in. I thought you were

raking hay today," she said as she handed me a steaming mug of coffee.

I sank down into my chair. "Oh, yes, I have." I changed the conversation. Everyone laughed at inexperienced ranchers and there was no way I would let Cherie know what had happened. She was such a capable hand with horses as well as cattle, and she would find this incident hilarious.

"I'm going riding tomorrow," Cherie said. "I want to ride to Prairie Chicken and see how the cattle are doing. Everyone is so busy haying and someone should check the cattle on the range. Would you like to go? Perhaps you could ride Bucky. We can take along a lunch, as we will be gone all day."

"I would like to go, and I'm sure John won't need me to rake hay tomorrow," I said, not admitting I had no intention of getting involved with any more horse rakes or wasps. After we had made our plans for the next day, I left in time to prepare the evening meal. No more mention was made of the day's incident.

Next morning I was excited about going to the range, and as breakfast cooked I busily fixed the lunches for the day. Chip had caught and saddled Bucky when he fed and watered Chub and Dan, and both horses had received their ration of oats and hay in preparation for their day's work.

I had only ridden Bucky a few times and just for short rides. I was excited to be making such a nice long ride. A smirk crossed John's face as I expressed my eagerness, and little did I know what this smirk meant.

John cautioned me about the do's and don'ts of horsemanship, although Bucky, the bay-blaze-faced horse we had acquired with the ranch, was absolutely foolproof. Several small children had been entrusted with this gentle horse. If you fell off, all Bucky would do was immediately stop dead still and look around as you picked yourself up off the ground. A horse of this type was invaluable to the inexperienced rider, and difficult to acquire, as I was to learn in later years.

Cherie's spirited horse, Bourbon, pranced along while Bucky

plodded along behind with his inexperienced rider, nipping at the tall, lush grasses, knowing he was in full command. Cherie's life revolved around ranching and she knew the livestock and could ride with the best cowboys. This young, energetic, playful woman was very versatile. She could fit in with any type of person or situation, equally at home amidst the blood, manure and smoke of branding and in the plush homes of the upper crust. Cherie's years at boarding school had given her the poise to behave as a dignified young lady when the occasion called for it.

When we reached Marguerite Lake, the aggressive bald eagles screamed and circled as we approached their territory. Cherie pointed skyward. "These bald eagles always nest here at Eagle Point. Been here since the first year I ever rode up here. Do you see the two eaglets looking over the top of their nest? Looks like they are about ready to take flight."

As we rode onward, the waters of the placid Marguerite Lake glistened under the summer sun. Cherie suddenly rode quickly off the road into a nearby clump of dark green shrub-like bushes. Dismounting and turning her back to me, Cherie called. "Come quick and try these." She pretended to be stuffing herself with berries. "Try them, they are so good!" She placed several in my outstretched palm. I put the bright, orange-red translucent berries into my mouth and hungrily bit down. My mouth began to pucker with a horrible, bitter taste as Cherie doubled over with laughter. I realized then she had played one of her many pranks on this unsuspecting dude. Amid outbursts of laughter, Cherie explained that they were soapberries. "Soapolallie" was the Native name for these berries, which made a soapy froth if you rubbed them between your hands. She knelt down and demonstrated. The Native people made "whooshu," or "Indian ice cream" with them, she said. "It's not too bad," she chuckled, as I continued to spit the harsh, acrid taste from my mouth.

"Ice cream! How could anyone make ice cream from these berries?" I said. "They're terrible."

We all learned to ride on a quiet horse called Bucky. If you fell off he would stand still until you could get back on. Later I graduated to Beauty (shown here). She was also a gentle horse to ride.

"When I was a little girl," Cherie replied, "I used to go to Alkali Lake Ranch and stay with my grandfather, Wynn Johnson, who owned the ranch. On the nearby reserve there was a very old Indian woman who often made ice cream. She would crush these berries, add sugar and beat until they were frothy. This elder claimed these berries were like a tonic." Cherie mounted her horse with ease, and Bucky stood patiently while his rider struggled into the saddle, still spitting from the taste of the soapolallie berries.

The rest of the day was uneventful, and we stopped only to eat our lunch. Cherie told me about the pranks she had played on other unsuspecting people when she was younger. She knew the cattle range as well as anyone, and she knew the cattle and what to look for. To those who enjoy riding and are experienced, riding is relaxing, but being inexperienced I was glad when Cherie announced it was time to start home. After a while I doubted I would be able to make it back, finally realizing what the smirk on John's face had meant that morning. I was exhausted that night, turning in immediately after an easily cooked dinner of bacon and eggs.

Summer passed quickly, but it seemed as if it had taken weeks and weeks to finish haying. There were delays caused by the rains, which often plagued the Cariboo, but when one looked at the succulent green growth and the vast lakes and streams, one had to realize that the bitter must be taken with the sweet. These and other delays just naturally went with ranch life.

The barley crop John had planted earlier in the year on the newly cleared ground was now turning a golden colour. The crop was better than four feet tall and heavily laden with plump kernels of grain. Barley had not been grown in this area before so it was pleasing to see John's efforts producing such an excellent crop. A touch of fall was in the air, the mornings were getting cool and the autumn colours were showing themselves amid the dark green of the spruce and fir forests in the distance.

"I want to make a deal with you," said John one morning. He put his arm around my shoulders as I stood over the fresh ranch eggs cooking in the heavy iron skillet.

"What now? Is this something for a dude?" I asked pleasantly.

"I must get the heavy crop of barley cut," he said. "There are so many things to do and not enough time to get it all accomplished. Have to fence the stackyards, gather the cattle, cut our winter wood plus a million and one small jobs. I want to get some hunting in."

"Come on, let's have your deal," I said. "I have heard nothing aside from all the work you have to do."

John's eyes twinkled. "I thought maybe I could get you to help me harvest the grain, and when we get finished, we could go on a camping trip for a few days. We could take some pack horses and go north of Prairie Chicken. Should be really good hunting out there along Long Lake."

"Camping?" I replied sharply. "I'm sure the camping part would be worse than helping with the grain. You know I hate camping—it's so dirty!"

"Really?" said John. "You told me once you didn't like camping, but I didn't realize you were serious."

"When I was a little girl, six or seven years old, my parents took me and my brother camping in the Modocs in northern California to go deer hunting," I said. "It was near Quaken Asp Springs, and all I can remember is I hated every minute of it. It was dusty, dry and hot and we had to haul water to our camp from a spring several miles away. I can't remember much except there was nothing to do out there in the lava beds. There were rattlesnakes, dust and more dust. That quelled my desire to ever go camping again."

The disappointment showed in John's eyes, for he loved to hunt and camp.

"Regardless of whether we go camping or not, I need you to help me. You wouldn't mind helping, would you?" John asked. "I have to repair the canvasses and check the rollers on the old binder so I can start binding the grain next Monday, providing the weather holds." I had never seen a binder but agreed to help whenever the time came. But as far as the camping trip, I would have to do considerable thinking about that.

It was a warm Indian summer day, and the hazy atmosphere dimmed the brilliance of the fall colours of the deciduous trees. I could hear the Ford tractor as I finished the morning dishes. Soon John appeared. "Your chariot awaits you. Are you ready?" he asked, grabbing a freshly baked cookie.

I poured him some coffee to have while I changed my clothes. "Be just a minute," I said.

Near the ranch house just outside the fence sat the tractor, and behind it was attached an ancient-looking piece of machinery. The binder was far more formidable to my eye than the horse rake. Had I made another stupid mistake?

"You drive the tractor until we get to the field and I will stand back here on the draw bar and open the gates," said John as he stepped on the tractor.

The old, horse-drawn binder had been cut down and the long tongue had been replaced with a snub tongue to be pulled behind a tractor instead of a team of horses. It had a high revolving reel and what they called a platform in which the canvasses rode, and yes, another precarious, high-placed seat. When we reached the field I realized I would be riding on the binder and not driving the tractor. What a disappointment!

John began to tell me what I had to do, saying that since it was newly worked ground, I had to be very careful of the rocks and sticks, despite the tons we had already picked. I would also have to watch very closely and raise and lower the reel. There were levers and handles and what have you, and they all seemed so complicated. My brain was crammed with instructions as I stepped up on the binder.

Away we went, with John driving the tractor, as he knew more about the field and how to avoid serious equipment damage. Well, let me tell you, the horse-drawn rake was nothing compared to this piece of equipment! The ground was rough, and occasionally one wheel would ride up onto a hidden stump or rock we had missed in the initial ground preparation. It was a tough job to stay balanced while raising the reel, looking for the rock or stump, tripping the sheaves, and watching the string supply that bound the grain together. I became confused with my directions, as all my concentration was devoted to just staying on the binder. I lowered the reel instead of raising it, and from there it was one thing after another. I neglected to see a rock, which nearly caused me to fall off. John had to stop several times to give me further instructions and words of encouragement. As we continued round and round the field, I became more and more frustrated. It was a horrendous experience! But by the time the day was over I had learned the basics of a binder and was able to join John in laughter. To this day it is a memorable event in my life.

After the binding came the stooking of the grain sheaves, which consisted of standing each shock on end in groups of six enabling the air to penetrate through them. It was most important the sheaves be completely dry for thrashing later on. I volunteered to stook the grain, another task that was much bigger than I anticipated. But at least I could have my feet on the ground where I felt much more secure, and I didn't mind walking. Stooking didn't require any talent and your compensation came with the final results as you looked out over the field to see the stooks row on row. When one project was finished it was time to start something else. The days grew progressively shorter, each day bringing winter closer. The cattle had to be gathered and brought off the range, which meant considerable riding for all involved. John loved this part of ranching, and looked forward to riding over the range and perhaps seeing one of those big bucks he had heard stories of.

After gathering most of the cattle, it was time to get them ready to sell at the Williams Lake stockyard. This meant another big day or two. John's patience was easily taxed when working with the cattle, more than any other time. He would often get me to help when there was no one else available. I was certainly no help on horseback, and really not much better doing the groundwork. "If you look at a cow, you can nearly always tell what they will do next," John would say. But although I looked, I never related to the cows. They never gave me any messages except when it was time to run from some critter on the prod. I did not understand their thinking. "What are you doing on that side of the gate? The cattle can see you standing there and they will never go through," John called once. Just when I thought there was some improvement in my cow sense, I would either crowd the cattle too fast or not fast enough, causing them to break back or scatter in different directions. When cutting out steers from heifers while trying to determine their sex, several head would shoot by me.

John was a quiet man, never making unkind remarks, but I always knew if I was doing the right thing or not. Sitting astride his saddle horse, he would shake his head and say, "Hard to work cattle with anyone who doesn't know stock." There was still so much for me to learn. He was a natural-born stockman, and he had always lived on a ranch. I often thought he must think like one of those animals, always seeming to anticipate their every move.

John rode his favourite horse, Banjo, a docile animal except when ridden into a herd of cattle. Banjo's erect ears bent forward as he swayed first one way and then the other, untouched by the reins. This lightning-quick gelding came to life among cattle, and cutting them from one corral to another was indeed a pleasure if one had a good horse. John knew what he wanted to sell and what he had to sell to meet our financial obligations. The cows that were poor producers or failed to raise calves, and the bulls that came home lame, definitely had to be sold.

It could be a depressing time of year, with current cattle prices usually a deciding factor. There were other circumstances controlling what cattle you could keep as well. Sometimes the cattle buyers wanted just the opposite of what you had to sell. The winter hay supply was of utmost importance, although no one could predict the cold or the length of the feeding period, and we had to make a realistic estimation.

After selecting the cattle to sell, John would make arrangements to ship them to the sale. The cattle sales were held at Williams Lake, which was known as the cattle capital of British Columbia. At that time as many as twenty thousand head of cattle were shipped through the sale. To the south and west of the small village were some of the province's largest cattle ranches, some well over 100,000 acres. It was a good time for the ranchers to meet, but often a disappointing time, depending upon the current cattle market. The rancher received the money from his cattle sales only once a year, and he had to make enough money to cover his operating costs until the following year. This was certainly new to me, as I was used to a monthly paycheque.

The sales yard at Williams Lake was much different for John than those in California. There were three cattle sales a year here, compared to the many sales he was accustomed to. The cattle were weighed off the truck as they arrived, plus a three-percent pencil shrink, and sold in carload lots. John shuddered at the thought of the losses taken by cowmen through these methods of selling. He was more concerned about shrinkage than price per pound. The sales ring and pens were all out in the open, and the only parts under cover were the bleachers, the kitchen and the auctioneer's box. In late fall the raw, cold winds whistled through the bleachers, often making the wait unbearable, and calling for the occasional swig from your neighbour's jug (known as anti-freeze) stashed in his car. Drinking in a public place was a violation of the law, a law that we were unfamiliar with in California.

When we got back to the ranch, the cows bawled constantly and walked aimlessly for three days and three nights searching for their calves, which were now on the way to their new homes. It was disheartening for me to watch them; how could they understand? Eventually the cows gave up and all was quiet.

Autumn is many things to many people, with the coloured leaves a magnificent epitaph to summer. The season of harvest is for meditation and a time for being thankful. It is a glorious, serene time, with each sunny day heaped with rewards for another year. It is the gold of the distant hills and the shimmering waters of Big Lake stirred by a restless, uncertain wind and the sigh of the trees as they prepare themselves for yet another winter. It is the honk of the goose fleeing the north for an easier climate and the coyote's snout pointed to the harvest moon as it utters its forlorn-sounding howl. Autumn is the season for tidying up and settling in for the approaching long, cold winter.

The rancher has fences to repair, equipment to store away, horses to be shod with ice shoes, bobsleighs to be repaired and the cattle to be counted and separated according to category for the long feeding period.

"Have you thought about the camping trip I promised I would take you on?" asked John as he slid into his easy chair one evening. "I would sure like to show you camping in British Columbia. I will help get our supplies together." John tried hard to keep me from getting homesick by keeping me interested in ranch life and hunting. A successful marriage meant consideration for one another, and it could not be one-sided. The California camping trip was years ago, I thought. At least I should go and give it a fair trial.

"Yes, John," I replied, "I have given this camping trip careful thought and I have decided I'll go camping providing the offer to help get the necessities ready stands. I have never gone on a pack trip. I've never seen a pack horse other than in pictures."

John laughed. "Yes, it will be different, but I promise if this weather holds out you will have a real good time." He said I might get a chance to shoot the .30-30 Winchester rifle he had given me before we were married. "We can take along your .22 Winchester pump for grouse, and maybe even do a little target practice." John had given me these two guns in hopes I would take to hunting. I had some experience with guns, mostly the safety aspect, but had never done any hunting on my own, so I had lots to learn.

The golden cottonwoods quivered in the chilly fall breeze as our saddle horses walked briskly along, each of us leading a pack horse loaded with supplies. The packs consisted mostly of food, a tent, a few extra clothes and our bedrolls. John had chosen the white saddle horse for me, called Kid. He was another foolproof horse we had acquired with the ranch, and he had a little more speed than Bucky. John showed me how to lead the pack horse, making sure not to get the horse's lead rope underneath the tail of my saddle horse. "Horses are not all gentle," he warned me. From my saddle hung a scabbard equipped with my new .30-30 rifle.

Willow grouse spooked our horses, flying from the heavily laden wild rose bush where they had been gorging on the brilliant red rose-

John was a master at setting up camp. He would make us a mattress from the cedar and fir boughs, which was surprisingly comfortable.

hips. We arrived at our camping spot in plenty of time to get our tent set up before darkness fell. It was a beautiful spot, with the now over-ripe grasses waving in the slight breeze surrounded by the grove of cottonwood overlooking the waters of Long Lake.

John busied himself cutting boughs from the nearby firs, placing them inside our tent as a mattress for our bedrolls. They were comfortable if properly placed. I walked down to the shore of Long Lake with the sun slowly sinking in the west, leaving its last rays of rose and gold on the high points of the surrounding hills. A loud, sharp sound broke the silence, although I saw nothing that could have made the noise. I stood still and watched. Could I have imagined it? There were no roads and it was miles from the nearest house.

The gorgeous sunset was flaming streams of colour against the last wisps of clouds as I returned to camp, unable to solve the mystery of the loud noise. John had completed setting up camp and brought a pail of water from the nearby creek. "What did you see?" he asked as he sliced the newly pared crisp potatoes into the heavy cast-iron skillet.

"It's beautiful down there, just like a park. It is so peaceful and quiet. I just can't believe the difference compared to California. I'm sure I heard a loud sharp sound, almost like a shot. Surely there can't be anyone around out here, can there? I didn't see anything."

John chuckled. "Perhaps what you heard was the slap of the beaver's tail, warning other beavers that danger is imminent. The beaver dives with a loud slap of his tail, and that's usually followed by a series of slaps from other beavers in the vicinity and then they all disappear. Did you notice the beaver lodge as we rode along the lake? Next time we'll stop so you can have a look."

Soon the potatoes had fried to a golden brown, along with bacon and eggs, which had never tasted so good. Something told me I was going to like camping. Perhaps I had been missing plenty.

Darkness fell, and the sparks of the campfire danced merrily into the star-filled universe. We rested back against our saddles and listened to the tinkling bells of our horses as they grazed. We could also hear the nicker of the horse left tied up should the loose horses decide they were homesick and leave us here in the wilderness.

It was not cold as we sat around the campfire. We drank numerous cups of coffee from the billycan, which John had placed on a forked stick hovering above the red coals of the campfire. He told me stories of the many camping trips he had gone on since he was a small boy. Each fall after haying, he used to go to the mountains where they ranged their cattle in northern California. They would ride and hunt and tell big buck stories around the campfires. It was like a vacation.

John rose slowly to his feet, stretched and yawned. "I think it's time to hit the sack. Tomorrow we will be busy packing your deer in," he joked.

With the embers of the campfire fast dying, we crawled into our bedrolls. Soon I could hear the deep breathing of my husband telling me he was already asleep. Try as I might, I could not sleep. It was just too exciting. The incense of the cut fir boughs beneath me filled my nostrils, and frequently a whiff of smoke would drift in from the campfire outside. From the tent door I could see the luminous band of the Milky Way with its innumerable stars. In the distance I could hear the honk of the most beautiful geese of all, the Canada geese, winging their way southward from their northern nesting grounds. Realizing daybreak would soon come, I snuggled deeper into my cozy bedroll. At last sleep came.

I was awakened by John's insistent shaking. "Wake up, wake up, I hear the grunt of a bull moose," he said. "It's somewhere close to the lake. Listen, hear him?" Sleepily I raised my head, and in the distance I could hear the call of the amorous bull searching for a mate. Finally all was still. "Maybe we'll see him tomorrow," said John. He turned over and was soon sound asleep.

Wanting to get started early, he rolled out before daybreak and soon had the campfire crackling and snapping. The smell of coffee brought me from the tent. To the east the horizon showed it was almost dawn.

After a breakfast of bacon and eggs, and coffee made in the billycan, we prepared to catch our horses. We gave them their ration of grain, then saddled them, leaving the pack horses tied at camp, not wanting them to follow us or head homeward. With our guns in our scabbards, we quietly wound our way northward along the shore of Long Lake and into the rolling hills.

Some time had elapsed since we left camp, and soon I started to think about the extra slice of bacon we had left in the skillet. It seemed I could smell the aroma of coffee; a cup right now would really hit the spot. The outdoors inspires an appetite and makes one especially hungry.

Suddenly I was brought out of my daydream by the crack of my husband's .300 Savage. Below me, at the edge of the fir thicket, I spotted him sharpening his pocketknife on the whetstone he always carried with him. On the ground lay a fat, slick, four-point mule deer.

"We will have to go back to camp and get the pack horses," said John as he lay the heart and liver on the nearby low green mat of kinnikinnick.

"Sure sounds good to me," I replied.

A worried frown flashed over John's handsome face. "What's the matter?" he said. "Don't you like it out here?"

I began to laugh. "Of course, I'm really enjoying this trip, but I'm starved."

"I guess you like food cooked over the campfire. There is nothing like food prepared in the great outdoors, as far as I am concerned," John replied as he continued dressing the deer. "It won't take me much longer. We won't skin it out until we get back to camp. The hide will help to keep the meat clean. Look at the fat on this fellow, so much fatter than the deer we get in California."

The branches of the mountain alder, with their small brown cones, seemed to reach out and greet us with a slap as the horses moved along quickly, nipping at the abundant feed. As we approached our camp, the nicker of the pack horses greeted us.

Then we came within sight of Long Lake, so appropriately named, and a flock of quacking mallards rose into the air from behind the dense jungle of flat-leaved common cattails. The dark brown female spongy spikes were ready to break open and spread their cottony white pollen grains to the four winds. The ducks soon vanished from view. Had this beautiful lake, so peaceful and serene, been their home for the summer, or only a feeding stopover on their annual southward journey?

The sun was high in the sky, indicating it was time for us and our horses to have something to eat. John busied himself feeding each horse its share of oats and releasing the horses that had been tied, giving them an opportunity to graze while we had lunch.

"We will have a quick lunch," said John, "and then take our saddle horses and one of the pack horses, along with plenty of extra rope, and pack the deer back to camp. We must get the deer back as soon as possible so we can get it skinned before dark." He pulled his pocketknife from his Levis and crouched before the charred embers of our morning's campfire. "A few sparks left. I'll whittle some shavings of kindling for the fire, and perhaps it will take off. I believe we could use a cup of coffee and a sandwich. Might taste pretty good along with some of those homemade cookies." He was hoping I would take a hint and prepare a sandwich or two, but he needn't worry, as I was starving too! Soon the contents of the billycan had reached the boiling point and the smell of the dark, rich coffee told us the brew was ready.

John finished his lunch quickly and leaned back against a nearby tree. "There is nothing as flavourful as campfire coffee," he remarked. "Guess we had better get back to looking after our deer." He tightened the cinches on our grazing saddle horses and threw the pack saddle on the horse he had chosen to take, tying the remaining pack horse to a nearby spruce tree.

John, leading the pack horse, was well ahead of me as I poked along behind. falling back farther and farther as Kid took advantage of his rider by stopping and having a mouthful of feed at his own convenience. Experienced riders did not allow their horses to eat as they travelled along—it was better to feed them well before leaving and again upon return.

Underneath the upturned roots of a fallen spruce tree sat the nearly snow-white varying hare. I was so close I could see the small animal trembling with fear. His long ears were laid back on his neck and shoulders and the large dark eyes stared as he sat prepared to spring should I come any closer.

This animal's "snowshoes" have given it another name, "snowshoe hare." The long toes spread wide and the soles of the big feet are covered with coarse hair, which is longer in winter than in summer. The snowshoes prevent it from slipping on icy crusts and hold the rabbit up in the snow.

Finally the hare could not stand my presence any longer and burst out of a sitting position into a dead run, dodging bewilderingly at full speed. His long hind legs pushed him over the ground at an amazing speed.

John was off his horse and preparing the deer to be packed out when I caught up with him. Although the pack horse was certainly not new at packing, he was trembling and snorting, not appreciating the smell of fresh blood from the dead deer. "We will tie our horses and lead the pack horse closer in to load him," said John. "We will let him stand a few minutes before we load while I get everything squared around." Taking the extra rope, he got ready to lash the animal on the pack saddle designed to support the load. I knew nothing about packing, and it was interesting to watch John place each rope in its proper position.

Back at camp, John cut a small pole, roping it between two closely spaced spruce trees, providing a place to hang the deer for skinning and to cool until we were ready to head back to the ranch.

John tended the horses, getting them their grain and rotating them for the fast approaching night, and I went about getting the evening meal. Fortunately, I soon had a supper that would satisfy the hungriest of hunters. I was amazed at how few dishes I used here in the camp—to make the same meal at home, it seemed I had every dish in the house dirty. John busied himself getting wood and water for the camp.

The sun sank behind the hovering hills with another magnificent Cariboo sunset. I was tired from riding, but found sitting around the campfire relaxing, the hanging billycan steaming with hot coffee. What more could a person wish for? I was lucky to see these gorgeous pristine surroundings. The barest sliver of a crescent moon climbed slowly over the surrounding hills. The night was dark, and the sky a glorious array of stars. The air was cool, and fingers of flame in the campfire lapped savagely at the dry firewood. Out of the hushed silence drifted the yap of the red fox, perhaps in search of an unsuspecting mouse, as he scooted between grass clumps.

"It's getting late," John said. "Tomorrow I will send you to a place where you can find the trophy buck. I noticed plenty of deer sign today. Just remember, if you become turned around, Kid will bring you back to camp." He laughed. "Don't you do like this guide Shelly Nicol told me about." Shelly was a long-time guide and neighbour with a great sense of humour. "If I remember right, it was one of his own hunters. The guide and his American hunter were out hunting and the guide knew a good place to send his hunter. After fully explaining all the details to the hunter, as an extra precaution he told his hunter, 'If you get lost, just get off your horse, wait a few minutes, give him his head when he starts out and he will take you back to camp'." As the story goes, it wasn't long before the American hunter figured he was lost in the wilderness. He dismounted his horse as instructed, and removed the bridle, and with that the horse took off, leaving the hunter holding only the bridle. The hunter learned a lesson, and had to spend the night out, to be found the next day by his anxious guide. "If you get off your horse," John went on, "wait a few minutes but don't take off the bridle, always hang on to those reins. When you start out again hold the reins loosely in your hands and let the horse lead the way. The horse will take you back to camp, the shortest and quickest way, for these animals have a wonderful sense of direction. Strange thing about horses." He stared into the campfire. "They get homesick, and lots of times in the spring will return to their place of birth, which may be several hundred miles away." He paused. "Guess we've talked long enough. Time to get to bed. Tomorrow will be a big day."

John was a great horseman and a patient teacher.

Coming from behind me I could hear the branches of the forest rustling with a slight tremor of rising wind. "I could sit here all night and enjoy the peace and quiet, but I know how tired I would be in the morning," I said. "Horseback riding is not relaxing for me like it is for you. It's hard!" John ducked into the tent with me close on his heels. Soon we were both fast asleep.

I awoke as rays of light poured from the horizon, first red, then orange and then shining gold. Outside the tent I could hear sizzling bacon as John prepared breakfast. I dressed quickly. "About time you're getting up," said John, smiling, as I emerged from the tent. I felt sheepish as I washed my face in the pan of warm water he had prepared for me. He was such a thoughtful person and I knew how hard he worked in his quiet way to help me during the difficult transition period.

I heaped my plate with crisp brown fried potatoes, along with bacon and eggs. John had even made me toast, on a forked stick over the campfire. It was delicious, spread lavishly with my favourite wild strawberry jam that I had canned earlier in the season.

John had an amused expression on his face, and finally he could no longer contain himself. "Sorry you don't like camping. It's pretty dirty, you know. I guess mostly you don't like the food." I looked at my plate, realizing I had taken very substantial helpings. I knew then I was in for plenty of teasing and soon we were both laughing.

Finally, after many cups of coffee, John rose to his feet. "Better get ready to go. I have fed and saddled the horses already. Today I hope you can get a chance to use your .30-30. There was lots of deer sign over toward White Stone Lake." Besides that, John hoped to move at least a few of our cattle into the area during the next summer. There was plenty of feed and he wanted to get to know that part of the range better. "I was only in this area once. When I went over the range with Jimmy Weber before we bought the ranch."

He fastened his chaps as he continued. "If time permits I would like to ride over to Canyon Lake and around Camille Lake. It's nice country but I was only there a couple of times when gathering the cattle last month. Nice to be able to take this camping trip, so I can see the range and to take full advantage of its potential. Looked as though it might be good deer and moose country, although we're not hunting moose now."

We mounted our horses and were soon on our way, toward the lower end of Long Lake. John pointed toward a small object swimming in our direction and placed his finger over his lips, warning me to be quiet.

I could see it was an animal. My horse, Kid, stepped forward to reach a clump of grass, and with the snap of a small twig we heard a loud slap of water. It was the sound I had heard the first night out, a warning given by the beaver when it sensed danger. "We won't see that beaver again," said John. "See that pile of sticks? That's a beaver house. Notice to the left there are those willows and cottonwoods? That is where he's cutting trees for his winter food supply. Let's ride up there and I will show you." I could not believe the chips left at the base of the trees made with the beaver's sharp incisors. It looked as if they had been made with an axe, and certainly larger chips than the ones I could make with an axe. "You remember the pictures of the early fur traders with those flat, round caps and those tall cylindrical hats for men you see so often these days?" John continued as we rode on. "Those hats are made from beaver fur. Beaver pelts were very valuable for the early fur traders."

The area was absolutely gorgeous, and it seemed no one had set foot here for years. There were no beer cans, no candy or gum wrappers. The only sounds were the gossip of the squirrels and the occasional whir of the wings of the grouse taking flight as we invaded their domain.

"We will separate here," said John, pointing to a nearby ridge. "I'll meet you over at the lower end. Looks like an ideal spot to find a nice buck. Remember what to do if you get lost; be sure and tie your horse if you get off to shoot. Good luck," he called as I rode away. I was excited thinking about the prospect of my first deer. Little did I know there was much to learn about hunting. Oh yes, I had heard many stories by this time, but never could they compare with the hunting stories of my own in the years to come.

Adrenalin raced through my veins. I set off eagerly, and after nearly an hour's ride, there before me was a buck that would stir the blood of any trophy hunter. Looking straight at me in wide-eyed vigilance, supporting tremendous antlers, was the deer I had dreamed of seeing. Experienced hunters had told me about "buck fever," a nervous excitement when a hunter spots game, and now I was apparently suffering from this malady. My heart pounding, I dismounted quickly, tying my horse to the nearest cottonwood. My fingers became all thumbs as I pulled my .30-30 Winchester from its scabbard, taking rest against a nearby tree. I was shaking from head to toe. Just as I was ready to pull the trigger, I thought about my horse—had I tied him securely as John had instructed? I was in the wilderness, far from home and the surroundings I knew. John had cautioned me many times, so perhaps I should check. I sneaked quietly back to my horse. The tall brown grasses brushed against my heavy leather chaps. When I turned back, the buck had disappeared, almost phantom-like. I was very disappointed. I would have given anything to show off this trophy animal to John.

We saw twenty-one deer during one day of the camping trip, but none could compare with the buck I had held within my sight. John was an excellent shot and easily could have killed other deer, but he had already bagged his deer and was only interested in me trying my luck. When we returned to camp in the late afternoon after a long ride and much excitement, I was exhausted.

John sensed my disappointment. "I will get the fire going and make a pot of coffee. Maybe even show you how to make some bannock. I used to make a lot in the hunting and cow camps in California." I tried not to think about my failed expectations and instead thought about the next time. As time went on, I would suffer badly from buck fever. I wondered if I would ever get over this nervous reaction, but I found some consolation knowing the most experienced hunters often suffered from it as well.

John took care of the horses while the blazing fire died to a bed of coals for cooking. He hustled around preparing the evening meal, making a biscuit-like batter and pouring it into an oiled frying pan with sloping sides enabling him to flip it upside down after browning on one side. I held my breath as he grasped the long handle of the frying pan in both hands and flipped the biscuit into the air. Just like a professional, down it came with the golden brown side on top, and soon the bottom side of the two-inch bannock was also golden brown. It was delicious. "If you don't have any butter," said John, breaking off a good-sized chunk of the hot bread, "you can put bacon drippings on it along with some sugar, just like a dessert."

Although I was enjoying my evening meal, my thoughts kept going back to the buck. I wished I had taken a chance on my horse being tied securely, which it had been. After the dishes and the evening camp chores were done, we again sat around the campfire and I retold my buck story, and each time I told it, I wished I had handled the situation differently.

"One thing, Doris, " John said. "You must never waste any time when you see one of those big bucks. They never achieved trophy size by being foolish. Don't feel too bad, you will learn."

John glanced at his watch. "It's getting late and I guess you are anxious to get home in the morning. We are running short of food and we must get the deer home before it spoils. I am against killing any kind of game and not taking care of it. The motto in my home when I was growing up was 'Waste not, want not.' Hunting is a great sport and you will find it is a battle of wits between man and beast."

The stars in the clear night sky overlooked the slowly dying campfire. I felt a twinge of sadness as I thought about leaving camp. I had to admit it had been a tremendous experience, far different than camping in the lava beds of northern California. I had been a little girl then, and now that I was a mature woman, my thinking had changed.

John had already retired to the tent. Nothing stirred; all I could hear was the sound of darkness. I sat quietly mulling over my experiences of the past few days.

The chilly night air crept around my shoulders, making me shiver. I snapped back to reality. Yes, it was getting late, and tomorrow we would be packing up for our return to the home ranch. As I slid into my sleeping bag next to John, he mumbled sleepily, "Did you finally decide to come to bed? Guess you are still thinking about the big buck."

"I will never forget the big buck as long as I live," I said, "and the points on those antlers." I was answered by stillness and deep breathing, which told me John had perhaps heard enough about my buck. He was sound asleep.

When I awoke the next morning, the landscape shone. John was busy breaking camp in preparation for our homeward trip. The horses had to be fed, saddled and packed with the deer and remaining camp gear. John prepared a swift and simple breakfast. Soon, with our bedrolls and tent dismantled, we packed up and left the impressive peace and quiet of Long Lake.

Back home, John had started preparing for winter. This was Canada, and winter could strike at any time. "It's November and for sure the snow cannot hold off much longer," he said. "It seems I just cannot get around to all the things I have to do before the snow flies." He dropped into his easy chair, exhausted.

"I have to get as much land as I can into production, which means operating the bulldozer more than I have. We need more hay land if we are to increase our cattle herd, and time is important. Doing the bulldozer work is just the beginning. You already know about those roots and rocks!" He said that Al Zirnhelt, who lived in Beaver Valley, was capable with equipment and also a good mechanic. John seemed to be looking for ways to justify the extra expense of another man. "More hay means more cattle and more income. Wages are so much cheaper here than in California, and I can probably hire Al for about a dollar an hour. I would much rather be looking after the ranching part. Maybe I should send word for him to come and see me if he is interested in working."

News travels fast, and within a few days, a big, jovial, heavy-set man knocked on the kitchen door. "I'm Al Zirnhelt," he said, extending a huge hand that showed he knew all about the toil of the Cariboo. "Is John around? I heard he might be looking for someone to work."

"John is down at the barn," I replied. "He has been working the cattle this morning and has gone to unsaddle his horse. Come in and have a cup of coffee while you're waiting."

Al started work the following week, and he worked for us for years. He was a practical man, able to improvise something out of nothing, and he could get the most stubborn of engines started when all else failed. A rancher needed a man who was resourceful and knowledgeable about ranching. This was the beginning of a long friendship with the Al Zirnhelt family.

By this time, fall was quickly giving way to winter. During the summer, which now seemed like a distant memory, we had spent all the hours we could find tending the large vegetable garden between the ranch house and the shore of Big Lake. The garden was one of the centres of ranch life, contributing much to the filling of the root cellar. Whenever time had permitted, I processed and canned jars and jars of fruit, vegetables, fish and meat. We had brought a big upright deep freeze, but we found it unsatisfactory. If for some reason (and there seemed to be many) we could not start the army surplus lighting plant, everything would thaw and spoil. Replacement parts took weeks to receive, and after a couple of costly experiences we sold the deep freeze.

I had learned to cook and can from my mother, who utilized food to the fullest. We did not have a pressure cooker so it took many hours to process some of the food, particularly meat and fish, by the open kettle method, but now it was indeed rewarding to see the results in our root cellar. Within the thick double walls filled with sod, and protected from the elements of the Cariboo winters, the root vegetables that

Al Zirnhelt lived in Beaver Valley and did some work for us. He was good with mechanical equipment and could fix anything. He was also a very compassionate man. In this picture he is digging out a moose that was trapped during a snowstorm.

My little pig "Dirty Face" was a troublemaker from the beginning, but I was really fond of her. John was not so fond of pigs, especially this one.

had grown so profusely in the dark, rich soil of the garden were arranged in sections for our winter food. The bins were filled with rutabagas (Swede turnips), carrots buried in sand to keep them crisp, and piles of the large, versatile netted gem potato. Hanging from the heavy log rafters, suspended by its root system, was the Danish ballhead cabbage, an excellent winter keeper.

On the shelves were our many jars of home-processed vegetables, fish and all types of meat, including moose, deer, bear, chicken and grouse. The meat had been prepared as meat balls, stew, Swiss steak, mincemeat and other ways. No meat was ever wasted, and all of it, including the less-tender cuts of game animals, was tasty and tender from the hot-water bath method of canning.

Bear stew, consisting of bear meat plus carrots, peas, green beans, potatoes, turnips, garlic, onions and other assorted vegetables from the garden, could be quickly prepared by just opening a jar and heating the contents. Other jars contained all types and combinations of vegetables in various forms, from pickled beets to sauerkraut to carrot marmalade.

Commercial fresh fruit was not available during those early years in the Cariboo. In a very special section of the cellar were jars of wild berries, Saskatoons, raspberries, blueberries, strawberries and gooseberries, which were all available for the picking. These berries could be made into excellent pie fillings, jellies, jams and marmalades.

One of the tastiest jellies, delicious on hot biscuits slathered with fresh homemade butter, was made from the tart, red highbush cranberry, which was difficult to find in its limited damp, bushy habitat. A close tasty second was the wild strawberry—tedious to pick, but

Our Danish ballhead cabbages were a staple. I hung them in the cellar and then we could eat them all winter.

no berry ever developed by the "plant wizard," the botanist Luther Burbank, could compare to it for flavour and sweetness. When I cooked or baked with this berry, I often stretched the recipe with the addition of rhubarb, which grew abundantly at the garden's edge. I also made rhubarb into a fresh sauce, a delicious summer drink, pies, jelly and marmalade.

The walls of the root cellar were chinked and surrounded by rows of burlap sacking to keep the penetrating frost from entering. Proper ventilation was important, helping to maintain a balanced environment for storing the food through the winter. As I surveyed the harvest of the seven or eight hundred jars of assorted preserves, neatly shelved, and the vegetables arranged in their bins, a feeling of accomplishment swept over me. At the same time I could not help but think of the many less fortunate people of the world. Mother Nature had bestowed British Columbia with many blessings, ours only for the effort. I closed the cellar doors tightly and headed back to the warmth of the kitchen stove.

The last task of canning season had been to prepare mincemeat from the neck and poorer cuts of the moose John had recently killed. "Sure looks nice, all those jars of mincemeat in the cellar," he said now, pulling out a chair from the kitchen table. "I think a mincemeat tart would be pretty tasty, don't you?" He winked as he raised his hot coffee to his lips. "I have been doing some thinking," he said. "Chip and I should have the winter wood in by the end of the week. I think we should have a party so we can get to know the neighbours better. Sorta celebrate when the work's all done, or perhaps I should say about as much as we are going to get done this year. Would you like to have a party?"

"Sounds like a great idea," I said. We laughed, recalling the parties and events of Stampede time. "I will start preparing right away." Although I was known as a schoolteacher and a dude, I longed to become a part of this small community. I had my accomplishments in the field of education while the local people had theirs. I thought with determination and effort I could master their skills. Not everything comes from books.

The people of the Cariboo loved a party, and since there weren't many people living around the Big Lake area, entertainment was self-made. Those who were musical brought their instruments, some brought food, and everyone brought their own spirits, whether purchased from the government liquor store or home-brewed.

The first to arrive was Al Zirnhelt, along with his wife, Ida, and their only daughter, Cathy, who was about twelve years old. Ida's maiden name was Patenaude and she was a true Caribooian, born and raised in the historic Horsefly area. Ida was a delightful person, versatile and hard-working. She provided music for many occasions and was one of the very few who did not indulge in alcohol.

After many hours of preparation, the neighbours started arriving and I was excited. We welcomed the Crippses, McKenzies, McDougals, Huxtables, Hutchinsons, Bryces, and the Schultz brothers, Bill and Bert, who were bachelors, and the Jefferson brothers, who were all single as well. The Jeffersons were descendants of pioneers who helped to settle up the Big Lake area years before. They were a shy group, except Dan, who, when after only a few nips from the bottle, was a real comedian. The more nips, the more toe-tapping music of "Soldier's Joy" came from the bow and his four-stringed, treble-pitched violin.

The party was also my first opportunity to meet the notorious character Phil Ramsden, known to all as the Potato King because of the fermented beverages he made from potatoes, better known as potato champagne.

"I am glad to meet you," I said as I clasped his outstretched hand. "I hear you are the Potato King."

"Where did you hear that? I just brew the bastards," he retorted in his English accent. I was rather taken back by his gruff tone of voice. "I didn't know if you newcomers consumed 'goof.' Sometime people call it 'jungle juice.' Want to try some?"

He grabbed my hand and pulled me toward the kitchen door. Outside the night was dark and the wind swept raw and cold. As we left the fenced yard, Phil leading the way among the parked cars, he suddenly fell to the ground. Was he hurt? Was he having a heart attack? Then he bounced up clutching a jug of homebrew he had stashed near the rear wheels of his pickup. I had never experienced the drinking of homebrew but I had heard of bad batches and the results. Phil removed the cork, passing the chilled jug to me and insisting I try some. I was skeptical. Should I refuse? Phil might take offence and I would be considered too uppity for the Cariboo. I did not want to be regarded as snobbish, so I raised the jug to my lips and took several swallows. Handing the jug back to Phil, I did have to admit it was tasty.

"Potatoes are better fermented in a jug than any other way," said Phil as he gulped down the potent liquid. "Better get back in there and have a dance." He returned the jug to its secret hiding spot.

Phil was an exceptionally good dancer, and away we went circling around the tightly packed living room. I thought back to the story I had heard about him before moving to the Cariboo. It was hunting season, as the story goes, and late one night Phil was returning home from a Cariboo party, with much too much potato champagne under his belt. There before his eyes was what he thought was a moose, which would have been his winter's meat supply. Down went the animal with the crack of Phil's rifle—but it was his neighbour's milk cow. The police were called and Phil owned up to the offence. The neighbour did not press charges, but Phil reimbursed his long-time neighbour for the loss of the cow.

I had heard much about this very intelligent man, who had been an officer in the armed services during World War II. He had been married to a beautiful woman, but during the solitary war years his wife had chosen other paths. After Phil returned from the war, amid memories and loneliness, he found consolation in his crock of homebrew.

No party was complete without the Hamiltons, who were well liked and respected in the community. This large family was soft-spoken and hard-working. The men were true outdoorsmen and the women were excellent cooks and homemakers. British Columbia as we know it now was founded by people like these, their ancestry dating back many years. After the Civil War, a Pennsylvania man by the name of Charles Eagle worked his way northward and acquired what is now known as the Onward Ranch, situated near Williams Lake. Here Christine (Toppy) Eagle met Gavin Gaston Hamilton, and they were later married by a priest at the Mission. Christine, better known as Toppy, acquired the Beaver Lake Ranch after her brother Willie Eagle was killed by a lioness while serving in the Boer War.

Beaver Lake Ranch was still important in the community, although the owners no longer provided necessities for the miners. They now catered to American hunters and kept busy with their ranch and other varied interests. No one was ever turned away from their door.

Tommy, the third-eldest son of Toppy and Gavin Hamilton, was well known throughout the Cariboo and became a legend within his own lifetime. He was a good-looking man, extremely quiet, but after a few nips from the bottle he was one of the most comical people one could ever hope to meet. He was an entertainer who told wonderful anecdotes and engaged in humorous repartee, but he did like to over-indulge in drink. During the later part of the evening, during which he had been his usual entertaining self and consumed more than his share of spirits, he asked John if he could go up to the bunkhouse where Chip stayed and grab a few winks of sleep. Tommy was weaving to and fro as he shut the door behind him, supposedly leaving for the bunkhouse as the party continued. In the wee hours, when the party was nearly over, members of his family started searching for Tommy, but he was nowhere to be found. Temperatures were hovering far below zero, and fear gripped the revellers. Where had Tommy disappeared to? The danger of hypothermia, the silent killer of the North, was of concern to all. It turned out Tommy had gone to the chicken house instead of the bunkhouse. He was fast asleep when the searchers found him stretched out nearby the roosting chickens.

Daylight was fast approaching when the last partygoer left, and soon we were fast asleep. The walls had held music, noise and laughter—it had been a successful Cariboo party.

Christmas is devoted to family reunions and merry-making, and as the Christmas season was fast approaching I became very depressed. It would be our first Christmas away from our families. Although it was a winter wonderland outside, and friends were coming to call, it was not like our very own family. John and Chip kept busy feeding the cattle and doing other wintertime duties, but men are not so sentimental. I cried with loneliness.

On Christmas Eve the kerosene lamp flickered and the warmth from the stove made our batten-board home cozy. The temperature dropped steadily and by early morning it was well below zero. The deep snow drifted with a gentle motion out of the north. John and I exchanged gifts and listened to carols on CBC Radio. John was up early on Christmas day to feed the animals, as well-fed animals can withstand the cold much better. "Merry Christmas, darling," he said. He reminded me that Paddy and Harold had invited us to Christmas dinner. "It's so cold out today, I doubt if we can get the car started, and with the snow drifting like it is, we might not make it anyway. I could keep the team harnessed or, if you don't mind, we can ride our saddle horses down and put them in their barn."

"How can I dress up for Christmas dinner and go by saddle horse?" I asked tearfully.

John put his comforting arms around me. "I know you are homesick and all," he said, "but please don't cry. It's not as bad as all of that.

Your friends in California would think it exciting going to Christmas dinner on horseback."

"What can I wear?" Wiping the tears from my eyes, I realized I was being ridiculous about the whole situation. I was just feeling sorry for myself.

"You know the dark suit you used to wear when you went off to conferences when you were teaching?" he said. "What's wrong with that? You can wear your Levis down and change once you get there. Your red blouse looks nice on you and it's a good Christmas colour." I spent the day doing my regular household chores, washing and setting my hair and looking over the nice gifts from my husband and family far away. I knew I should thank God for my blessings. I picked up one of the nice shearling-lined slippers John had given me, brushing the shorn wool first one way and then the other. John hated Christmas shopping. Perhaps he had stopped by Lil Crosina's 153 Mile Store and she had given him some suggestions.

It was late afternoon when John returned from the feeding. "It sure is cold out there," he said. He poured himself a cup of hot coffee. "Chip will be in soon. He's saddling the horses and we should be on our way before it gets dark."

As Chip led the way through the freshly fallen snow, the clouds hung heavy, promising more snow.

John rode beside me. "It's pretty cold, all right, but just feel that invigorating air. Not so bad after all, is it?"

The extreme cold bit at our faces as we rode across the windswept open field. In the distance I could see the homey two-storey ranch house, a ringlet of smoke unfolding from the chimney into the winter night.

I stepped into the back room and Paddy opened the door and threw her arms around me. "Merry Christmas, my dear, Merry Christmas! Where's John and Chip?"

"We came up with our saddle horses so they have taken the horses to the barn."

There was lots of noise coming from the house. "Come in," said Harold. "What you need is a good hot rum." The house was full of neighbours and Christmas spirit. A short time and a few hot rums later my thoughts were far from California. Everyone was having a great time. Wade and Clint were excited with the gifts Santa had left for them, and they roared around the house while Julie gave her mother a helping hand.

I was used to a big family and a traditional Christmas dinner, and I poked at my appetizer. Yes, before my eyes was a fresh oyster cocktail, which I had seen on the menu at Fisherman's Wharf in San Francisco many times. Who would expect to see it on the table in the Cariboo?

Paddy noticed me looking at my slippery mollusks. "Try them, Doris, they are delicious. We always make a point to have fresh oyster appetizers for Christmas. We can't get fresh oysters here in the Cariboo, so my sister Ruth Woodward in Vancouver sends us a treat each year for our Christmas dinner."

The hot rums I had were not enough to help me eat those fresh oysters—they were like yo-yo's in my throat. I pushed them over to John as discreetly as I could.

Hours later, after the children had long been tucked into bed, we departed for home stuffed with Christmas goodies. It was our first Cariboo Christmas, and one that I shall always remember.

Adopting the Cariboo

Success does not come quickly, nor does it come easily. But after a year or two of being very homesick, I had to secretly admit I was starting to adapt to my new life.

I had realized our living accommodations would never be very fancy, and that isolation was part of every day. Our water and electrical systems rarely worked, especially when we were in desperate need. Sleeping late was indeed a luxury, one that I would never again enjoy, and with lack of conveniences and money, life was indeed stressful.

Although there were plenty of tears of frustration from this greenhorn, looking back, I see many, many more happy times than the ones I found so hard, and I treasure every moment as a precious prize. During the very hard first two years after our arrival, the old-timers told me, "There is something about the Cariboo. Once you live here you will never want to live anywhere else." How true this statement proved to be!

A dude or not, I had a few things going for me. I thrived on work and there was no way I would admit to defeat, giving friends and relatives the opportunity to say "I told you so!" And I had a compassionate man for a husband. As a team, we worked very hard to develop our dream ranch. Every year we cleared more land to grow more hay for additional cows and more profitable returns.

Those unfamiliar with ranch life can get a false impression, thanks to the romantic fantasy portrayed in stories and movies. The working cowboy, casually riding horseback among the cattle, wearing his wide-brimmed hat and distinctive western boots, seems not to have a care in the world. But real cowboys shoulder great responsibilities. Much depends on the herd, large or small, for they represent the rancher's yearly income and must be as carefully managed as any other business asset. There is little time to sit around the campfire strumming a guitar and singing songs under the stars. For real cowboys, there is very little time even for just plain rest or relaxation. All ranchers are gamblers, trying their luck from year to year with an often unreliable Mother Nature.

I was willing to work hard with John, to give up a dependable income and regular hours and holidays, but other changes were harder. During those early years, it was always upsetting for me when animals had problems giving birth. I just couldn't stand to see an animal enduring such pain, or sadly standing guard over the motionless body of her dead calf. John was very proficient in helping animals give birth. I wanted to help, but he needed to call on extra patience when this dude came along. The sight of blood and the sound of a cow bellering with pain and fear would leave me vomiting with tears rolling down my cheeks. Why did anyone bother to ranch? Would I ever adapt to this life?

In time, I learned to accept this part of ranching life. To help a cow, to save her or save both her and the calf, was indeed satisfying. It brought the greatest reward of all—the gift of life! To revive a nearly frozen calf, or to give it a bottle of warm milk, finally paid off with a wobbly-legged but healthy little critter following along behind you.

Weather was always a concern, at any time of year. It was a constant worry whether we would get the rains at the right time to promote growth for a sufficient hay crop for next winter's feed. If it started raining in the late summer, would it stop long enough to get the hay cut and cured before winter set in? If the hay was lacking necessary nutrients, we would have plenty of calving problems when spring came.

Mother Nature was often relentlessly severe, dropping temperatures to 50 or 60 below zero (Fahrenheit!). When temperatures plunge to that level and hang for days, cattle need more feed than usual. Snow and ice cling to their backs for weeks, they become short of breath and often their noses bleed. Nature provided Cariboo cattle with hides more like fur than hair, different than those in warmer climates, but they needed extra care in extreme cold. They were fed in protected areas on a different patch of snow, moving farther afield each day, to keep their hay clean from the manure of the feed ground. The cattle themselves knew where to go, seeking out the warmest places for shelter from the penetrating snow-laced polar air masses from the North.

There were many comical aspects to ranch life—sometimes only for me, not for John, when I didn't grasp the seriousness of a situation. This was especially true when the team ran away. I thought it hilarious when the rubber-tired farm wagon bounced wildly over the uneven ground, but John didn't see anything funny about the incident at all. The so-called "teamster" (a dude also) could have been seriously hurt when he was thrown to the ground, and the damage done to the undercarriage of the wagon was extensive and certainly no laughing matter.

Another time, during a long, cold, hard winter, we were hauling hay with a four-horse team and sleigh from Peavine Ridge—Kirbys, to be exact. John had shovelled the pole gate free of the deep snow, opening the gate and stretching a cable across the opening, leading from the home ranch, to keep the livestock in. This was easier than shovelling the gate out each time it snowed—I could at least open the gate, or so I thought! I looped the cable back solidly to the nearby post with a loop drooping into the new fallen snow. It took nearly all day to go to Kirbys to get a load of hay and make it back home within the now short daylight hours. John hurriedly pitched the loose hay on the sleigh, showing me how to build up the outside edge with hay, gradually pulling the hay to the centre. These techniques gave one a monstrous load, never to slip off. John could certainly get more hay on a load than I thought humanly possible, but as with all ranch work, there was a knack to getting a proper load. Soon we were homeward bound as I burrowed down into the hay next to John. It was fiercely cold and the runners of the sleigh creaked in the snow under the heavy load.

At last we were back at the gate entering the home ranch, when the sleigh of hay stopped dead still. John, hanging tightly to the lines of the team, went flying from the load of hay. Luckily his landing was cushioned some by the freshly fallen snow, and he barely missed the double runners under the sleigh. John dragged along, sliding his full length, until he brought the team to a halt. After I saw he was not hurt I began to laugh, not knowing what had happened. It turned out that the hidden cable I had looped so solidly had caught the runners of the sleigh, pulling them out from underneath the load. Here came the bawling cattle, pulling mouthfuls of hay from the load, the stronger and more aggressive cattle knocking the younger and more timid animals away. It was impossible to put the runners back under the load of hay with all the cattle crowding around to get their much-awaited feed.

"What happened?" I asked.

"Just something a dude would do," he replied snappishly, shaking his head. I knew then I had said enough.

Dinner and the remainder of the evening were very quiet. It seemed when I should be laughing I was crying, and crying when I should be laughing.

As with all marriages, those first few years were sometimes difficult. John was a very tolerant person who hated confrontations, but I could get upset quite easily. Rather than argue, he would saddle up his horse and ride up the gentle sloping hills of Big Lake and drift among the cattle he knew so well, meditating in solitude in this great expanse of beauty. After a few hours he would return, and by this time my mood had changed and all would be back to normal.

Before our wedding we had made an agreement that no matter how annoyed we got with each other, we would never go to bed angry. Sometimes it was very hard to swallow one's pride, but the agreement paid off in a very successful marriage of many years. Even in our later years, if one of us got aggravated, we would say, "Shall I get my horse and ride up the hill?" We would look at each other with fleeting thoughts of those early years, and laugh.

Some aspects of ranch life took longer for me to adapt to, and one of those was horses.

John was noted for his knowledge of all types of livestock, particularly cattle and horses, and his ancestors were well known for their horsemanship, dating back to the American Revolutionary War. Here was a man who truly knew horses and appreciated them, who always owned an excellent cow horse or two and took great pride and enjoyment in working with good teams of horses. My adventures with horses those first few years, on the other hand, were far more frightful than enjoyable.

Horses are very intelligent, and they easily sense any fear that an inexperienced rider might have. A horse will shy at the smallest thing, or jump over logs unnecessarily, catching the unskilled rider off guard. I could not get any horse to go or to stop unless it decided to do so. I was walked on, jumped on, bucked over, mired in muskegs, and run under hanging branches and pulled off horses. You name it and it happened to me astride a horse. Luckily I never suffered any broken bones, but I did have many scrapes and bruises, supplying many laughs to those familiar with what horses can do.

I tried hard to learn, because Cariboo ranchers need to know both saddle and work horses, and I certainly did not want to be a dude forever. But I didn't understand horses, and secretly I didn't enjoy working with them and was afraid of them. Had I grown up around horses, it might have been different.

I dreamed of the day I would learn to ride and handle livestock like Cherie Harris and her mother, Paddy Cripps, but as hard as I tried something always seemed to go wrong. Cherie teased me unmercifully, as she did every other dude, and it seemed whenever anything to do with horses or cattle was going on, she showed up. John was always glad to see her, saying she was as good a hand as there was in the area, and I knew he needed someone other than this greenhorn. When he was trying to teach me, I learned to watch his reactions and to sense when I was making the wrong move. If he shook his head or pulled his hat down tightly on his head, I knew I had cut the wrong animal out, or was on the wrong side of the gate, or had made one of many other dude mistakes.

As the summer came to a close there was always so much to do, bringing in the catlte, putting up the hay. It was a busy time on the ranch.

One morning, when the summer of 1952 was winding down, still so beautiful with the early fall colours reflected on the quiet waters of Big Lake, John lingered longer than usual over his last cup of coffee. "You know, I just don't know what I should do first today," he said. He talked about how frustrating it was that the seasons were so short and everything had to be done at once. "I want to get those steers from the back pasture," he went on, "and we just have to get the last of the hay up—every potential mouthful is important. Well, nothing is going to get done sitting around this table."

There was a knock at the kitchen door, and there stood Cherie. Before we could even say good morning she busted energetically through the door, dressed in her usual cowgirl attire. Spurs jangled as she removed her batwing chaps and tossed her well-worn black hat into a corner.

"What are you doing today, going to the range?" asked John.

"You mentioned last week you might move those steers from the back pasture," Cherie said. "Thought maybe you could use some help."

"That's really nice of you, Cherie," John said. With the unpredictable weather he had planned to finish haying first, but the mower had broken down and there had been rain, and now he was way behind.

"Haven't had much time to ride my new horse lately," Cherie said. "He wanted to buck with me this morning—he just needs lots of work! Do you suppose Doris and I could get those steers in?"

John hesitated. "Sure would like to get those critters gathered, but I don't know…"

I knew what both were thinking, but John knew Cherie would be able to handle the situation and it wouldn't make any difference if I was along or not. I rose from the table with my hands full of breakfast dishes. "I sure would like to go," I said. "Won't take me long to get ready. I could ride Bucky."

Cherie pushed her chair from the table. "John, go ahead haying. I will saddle Bucky for Doris and we'll see you when you get back."

It didn't take Cherie long to get Bucky saddled; with quick and efficient movements she was soon astride her mount, eager to get started.

A sheen of sunlight touched the ripened summer grasses with gold as Cherie's horse pranced along, leading the way while I followed behind—with Bucky in full command. We had gone only a short way when we saw several steers, in prime condition, fattened on the succulent grasses. They stared, wild-eyed, as we approached. All of a sudden they switched their tails, kicked and twisted, and exploded into the timbered pasture, each going in its own direction.

Spurring her horse, Cherie took chase. She darted between the trees and jumped downed logs trying to head these critters off, and quickly disappeared from view. I wouldn't see her again for some time. There was no way I could ride with that degree of skill. Here I was, not knowing which way to go.

Saddles never felt comfortable to me, so I dismounted. Bucky was not the least concerned as he dragged his reins, nipping at the grasses.

Letting go of the reins was something only a dude would do, as John had told me many times, but Bucky wanted to eat and I soon became enchanted with my surroundings.

Overhead was a chorus of jeering *caws* from a flock of crows with their lustrous jet-black plumage. A small, green, smooth-skinned frog leapt into the grass surrounding the clump of native wild roses, which had long ago dropped their roundish pink flowers and replaced them with red rosehips.

Nearby a thick trail of red ants was marching off to somewhere, but where? Watching these very social insects, carrying loads much larger than themselves, I thought about the marvels of the anthill, a large mound at the base of the Douglas fir snag nearby.

Much, much later Cherie came back. "Where have you been?" she asked, bringing her sweat-lathered horse to a halt almost at my feet. "Thought you were going to help me. Finally got those critters to the gate but needed someone to open it. Didn't know what happened to you."

Sheepishly, I looked at the ground, sensing that Cherie, normally good-natured, was a little annoyed. I had never thought about opening the gate. Little did she know how I had whiled my time away; I wouldn't dare tell her, or anyone else. This dude would be in for plenty of harassment if they found out I had been watching the ants.

Hurriedly I mounted Bucky and we were soon homeward bound, close behind Cherie and her horse.

The pleasant aroma of the freshly brewed coffee greeted us as Cherie opened the kitchen door. I was keeping a pretty low profile.

"Made it back already?" asked John, who was preparing a noontime snack. "Didn't expect you so soon. Did you get all the steers in?"

Cherie's voice faltered with defeat as she looked briefly toward John. "Have to admit, I only got three steers in *but I did get back with Doris*," she said. "If you think you will be finishing haying tomorrow, I will come and give you a hand."

Cherie Overton (née Harris) displaying her riding skills.

The conversation ended abruptly.

"Will have to see how the rest of today goes," said John, "but I will let you know."

I had heard John say so many times that there was nothing worse than handling cattle with a dude along. He didn't have to say it again.

Most greenhorns think they have mastered the skill of horsemanship, if after a few jaunts, they can manage to stay in the saddle. They tend to develop a false sense of security, and I was no exception. One late summer day, as white clouds rushed through the blue of the sky and I was returning home from a ride to prepare lunch, I felt confident. After all, hadn't I graduated from Bucky to Kid, the big white gelding? This horse was considered safe for inexperienced riders but not quite as docile as Bucky.

Faster and faster we went, the rolling and eddying wind currents fresh against my face. As we raced across the hayfield, I imagined that someday I would ride a much faster, sleeker racehorse, maybe even get to the racetrack.

John had brought his hay baler with him from California and it was the only baler in the area. Kid, being a Cariboo-raised horse, had never seen a bale of hay, only loose hay. I gave him a slight kick to prod him along even faster—it was so much fun to race along! Then right before his eyes, nestled in the tall, second-growth grass, were two badly weather-beaten hay bales that John had neglected to pick up. This spooked him, and although he was a gentle saddle horse, he jumped quickly to the side, which I was not prepared for.

I picked myself up from the ground wondering what had happened. Apparently the only injury was to my ego. Looking around, I gathered myself together, hoping no one had seen me hit the ground, especially Cherie. What a teasing I would have taken! No one would ever know my dreams about having a racehorse, and after this episode, it didn't take me long to abandon that idea.

One day John suggested we ride to Prairie Chicken to check

the cattle on the range. "How about fixing a sandwich or two while I saddle our horses," he said. "I want to go and maybe move a bull or two around to assure a good calf crop and see if the bear have been molesting the cattle. Chip has plenty to do getting the haying equipment ready to go. Plan to start haying the alfalfa field next week if the weather holds."

Remembering how sore and tired I was the first time I made the long ride, I began making excuses to stay at home. Not many men would want to take such a tenderfoot along, and I definitely would restrict John's activities. But I got a bit disgusted with myself for the feeble excuses and finally relented.

We were soon on our way, crowding the horses briskly, as it was an all-day ride. The government range land stretched for miles, and our white-faced Hereford cattle left only a minor impression as they ambled along seeking the nutrients of the prolific native grasses.

It is hard to convey the solitude and silence we experienced as we moved through this unspoiled beauty far from the smog-filled freeways and crowded cities of California. The aroma of the great outdoors permeating our senses was invigorating, and the stillness, broken only by one or another of God's many creatures of the wilderness, brought an atmosphere of serenity.

I was relieved when we reached one of the several salt grounds scattered in various areas of the range. It contained the best feed and was close to a good water supply.

"Too early to eat our lunch," John said. "You can wait here and take a break while I check on a few of the cattle hanging around in this area. Won't be gone long." He shoved his feet in the stirrups and rode quickly from sight.

Appreciating the opportunity to rest, I thought about the lunch tied behind the cantle of John's saddle. I was already ravenously hungry thanks to the uncontaminated refreshing air. Dropping the reins of the gentle bay horse, Dusty, to the ground, I loosened his cinch as I had seen the experienced horsemen do.

Stretching out on the grass, I watched my horse as he cropped the green feed nearby. Above me was a golden eagle, soaring in a cloudless azure sky as it searched its domain for food for its insatiable eaglets.

From my left came a loud, slow, rhythmic hammering sound from a snag of a huge Douglas fir. From the far side of the tree came the uncommon wary bird of the mixed forest—the crow-sized pileated woodpecker with its fiery red crest. Using its tail for stability and clinging with its sharp claws, the bird chiselled rectangular holes in the wood, searching for insects.

Suddenly, all hell seemed to break loose. Startled white-faced cows took flight in mad confusion, their heavy udders swinging wildly side to side, their wide-eyed calves stumbling closely behind as they hurried into the timber.

It took me a few minutes to comprehend what had happened. Gone was my gentle saddle horse pounding away with the saddle directly under his belly. Too late, I realized I had loosened the cinch too much and the weight of my .30-30 rifle and its leather scabbard had pulled the saddle off balance. The once-docile animal bucked and kicked like a rodeo horse as his powerful hooves struck again and again at the well-crafted, flower-stamped saddle. As John had told me more than once, if a horse gets a saddle underneath its belly, it can be kicked to pieces.

I trembled with fright as the horse kicked unmercifully at the saddle, and my treasured gun and scabbard, with its straps ripped off, lay on the ground. The horse headed down the homeward trail, running, bucking and kicking the saddle every step of the way. Attempting to catch him, I found there was not a chance. The saddle came off, busted and badly marked from the striking hooves. The crazed animal had stepped on the reins, breaking them as well—not once, but twice.

How could I explain what had happened? Foolish thought! I wouldn't need to explain. Just one look would tell John the whole story.

When he arrived at the scene of the pandemonium, he was

shaking his head in disgust at the damage done to one of his favourite saddles. "Cost plenty to get this saddle repaired," he said bearishly. "Looks like you'll have to walk home. Can't ride a saddle in this shape. You always want to keep the cinch snug so this predicament doesn't happen." Few words were exchanged for the remainder of the day. I did walk home, leading my horse quietly and briskly, telling myself that I was better off on foot than trying to learn anything about these so-called domesticated animals.

One of my most important objectives living in the Cariboo was to learn to hunt. In my opinion, it was the most demanding of activities and required the greatest level of proficiency. I felt sure I could accomplish all other tasks fate handed me, but I wasn't so sure about the skill of hunting—that is, if my future ventures in this area were no more rewarding than my many past experiences.

I suffered acutely from buck fever, an anxiety condition well known to hunters and having various symptoms, all which I experienced during my early years. The more I hunted, the more I liked to hunt. The very sight of any deer, regardless of gender, size or time of year sent thrills of excitement surging through me. There was no problem finding game, and the opportunities I had were incredible, but bringing down the animal and taking the carcass home was another story. Without a steady rest for my gun, I shook so badly in aiming that I either overshot or undershot, rarely coming close. The animals were either too fast or I was too slow, searching for a suitable gun rest or a tree to tie up my horse.

Sometimes, after taking deadly aim at an animal and confident that I couldn't miss, I would find to my chagrin that I had not pulled hard enough on my rifle's lever action to pump the shell into firing position. On more than one occasion, I even forgot to shoot. I always had a "deer story" to tell and, the moose or deer always ended up winning. Of course, this provided many laughs for the more experienced hunters who had conquered the affliction of buck fever.

The hunting we did was not for the thrill of killing. It meant food, one of life's basic necessities. Mother Nature has provided animals and birds for even the earliest species of mankind. The human being, so physically insignificant, lacks the keen sense of sight and hearing, the natural camouflage and the reflexes and speed of escape that have evolved in our prey. The "hunting game" is a contest of intelligence and ability between man and beast—the trophy-size animals that I have encountered did not acquire those eye-catching antlers by slowness or stupidity.

The confines of our ranch property, an excellent hunting area, were heavily populated with moose and deer, and hunting soon became a source of relaxation for me. Hunting on horseback was never as tiring as ranch duties that required me to ride horseback. I often wondered if I was prejudiced, or whether the adrenalin of buck fever had something to do with it. It wasn't long before I knew the answer: I would rather hunt than do anything else!

It was early autumn as I rode over the rolling hills of our 640-acre back pasture. The air gave signs that summer was now behind us, with the fluttering leaves of the cottonwoods and birch barely touched with colour. The tall, overripe native grasses among the trees and shrubbery bent slightly with the breeze. It had not been a successful hunt, but we could not expect to see game every time we went hunting. No doubt the animals had heard or seen me with their keen senses and fled to safety; little did they know how safe they were from this hunter.

The sun was dropping quickly to the west as my gentle horse Bucky stepped briskly homeward. The air was cooling fast as I hurried home to prepare the evening meal. There was always some apprehension for anyone in the woods alone, particularly a person in my category, and I did not want to cause John any unnecessary worry.

To my left, not fifty yards away, was a sleek, antlered mule deer, feeding on the rich orange-red rosehips. There it was, standing broadside to me, paying little attention to this intruder—the deer I hoped to take home. John's voice reverberated in my mind: "Just try and control yourself." That was easier said than done. Remembering to hang tightly to the reins, I quickly dismounted, mentally scanning an invisible list of successful hunting do's and don'ts.

My .30-30 was in its scabbard on the opposite side of the horse from where I stood. The trail sloped downward and I was on the high side. I tried to reach over the horse's back with my right arm to free the gun while keeping one eye on the deer. Of course, buck fever set in. My heart began to palpitate, my body quivered, my fingers turned to butter and down went my gun, barrel-first into the soft, gooey mud of the trail. The heavy-horned buck must have sensed that he was safe, as he continued to stand there and graze. Around the horse I darted, grabbing my gun from the mire and quickly checking it, only to find the barrel jammed full of sticky black mud. As hard as I tried, there was nothing I could do to clear the barrel. The buck finally turned, with head held high and nostrils pointed into the wind, and moved away in a slow, stiff-legged gait, slipping majestically into the heavily forested fir ridge. He would be well hidden there. I shoved my rifle back into the scabbard and hurried home with nothing more than another deer story to add to my collection.

Later in the fall, John and I went on the last ride of the season to a particular area of the Tyee and Marguerite Lake range. Most of the cattle had already been gathered but we were still short a few head. Knowing time was of such importance in the Cariboo, John decided we would combine pleasure with work, and do some hunting along the way. The gentle slopes supported flourishing native grasses for livestock, as well as feeding areas for both moose and deer. Nearby were several swampland meadows from which trickled the brownish waters of the small, gravelled May Creek. The stream had already slowed as ice formed along its edges, and until total freeze-up it would empty sluggishly into Marguerite Lake. Our cattle did not often find their way into this particular area, but with a few still missing and winter fast approaching we had to exhaust every possibility, searching every corner of our range.

The chilly northern wind whispered through the branches of the regal spruce and fir. The bare branches of the deciduous cottonwood and birch stood stark naked against the leaden grey sky. My feet tingled from the cold despite my shearling-lined winter boots. I wondered if it would snow.

Darkness would come early, and we still had a long way to ride home. We had ridden for hours and not seen a cow, deer or moose. I was shivering with cold and somewhat discouraged.

John brought his sorrel horse to a halt beside me. "I want to take a small hunt and check out an area east of here. It won't take me long, I'll meet you at Cripps Cabin if you want to start home. Guess you're getting pretty cold and tired." He smiled, buttoned the top button on his denim jacket and turned his horse toward the timbered ridge close by.

John knew horseback riding was not as relaxing for me as it was for him, and I'd had more than enough riding for one day. I had only gone a short distance when I spied a dry, partly rotten fir stump and decided it would be a good place to start a fire and warm up. Although a non-smoker, I always carried a generous supply of matches, something John had taught me from the very beginning.

Stiffened from the cold and long ride, I slid off my black mare, Beauty. My chaps brushed against the solidified straw-coloured grass as I securely tied my horse to a tall lodgepole pine close by the well-worn game trail, only about fifty feet from my anticipated fire. Beauty pawed the frozen ground impatiently as I walked toward the chosen stump.

Fires require a great deal of effort to get started during the late fall in the Cariboo, often because of the humidity and poor availability of dry material. In my saddle bag I kept a good supply of birch bark, invaluable for starting a fire. I searched for small dry twigs and collected a generous amount of highly flammable pitch (a dark-brown resinous substance found on pine and fir trees) which is also helpful in fire building.

Trembling from the cold, I gathered the dry twigs and broke them over my knee. My small fire belched puffs of black smoke upward into the cold, dismal sky, and soon grew into an undersized warm blaze.

The forest was now deathly silent as I gazed into the fire, watching the flames increase in size as tongues of flame lapped around the branches. The cold had penetrated my entire body and I turned to warm my back. Then I turned back to the fire and, while warming my chilled hands over the blazing branches, I looked up and was startled to see a wide-eyed mule doe that had stepped silently out into the game trail, emerging phantom-like from the timber. Immediately behind her stood a considerably larger mule buck, proudly carrying his many-pointed, highly polished antlers. Perhaps these evasive animals knew that winter was near and were following their generations-old game trail to their wintering grounds along the Fraser River.

Here I stood, with a chance to try my luck and show John that I too could bring home the proverbial bacon. But I had no gun! It was hanging in the scabbard on my saddle. I was as close to the deer as I was to my horse, and to get the gun I had no recourse but to walk across the game trail in front of the deer, hoping they would stand still, which was a foolish thought.

Buck fever had already set in, and John's voice echoed in my mind as it had before: "Always keep your gun where you can get hold of it in case you need it!" Adrenalin raced through me as I tried to pull the .30-30 from its scabbard as slowly and quietly as possible. But the whishing sound of the metal against the rigid leather sheath sent the deer bounding away, disappearing into the trees. In the wildly surging excitement of the moment I had completely forgotten about the effects of the cold on the leather of the scabbard, stiffening it and making silent removal of the rifle impossible. Once again I was so disappointed! Was I ever going to learn?

I got my next opportunity a year later, in harvest season. The autumn-hued coloured fields of late September had been crossed by the modified grain binder, leaving sunshine-yellow sheaves to be stooked, and a few

John told me he would take me camping if I helped bring in the grain. I wasn't keen, but I helped anyway and found that I loved camping in the Cariboo.

field mice playing in the shadows of the stubble. It was a satisfying feeling to get the sixteen-pound sheaves stooked to dry for later threshing—a sacred symbol of the blessing of hard work and the knowledge that we were providing more nutritious food for the livestock than a straight diet of hay through the very cold northern winters.

When the stooks were fully dried, they would be pitchforked onto a farm wagon and hauled to the stationary thrashing machine owned by Harold and Paddy Cripps, and operated in a neighbour-help-neighbour situation.

I worked feverishly to finish stooking the grain, hoping I would have time to find a large bull moose that John had seen earlier in the week while moving the cattle. In this I was spurred on by the excitement of imagining a successful hunting trip. All week I thought about this moose, vowing not to get moose fever, since hunting moose did not excite me like the pursuit of the alert and graceful mule deer.

The moose, with its long, lanky, almost stilt-like legs, is a very tall animal. The male is a particularly awesome sight with its enormous palmated antlers, its great body mass and its long head, bearing a broad, pendulous muzzle and large ears. The moose can stand motionless longer than any other member of the deer family, having somewhat poor vision but phenomenal hearing and a keen sense of smell. Camouflage is the most significant factor for the survival of this spectacular animal. Despite its size, it can steal away through the brush and timber as quietly as a shadow.

The Cariboo is home to a variety of wildlife. Above is a cow moose and her calf, below is a spruce (Franklin's) grouse hen.

Like other Cariboo ranchers, we rarely butchered our own beef. We lived mainly on wild game, saving any income from the sale of livestock and using it to develop the ranch. The meat of a young adult moose is fine-tasting, much like beef.

When at last I finished stooking the sheaves, I still had several hours before dark to seek the elusive moose. John was working on the stackyard fences, a job that had to be completed before we could bring the cattle home from the summer range. I saddled my black mare, Beauty, and grabbed my .30-30 Winchester rifle, along with my lighter .22 Remington pump. John had given me two scabbards, one hanging from each side of my saddle, so that I could carry both weapons and hunt either game birds or larger animals. I was an accurate shot when hunting the tasty willow grouse, Franklin's grouse and sharp-tailed grouse (often incorrectly called prairie chicken) that were abundant in the bush.

My horse sauntered along, grasping one mouthful after another of the plentiful feed. After some time I was getting discouraged, as I had not heard or seen a grouse, let alone a deer or moose. There were days like this, when it seemed that the animals were purposely hiding from us. I turned Beauty toward Parker Lake, an ideal feeding area for both moose and deer where John had earlier seen the moose. We had not gone far when I spotted a huge bull moose off to my left. I slid quickly to the ground, struggling to free my rifle from its scabbard.

But in my rush, I grabbed the far too underpowered .22 and, in my confusion—coupled with an attack of moose fever—dropped the reins. As I fumbled around, trying to replace my .22 and pull out my .30-30, Beauty suddenly decided she had had enough. She whirled around and headed for home, running flat out with both guns slapping at her sides. Here I was, nearly two miles from home, no gun, no horse and the moose still standing there. I set out on my long, frustrating walk home.

When I reached the cross fence of our property, there stood Beauty at the closed gate. I decided I should go and tell John my tale of woe. Hopefully he would go back with me to find the much-desired moose.

I found him busy in the shop. "Where's the game?" he called. By this time I had worked myself into such a state that I began to cry, even though a snivelling woman was one thing this otherwise patient man just couldn't stand.

"What has happened this time?" he said, pulling his cowboy hat down more securely and staring down at the ground.

"The moose was still standing there when I left," I said. "I never frightened him. Perhaps we can find him close by. He was huge. Please come!"

"There is no need to go back there now. You will never see that moose again. I have told you and told you, hang on to those reins. Aren't you ever going to learn?" He dropped his tools and walked toward the barn with Beauty and me following close behind. "Wasting our time!" he grumbled, throwing his saddle on his bay horse, Banjo. Just wish you'd learn to hang onto those reins. Someday you are going to find yourself left out miles and miles from home."

I led the way back to the timbered ridge, where I had last set eyes on the moose, but he was nowhere to be seen. We zigzagged through the surrounding area, searching. As John had predicted, we had just wasted our time.

It was the beginning of rutting season and the moose had probably gone in search of some lovesick cow. We never did see him again. He was a trophy!

In the fall of 1952, when the season's work was done, Chip decided he'd had enough of ranching and left in search of a more lucrative job.

John spent weeks debating whether to hire another man for the winter months. With his many plans for developing the ranch, he disliked spending those scarce dollars on anything he could not fully justify. In winter, snow and extreme cold sharply limited extra projects, and the care and feeding of the livestock would take most of the short daylight hours.

"There is no reason for the extra expenditure when I can do the feeding by myself," he finally decided. Then, with a wink: "Just once in a while maybe you could give me a hand."

This was going to be my third winter in the Cariboo. I still had plenty to absorb as an all-around rancher's wife, but I had learned a lot about ranching. I often thought about my first Cariboo winter, and all those tears. Had the Cariboo changed, or had I?

Several weeks had gone by with the routine of winter feeding well established when John was suddenly called to California for unexpected urgent family business. His absence was something we had not planned for. After much coaxing, I persuaded him to leave the two hundred head of cattle and other livestock in my care.

John was most hesitant, but he knew there was not much choice. He would be away for at least ten days. But he knew how determined I was, and he trusted me to get the job accomplished. It would be plenty of hard work, but we were feeding baled hay, which should not be any trouble. "I know you can work and you are a problem solver," he said, "so I have no qualms about leaving you alone—other than the possibility of an accident." He began to gather the necessary papers from the desk. "Must have had an omen yesterday when I started the HD-7 and bulldozed our road open to the main road. With all this snow, wouldn't get away for another day or so and time is important."

After numerous words of caution, John put on his hat and coat and pulled me close, kissed me, avowed his love and promised to come home as soon as possible. With a wave, he slipped the Chrysler into gear and disappeared into the dusk.

The drone of the vehicle faded out of hearing distance as I stood there, the wind sweeping coldly down over the snow. Reality hit me, sending a surge of apprehension throughout my body. Here I was alone. Yes, really isolated; no telephone, no close neighbours and no vehicle. Had I been overconfident?

Scoffing at myself, I briskly walked to our pole-framed woodshed to get extra wood for the fast approaching cold winter's night. I enjoyed chopping the kindling, but after many warnings I had become wary when handling an axe. Being alone made me extra careful, my fingers retreating even further back as the sharp blade of the hatchet bit into the dry fir.

I could not keep from thinking how merciless the North could be for the inexperienced and even the experienced person, should they become incapacitated. Hypothermia is the number one killer of people outdoors. Cold kills in two distinct steps: exposure and exhaustion. The moment your body begins to lose heat faster than it is produced, you are experiencing exposure. If the process continues until the cold reaches your brain, you are deprived of judgement and reasoning power, and you do not realize what is happening. You also lose control of your hands as your internal temperature drops, and this condition soon leads to stupor, collapse and death.

The first line of defence is to avoid exposure, stay dry and understand the power of cold and wind. Wind chill is a winter phenomenon that is not always fully comprehended when one is working in a strong wind and freezing temperatures. I was not accident-prone, but I knew about hypothermia and I knew that extra precautions had to be taken.

During John's absence there would be no gas lights for me. I had grown accustomed to the illuminating burners of gas, but felt far more comfortable with the soft, warm glow of the kerosene lamp. Although our lamps were a far cry from the always available electric power generated by the huge Pacific Gas and Electric Company of California, I was now able to cope with these minimal conveniences.

As I hastily ate leftover odds and ends for my dinner, I became aware of how lonely it was going to be without John. Turning on the CBC for company, I picked up my knitting and proceeded to work on a very simple, plain sweater. I had just started knitting, thanks to Paddy Cripps and an Alkali woman, Celestine Rosette, who together had enough patience to teach me this skill. Chuckling to myself, I remembered my first knitting lesson. My fingers were all thumbs and I was nearly hysterical with laughter, *knit one*, *purl one,* as I watched the long, slim needles bob up and down and wondered if I would ever master this craft.

During the night a storm moved in, perhaps from Alaska; the wind drove hard and steadily out of the North as the storm's power intensified. Storms from this direction brought very cold temperatures and were often the most tempestuous. Up until now the weather had not been extremely cold, but a severe change in temperature would be very hard on me. Because of the effect of cold on people and animals, it would take me longer to do all of the jobs.

I slept intermittently, tense about the ten days ahead. I wasn't afraid of work but what if something unforeseen came up? There were many ranch-related situations I had never encountered. It was past midnight when I got up to refill the wood heater. I could tell it was getting colder by the popping sounds of the outside walls of the house, which contracted as the cold penetrated them. Rushing back to my cozy warm bed, I pulled the covers closely around me. Finally I drifted off into a deep sleep.

I awoke abruptly at first light. Dawn was arriving later each day, and the temperature had dropped far below zero during the night. I had plenty to accomplish. I started by loading the wood heater in the living room with wedges of split Douglas fir until the firewood crackled and popped. Soon the fire in the Home Comfort cookstove in the kitchen had the enamel-coated coffee pot sending forth the aroma of a fresh brew.

After eating breakfast with haste, I gathered up my warmest winter clothing and checked the wood supply in each stove before departing. It was hard telling when I would get back.

Dry snow was drifting gently from the north. Walking toward the log barn, its roof freshly covered with snow, I pulled my toque even farther down on my head, protecting my ear lobes from the penetrating cold.

I tried to do everything as I had seen John do. First thing was to feed the team of horses, Chub and Dan, so they would have time to eat their ration of hay and grain before starting the day's work. Then there was the farm flock of Rhode Island chickens to be tended. The box-type wood heater that warmed the log-constructed chicken house and kept their water from freezing needed to be replenished, and more wood had to be brought in for the evening filling. The fall grain crop provided the laying hens with sufficient straw and grain, bringing us a generous supply of fresh eggs.

I fed John's two special saddle horses and the milk cow, which was due to freshen within a few weeks. Good thing she hasn't calved, I thought. Along with all my other chores I certainly didn't need a cow to milk.

Grabbing the double-bitted axe from inside the barn door, I began chopping the thick ice from the livestock watering holes, exercising special care as John's numerous precautions echoed in my mind.

Filled with confidence, I walked into the barn to harness Chub and Dan. The cattle would be anxious for their feed and it would take longer to feed the livestock by myself, since I was not as skilled at these chores as John.

Carefully, I brushed first one horse and then the other. I placed the collar pad on, then pulled the harness from its wooden peg and swung it up onto the back of Chub. I'd never harnessed the team before but I had seen John do it every day. It looked so simple.

Before long I had a big mess of leather at my feet, boggling my mind. The harder I worked at trying to get the harness on the horse, the more hopeless the situation became. I tried putting the other set of harness on the remaining horse, exercising even more care, but was again unsuccessful. I had to get the cattle fed, so I had to find a solution, and by now I knew that I could not harness the horses. Maybe I could get someone to come and show me, step by step. I had taken the harness off many times, but had never before attempted to put it on. Why hadn't I paid more attention when John was doing this chore?

I had no transportation, so I decided to walk down to Harold and Paddy Cripps at Big Lake Ranch, and perhaps they would come and help me get the situation under control. After briskly covering the mile or so to the Cripps ranch, my heart sank—they were not there! Where had they gone?

I had no time to lose and certainly no time to feel sorry for myself. I knew I was welcome to go in and use the Cripps' telephone, one of the few in the area. The Hamilton Ranch had a telephone—I could try to call them, seeking someone to help me. Getting the livestock fed was of utmost importance. Gavie and Christine (Toppy) Hamilton and their family were always ready to extend a hand to help their neighbour and there were always other people there when they were not available.

To my great relief, Pete Hamilton, one of the four sons in the family, agreed to come up and help me. It was a ten-mile trip from the Hamilton Ranch to Big Lake, and in the extreme cold it was often difficult to get an automobile started. I walked back home, finding plenty to keep me busy while I awaited Pete's arrival. The cattle wandered aimlessly on the feeding ground. It was time for their feed and regularity was something that John insisted on, believing that livestock always do better on a schedule.

The Hamilton Ranch, originally called Beaver Lake Ranch, was rich in history. Once a popular stopping house, it was owned by Peter C. Dunley after he discovered gold on the Little Horsefly River in 1859, and it catered to miners on the way to and from the goldfields.

Beaver Lake Ranch passed down through the years to the descendants of Gavin Hamilton, Pete's grandfather, Chief Factor of the Hudson's Bay Company at Fort St. James. Gavin Hamilton, the father of sixteen children, bought the 150 Mile Ranch so his children could attend school at St. Joseph's Mission. Many tragedies befell the senior Gavin Hamilton family, and later they sold the 150 Mile Ranch to Vieth and Borland, of Keithley Creek. Young Gavie, as he was called from early childhood to distinguish him from Gavin, watched his future wife grow up at the nearby Onward Ranch. She was Christine (Toppy) Eagle, whose father owned the ranch.

Pete was a robust, happy-go-lucky type who never married and was always chuckling and smiling. When the older-model ranch pick-up came to a halt outside the front gate, I was very glad to see him! When he walked into our horse barn and saw the heap of harness on the barn floor, he could not contain his laughter. "You sure you never unbuckled any straps?" A bit embarrassed, I could not remember what went where. To this day I am sure I never unbuckled anything, but it seemed as if the harness just kept rolling and twisting! It wasn't long before we had Chub and Dan hitched to the bobsleigh and the cows hungrily munching their late but welcome hay.

Later I did learn to harness and capably work the horses, but I never came to enjoy working or riding horses; to me it was only a necessity. I just didn't understand those animals, or maybe horses just didn't understand me.

It was nearly dark when we finished the evening chores. Pete replaced the wood supply and I quickly went about fixing our evening meal. It had been a long day, with many joking reminders from Pete about the harness incident. We devoured the food, our appetites stimulated by cold fresh air and a good day of hard physical work.

After dinner, Pete slid forward in his chair, placed his coffee cup on the table and said, "There's plenty of help around our ranch to feed our livestock. If you don't mind, I will stay here and help out until John gets back. This country is no place for a woman alone."

I felt grateful, but had mixed emotions. I still wanted to prove that I was well on the way to being an all-around rancher's wife, but I did have to admit, with Pete helping me, I felt safe and secure.

Above: Florence Bosworth is standing in the middle.

Above: Walter Bosworth (left) pitching hay.

When John and I moved to British Columbia, we were part of an influx of Americans to Canada during the late 1940s and '50s, so we had numerous visitors in those first few years. Both relatives and friends were eager to see this country that held so much fascination for us. Shortly after our move to the Cariboo, Walter and Florence Bosworth, along with a long-time mutual friend, Merle Heaton, came to visit us, looking for new ventures away from the bustle of populated areas. Walter was a childhood friend of John's in California. Before long the Bosworths and their four children, Jim, Barbara, Lucille and Elsie, arrived full of exuberance about their new-found land. They settled first at Deep Creek and then at the Peavine Ridge, both in the Big Lake area.

Making a Family, Making a Living

By spring 1954, John and I had been married for nearly five years and we both agreed we had made the correct decision in selecting Big Lake as our home. We had far more dreams than money, we worked long, hard hours with many sacrifices, and we had our share of disappointments and failures, but we knew that to succeed one must look forward, building positively on experiences of the past.

One February morning I woke up very ill, vomiting continuously and unable to get out of bed. "John," I said, "I'm so sick. I must have the flu. If you have time would you please check my traps? I'll be better tomorrow. You know I'm never sick."

"I'll try to find time," John replied. "You've been lying on the ice too much while you're fishing and I've been worried about you getting sick. The cold seeping through your body is not good for anyone; you've probably caught pneumonia."

Three days passed and I was still vomiting day and night, with no symptoms of pneumonia. Paddy Cripps, hearing of my illness, stopped by and came to my bedroom. "Hear you have the flu," she said. "Are you sure you are not pregnant?"

"No," I instantly replied. "Never even thought of being pregnant." In California I had been told by several doctors that I would never be able to have children. I had always wanted to have a family, and I had shed many tears over this news, but finally accepted it.

"Do you have any cornstarch?" asked Paddy, straightening up the bed. "I'll make you a pudding. Maybe it will help to settle your stomach." Paddy was always there to offer a helping hand, whether it be illness, a cow having problems calving or any other crisis of man or beast. She disappeared into the kitchen and soon returned with a dish of warm pudding. Hoping it was what I needed, I tried a mouthful, but it tasted terrible. In spite of her efforts, the vomiting continued unabated.

Over the next few days Paddy managed to drop in frequently to check on me, even though she had more than her own share of work to do. With a cheery, "How are you today?" she would help herself to a cup of coffee. "Had my horse saddled to move some cattle this morning so thought I'd ride down and check on you," she said. "Nice out today. It's around zero degrees, so at least it's warmer than it has been." Pulling her chair to my bedside, she said, "You know, my dear, you're getting so dehydrated you will have to go and see Dr. Atwood. Can't let it continue, whatever is causing your illness." She reached over and touched my arm. "I don't believe it has anything to do with you lying on the ice while you were fishing. I think you're pregnant."

I could not permit myself to be hopeful, but hard as I tried, I couldn't erase the possibility from my mind. After all, Paddy was a knowledgeable woman, who had five children of her own.

The next morning, John got up especially early. I caught a whiff of the coffee he had brewed, and the smell of the aromatic drink I had once enjoyed was now nauseating. Soon the bedroom door opened and John said, "Going to take you to Williams Lake today so you can see Dr. Atwood. Will feed the cattle from the stackyard here at home so it won't take me so long. I'll go see if I can get the car going—hasn't been started for better than three weeks and it has been really cold."

He told me he had sprung my traps. He was so apologetic, but time just wouldn't permit him to walk my trapline every day along with the other ranch duties. I felt guilty making him do all the work.

It was late afternoon when we arrived at the small hospital in

Williams Lake where I was to be seen by Dr. Hugh Atwood. After checking me over carefully, Dr. Atwood said, "Doris, it's too early to be positive, but everything points to you being pregnant. It doesn't happen very often, but morning sickness associated with pregnancy can start within a few days after conception. What with your illness and your dehydrated condition, I am going to keep you in the hospital for a couple of days so I can keep a close eye on you."

John and I were overjoyed at this news. A house is not a home without the sound of a child's laughter, especially to those who have so desperately wanted children. The predicted two days in the hospital overlooking the village, situated where the city hall now stands, ended up being two months. Finally I was allowed to go home, but it was necessary to have someone stay with me for a few days after my return.

Although our ranch was isolated and had no real close neighbours, those in the small community were more than willing to give a helping hand. Bob and Dorothy McDougal had moved to the Big Lake area

Michael was born in 1954, and from the beginning he loved the ranch and the animals.

from the Lower Mainland several years prior to our arrival. They had a daughter, Marjorie, and later on another daughter, Valerie. Dorothy agreed to help out—something we have never forgotten.

Like his dad, Michael was a natural around the horses.

I was very ill and useless for the full nine months, and it was a difficult time for both of us. John had a full workload plus he had to help look after me. Because of my condition and my need to be close to medical attention, it was decided that I would go to California, where I could be cared for by a specialist. Approximately six weeks before my expected delivery date, I flew to the San Francisco Bay area to stay with old family friends. The doctor immediately ordered complete bedrest, and on November 6, 1954, our son Michael came to fulfill our greatest dreams.

It was more than two months after Michael's birth before we returned to British Columbia, where our lives took a new direction. I had no experience with small babies and we were far from medical attention, without a telephone if something went wrong. I panicked easily, but John was composed, having come from a large family.

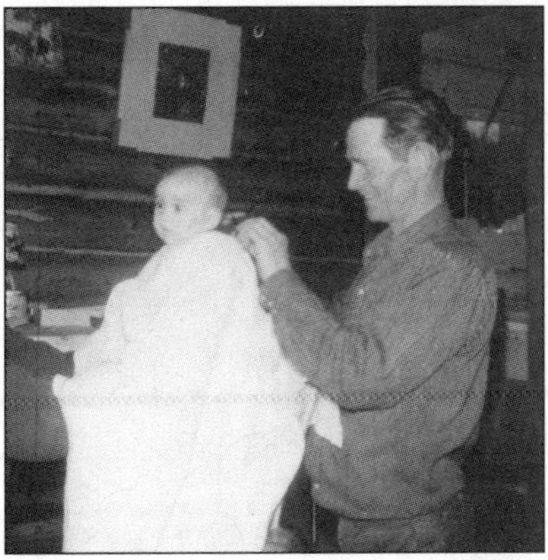

Ken McKenzie, owner of the Silver Horn Lodge, gave Michael his first haircut.

I received a book on children's diseases, written by a prominent children's doctor, as a gift. I was elated, thinking it was exactly what I needed. The book

Gary was born three years after his brother, in 1957. He liked horses but always preferred fishing and hunting. Today he is a big game guide.

described childhood problems from the simplest to the most advanced, but made every illness sound serious, and always recommended consultation with a family doctor. It was frustrating, and the final straw came after a couple of days worrying about Michael only to find out the problem was diaper rash, which was easily treated. I threw the book into the fire with great relief.

Nearly three years later, on May 15, 1957, our second son, Gary, came to complete our family. Gary was born in Redding, California, after another very difficult pregnancy. There I was close to medical attention and able to stay with my parents, who enjoyed looking after their grandchildren until I returned to British Columbia with the boys two months later.

Gary in front of Henry Grinder's bunkhouse showing off his new boots and hat. The chicken house is on the left.

Even when the ranch was doing all right, it was a challenge to make ends meet, especially once the children came along. If I could trap a few fur-bearing animals, I thought, it would help to supplement our limited ranch income, and I knew I would like the challenge. I gathered what information was available and talked to experienced local trappers such as Peter, Tom and Ray Hamilton, sons of Gavin and Toppy Hamilton, well known for their trapping and hunting abilities. Ray was particularly interested in trapping, giving me much useful advice, telling me many of his experiences, along with the ups and downs of the fur market.

Available along the shore of Big Lake and other lakes and waterways within our property existed ideal habitat for muskrat, mink, otter, and beaver; nearby in the more timbered areas were weasel (ermine), fox, red squirrel, wolf, coyote, bobcat, lynx and cougar. My first couple of months brought some success. I had trapping experiences that ranged from exciting to frightening, but "quit" was definitely not in my vocabulary.

One winter day, when the two- to three-foot thick ice on Big Lake was covered with a light skiff of new fallen snow, I briskly walked my trapline. The fine, swirling snow crept around my shoulder like a cape, and invigorating air filled my lungs. In a secluded spot where I had caught several mink, one of my traps now held fast to a long, slender, low-slung animal. It was not a fox, mink or cat. Had I caught something really exotic? The blood raced through my veins, although my first thought was an oversized Halloween cat.

The animal had rounded ears and a silky black coat. It was about three feet long from its nose to the tip of its magnificent bushy tail, and the tail made up better than a third of that length. Uttering a growling noise and arching its back, the creature lunged in an attempt to gain a foothold on the frozen bank with its sharp, curving claws. What an adventure!

The habitat around Big Lake was perfect for all kinds of wildlife. This lynx was watching me from the treetops.

I fulfilled the obligations of a trapper and completed the details. Then, forgetting the bitter cold, I returned to the ranch house. Breathlessly relating my tale, I threw my homemade gunny sack at John's feet and pulled the unknown animal out of my trapping gear. Did he know what animal it was?

John briefly examined the animal and said, "To be truthful, I don't know, as I have never seen one before. What I do know is, it's supposed to be much colder tonight and we had better get the livestock fed." I was secretly annoyed that he didn't seem to share my enthusiasm, although it was true that care of the livestock was far more essential than my mysterious catch.

Several days later Bill and Inez Crosina stopped to visit. Their Beatty Creek Ranch was eleven miles from Big Lake, by a commonly used shortcut, and they were good neighbours with seven grown children and numerous grandchildren. "Can you tell me what kind of animal this is?" I asked Bill, showing him the stretched pelt of my unknown catch.

"It's a fisher," he replied, "sometimes called a black marten, a very solitary animal. I have only seen a couple myself but I've heard about them from the old trappers. They were common before they were so heavily trapped, and now they are nearly extinct, at least in this area."

Inez told me that fishers were known as the fastest tree-travelling animals in North America, preying on squirrel, grouse and snowshoe hare, and also relishing the porcupine. "Despite its name," she went on, "the fisher doesn't care to chase after fish, but will eat fish when available. The fisher is as fierce as the wolverine, cunning as the fox and persistent as the weasel, and it has superior strength."

"I should tell you, Doris," said Bill, "the last time I heard, fisher pelts were bringing up to $350."

I was ecstatic. Just think—$350! I thought about the extras this money would provide, ignoring the proverbial "Don't count your chickens before they hatch."

My dreams were shattered when I received the current fur price list.

Fisher (small finely furred female): $75 to $100

Fisher (large coarse male pelt): $12 to $15

It didn't take long for me to realize that Bill had played a joke on this novice. My so-called treasured pelt would bring me twelve or fifteen dollars at the very most. By experience I soon learned that fur prices fluctuated from year to year, influenced by species and quality, but mainly by supply and demand. It was true that a fisher pelt did bring $350 at one time, but not in this day and age.

John, who always knew what to say, with a word of encouragement at the right time, said, "I know you are really disappointed, but I have an idea. Why don't you have the fisher hide tanned with a felt backing, and hang it on the living room wall, where you can enjoy it yourself? It will always remind you of a very exciting day."

He added that the Harold Harden family had just moved to the Peavine Ridge, and that their young son, Ron, was interested in taxidermy. John suggested that we go and talk to him, taking the opportunity to meet our new neighbours. "Scarce as this animal is," he added, "perhaps you will never catch another one." How true his statement was.

There was so much to learn, especially where to place my traps and what scent or other attractants to use for particular animals. Scents were made from rotten eggs, blood, urine, glands, fish heads and other malodorous items. The ingredients were a closely guarded secret of experienced trappers. It was also important to avoid leaving any human scent in the vicinity of the traps, for that would alert animals and frighten them away.

Trapping was rewarding in some ways, and each pelt meant extra money. But I did not particularly enjoy trapping. The animals had to be skinned with care, and the hide or pelt fleshed and properly stretched. I spent hours preparing the pelts for the fur market. The wild mink, with its thick, lustrous brown fur, had the most repulsive odour of any animal I knew of, even the notorious skunk of California.

The Cariboo, with its beautiful natural setting and wide variety of game animals—deer, moose, mule deer, black bear, grizzly bear and others—is a favourite destination for visitors during hunting season. John was an accomplished hunter and we both enjoyed hunting. We always needed extra income, so John jumped at the opportunity to become a licensed big game guide and to take hunters out to pursue the animals of their choice. Our clients were Americans, most of them interested in trying their luck at moose, the ungainly, long-legged, solitary animals whose features provided them with unbelievable camouflage.

Autumn, although gorgeous with its brilliant colours, heralded the approach of the long, cold winter months. But it also meant hunting season, a busy and exciting time of year as hunters came and went. We never knew what we would encounter with each new group of hunters. They varied in experience and attitude. We met many true hunters, and a few who were experienced but not conditioned for the vigorous physical demands of hunting in the Cariboo. Some hunters seemed more interested in saturating themselves in the serenity and beauty of the region, far from the hubbub of the overcrowded city they lived in.

Then comes the rare hunter who should have stayed home, known to us as the "Complainer," finding nothing enjoyable or right. Our advertisement read: "Get Back—Strictly a pack and tent camp. Hunt Moose, Mule Deer, Black Bear and Grizzly." The Complainer claimed to want to rough it, but expected all the modern conveniences of plush American resorts. Typically he was disappointed that there wasn't a trophy animal behind every tree, just waiting for him, and surprised to find out what a keen sense of sight, smell and hearing wild animals possess, and how fast they react and move.

By 1959, when the boys were five and two, we had a good autumn routine: I stayed home with the boys, and John went out to guide the American hunters. The milk cow and chickens were my responsibility, and I took the boys with me as I went about the ranch chores. The eggs and meat produced by the flock of chickens, along with milk, cream and butter provided by the family cow, and wild game, fish and produce from the large garden, supplied 75 to 80 percent of our needs, with amazing low-cost nutritious meals. We produced enough that I could sell milk, eggs and vegetables to the Silver Horn Lodge, whose guest list grew each year. One summer, long before we had children, I had cooked for guests of the lodge, earning enough money to enlarge my kitchen and add a big window.

One day early that fall, after John had left the ranch to guide a group of hunters, I worked in the kitchen and from the big window kept an eye on our two small boys. They took turns pretending to drive our old pickup truck, which was inoperable and had been parked in the machine shed close by. Michael was at the wheel and Gary stood next to him on the eat. I pushed the sad iron to and fro as I proceeded with my ironing, thinking about those before me who had perhaps considered this objectionable item a godsend.

Images passed through my mind. I thought of the electric iron we had received as a wedding gift, lightweight with temperature control, still packed away, impractical to operate with the electrical generating system we had brought with us. I thought about the large, dark, scorched iron shape on my husband's shirt, a memento of my first experience with the cumbersome sad iron. Every once in a while people need to stop and count their blessings and I did so now. Just outside were those two small boys God had blessed us with, beyond my greatest dreams.

I had little time to feel fortunate or sorry for myself, because the kitchen door suddenly burst open, and Michael shouted, "Mom, Gary is dying!" Complete pandemonium broke loose. Gary was crying, vomiting and wildly brushing his arm across his mouth. "We were pretending we were going on a picnic," Michael said, "and Gary wanted a drink."

Behind the seat of the pickup we had left a bottle containing methyl hydrate, a gas-line antifreeze. I could smell it on Gary's breath. Here I was all alone, with no phone, no vehicle that would run, a child crying and vomiting and no way to get help. I had to move fast.

I chose the high-wheeled International Farmall M tractor and somehow managed to get both boys on it, Gary on one side, still distressed, and Michael clinging to my other side. I succeeded in driving a couple of miles to where our current hired man was working. We then jumped into his car and raced off to the hospital in Williams Lake. It seemed as though we would never get there.

Dr. Atwood decided to keep Gary in the hospital overnight for observation, not knowing how much antifreeze he had consumed. Next day he was released, with no ill effects but a good lesson for all concerned.

Money was always in short supply, and any extra money from the sale of cattle was set aside and carefully budgeted to maintain the ranch until the next fall cattle sale. It was of utmost importance to estimate the cost of living and operating expenses for the coming year. Every possible corner was cut to save as much money as possible for the very expensive job of land clearing. I tried in many ways to help out financially.

When I heard there was money to be made in cutting Christmas trees and trucking them to large cities in the United States. I jumped at the opportunity. It would be my own project, and the deal sounded like nothing but money. First, I would have to buy a small chainsaw that I could easily handle, and when the Christmas trees were sold I would pay the balance owing on the chainsaw. Just think, a new saw plus all the extra spending money I'd have!

Cutting Christmas trees while caring for two small boys ended up being one of the most unforgettable experiences of my life.

What had I been thinking when I made this commitment? It was late October and I had a deadline to meet with lots of hard work ahead. Somehow I had to keep two small boys amused while I worked, although they had short attention spans like all children. I felt like a yo-yo as I bounced back and forth between cutting trees and looking after the boys.

Cariboo weather conditions were very unpredictable from day to day, and always a deciding factor as to whether I would be able to take the children out. When I did get the opportunity to cut Christmas trees, it seemed one child or the other was crying. They were cold or hungry or tired, or they had to go to the toilet, or they fought as siblings do. I could not leave them home, as John was either gathering cattle, taking American hunters out on guiding trips or working on one of his many other projects in preparation for winter.

At last it was time to sell the trees, and Ian Keith came to buy them. Expectations ran high as I thought about the money I would soon receive to pay for the new chainsaw and the other fanciful articles I had thought about buying. Mr. Keith, a real gentleman and a one-time resident of the Big Lake area (Keith Place), started two piles of trees, one for those he would take and one for those that did not meet the specifications. Needless to say, the piles were almost the same size, as I knew nothing about cutting Christmas trees for market. My heart sank

This buck was shot by one of our American hunters. I had been following him for years and when we finally got him he was so old he only had one tooth left. He would not have survived the harsh winter.

as Mr. Keith handed me the cheque. I did pay for the chainsaw, which I now had the skill to use. It would be useful on the ranch for many other projects. I also had a few extra bucks in my pocket, but nothing like what I had anticipated. And what does one do with rejected Christmas trees? I learned a lesson. Never again did I cut trees for market.

Later on, when the children were no longer babies, I acquired my Assistant Guide's Licence, enabling me to be more helpful to my husband. It had now been more than ten years since my first glimpse of Big Lake and I was no longer generally considered a dude. Despite the many tears and the exciting and sometimes horrendous experiences, I had slowly accomplished the feat of becoming a rancher's wife. My husband had provided me with strength and encouragement all along the way.

After many experiences of hunting and trapping, I even conquered buck fever. Now considered a good hunter as well as an excellent shot, I laughingly thought back to those many early hunting experiences and the shells I had shot with no results. I had always been well organized and independent, but now I was also a rugged individual who could strap on a backpack and compete with the best.

Guiding was something I could do well. I cooked, took out extra hunters, skinned and cared for their meat, wrangled horses and did whatever else needed to be done, although handling the horses was something I still did not enjoy. Taking hunters out brought added income, but it also brought gruelling hours of hard work. There were trails to cut, extra horses to shoe, and tents and pack boxes to repair before their expected arrival date. Regular ranch duties were curtailed, leaving me wondering if the extra money was actually profit after everything was taken into consideration. Ranching in itself was a full-time business that made very little money.

Our priorities were greatly influenced by the boys. Their welfare had to come first and there were many times when it was impossible to take them along on our excursions. As our work became more diversified we had to hire more help so we could both take advantage of other opportunities to make money.

But things were changing in the Cariboo, and ranch labour was becoming hard to get. The once-sleepy little village of Williams Lake was now awakening to the sound of newcomers seeking jobs in the lumber industry and starting new businesses. Who wanted to be confined to a ranch with low wages and isolation when there were new jobs available with much higher salaries?

Life can move slowly in a land as large as the Chilcotin-Cariboo, an area with only a few thousand occupants and the vast empire of open rolling grassland with forest glades, ideal for cattle, and miles and miles of dense coniferous trees. Williams Lake was the geographic centre of this area, approximately 38,000 square miles spread from the Cariboo Mountains west to the Coast Mountains. The face of the Chilcotin-Cariboo was veined with large, deep rivers, with many tributaries and countless lakes.

Fur trading was the first activity of newcomers to British Columbia, although the fur traders did not settle here. They traded with the local Native people, who had lived on this land for millennia, hunting, fishing, gathering and storing food for the winter. The next economic wave was the gold rush period of the 1850s and '60s. Some of these people stayed. In the area around Williams Lake, people took up farming and ranching, and others became merchants, selling their crops and animals to miners and other newcomers, and trading with the Native people. Williams Lake was well suited to agriculture, being a major supply centre and having the climate, soil and water for healthy crops.

The names of those early settlers are still rich with history in Williams Lake: Meldrum, who later moved west to the Chilcotin; and Borland, Pinchbeck and Lyne, a later partner, who influenced the growth of this area for the next sixty years. Among other businesses, Pinchbeck and Lyne had a store, hotel, flour mill, sawmill, brewery and distillery, supplying the miners and other new arrivals with most of their food and drink.

Economic growth was slow after the gold rush, until the end of World War I and the arrival of the Pacific Great Eastern railway in 1919. Williams Lake became a village, and once again new ventures were available to those who came in search of them.

Cattle raising was a major activity until about 1959, when the lumber industry began to bring dramatic changes to the area with big equipment, roads and higher wages than anyone had ever seen. Electricity, telephones, better roads and schools came to the town, and people living in rural areas started to plan for modern improvements. Electricity would be the most profound advancement, but money and time would be needed to electrify this vast area. It was 1967 before electricity came to Big Lake, and without a doubt it was the most beneficial development we could have obtained. Although the lumber industry did become predominant, Williams Lake continued to be one of the busiest cattle shipping points in British Columbia, and John and I did not want to quit ranching.

Still, we had to make some changes and try new ventures to meet our increasing financial obligations. Our business guiding American hunters was one way to bring in extra money, and John could do some logging on our property. This would generate some income and put more land into hay production. The rule of thumb was to allow at least two tons of hay per cow for each winter.

Our next project was already developing, unknown to us. It had started back in 1956 when Michael was very small. For his birthday, an American hunter and long-time friend had bought Michael six Suffolk ewes and a ram, from Kenneth and Jenny Peterson. The Petersons and their two daughters had purchased the historical Mountain House Ranch (158 Mile), once a stopping house along the Cariboo Wagon Road. The ranch had formerly been owned by the well-known pioneer Crosina family and later by William Parker, who lived at Big Lake. The Petersons had moved here shortly before John and I arrived. The Cariboo needed people like the Petersons, who worked hard to continually improve their ranch property.

The sheep were a nice thought, but what would this small boy do with them? They became my responsibility. Hardly knowing a sheep from a goat, I read every article on sheep that I could find. This small beginning launched me on one of the most challenging experiences of my life.

I liked the sheep. They were gentle, and they could be enticed anywhere with a bucket of grain. I felt I had control of these animals, something I seldom felt with cattle and horses. Gradually the flock of sheep grew, and ranch life continued, and we seemed to be working even harder than the previous year with less profit. John cleared more land, pushing the willow and cottonwood into heaping windrows. Here the most fertile land was found, the easiest to clear and put to production.

As we revamped our ranching operation, we decided to hire someone to look after the children, making me available to help out when needed. I had now graduated from greenhorn status to a person who could handle most ranching duties and who was always there come Monday morning. The lumber industry, with its higher wages, made it difficult to find good ranch hands—some of those we hired were not worth their wages, let alone room and board and the extra work they made for me.

One of the good ones, who also became a friend, was Henry Grinder. We were ready to start the haying season of 1961 when Henry

Shelley Nichol (left) was a big game guide in the Beaver Valley/Horsefly area and Henry Grinder (right) was one of the most knowledgeable ranch hands we ever hired.

Henry Grinder on the haystack.

and his wife, Violet, and small son, Thomas, came along to work for us. They moved into the nearby log bunkhouse, which became their home for several years. During this time their family grew with the birth of Lillian, Al and Johnny, and numerous other children who needed a temporary home.

Henry was a tall, slender, talkative and humorous man of German and Shuswap descent. His family were the well-known Grinders of Big Bar, northwest of Clinton, BC. Henry was one of the best men we ever hired, an all-around ranch hand knowledgeable about many facets of ranching. He was a hard worker, good with the livestock, a real hunter and a crack shot. He especially liked making pole gates and working with horses. Henry also liked to party, and John claimed Henry could do everything but get back on Monday morning. Violet, a Shuswap woman from the nearby Sugar Cane Reserve, was very shy but a trim, good-looking woman and a good cook and homemaker.

Having a married couple on the ranch was a great relief for me, allowing me more freedom. Michael and Gary and the Grinder children played together, and the boys are great friends to this day.

The children were too young to follow an adult all day, especially with the extreme weather of the Cariboo. Paddy Cripps suggested I hire a young Native girl to look after the boys and help with the housework. I took her advice, and this was a great help.

Sheep demanded far more attention than cattle, being entirely dependent on us for food and protection. The sheep would give us another source of income, in the form of two cash crops: one in the spring, when the sheep were shorn and the wool shipped, and another in the fall, when the lambs and any ewes failing to produce a lamb were marketed.

Winter came and went, and in the spring of 1957, I anxiously awaited lambing time. I had plenty to learn that cannot be learned by books alone, but by experience. I had never seen a newborn lamb, let alone help one during those first crucial hours of life. I had to chuckle as my thoughts flashed back to the tears I shed during my first experiences with the cows calving. Although I had never attended the birth of a lamb, I was knowledgeable about birth and felt confident, vowing to save every lamb. When we had only a few sheep it was easier to achieve a 100 percent birth rate, but as time went by and the flock grew, it was impossible to save every lamb. We never sold a ewe lamb and we purchased small home flocks whenever possible, carefully culling them and retaining the best producers.

Now, in spring, I had to learn to tag the ewes. This meant clipping any matted locks of wool from around the rear end and the udders in preparation for giving birth. If the wool was not trimmed, a lamb might latch onto a bit of wool hanging down, rather than to a teat. This could result in death, particularly in the cold climates.

Once lambing time came, we had to watch the ewes and their lambs day and night until all the lambs were born, and with the flock growing, my time was consumed with their care. After a gestation period of 150 days, a ewe gives birth to one or two lambs, and sometimes three. If the ewe had triplets it was a welcome sight, but it brought extra work—the ewe has nursing facilities for only two lambs, so I soon became the mother of the third. That lamb, known as a "bummer," would follow me everywhere and soon separate itself from the other sheep. If I didn't have enough work to keep me busy already, the addition of a bummer meant fixing a bottle of warm milk every few hours day and night. Should a ewe lose a lamb for one of many reasons, with care it was possible to graft a bummer on to a lambless ewe. I heard of many ways of persuading the ewe—placing scents on the ewe's nose and on the lamb, for instance, though I had little success with this method. The maternal instinct is strong, and even the cowardly, timid sheep are not easily fooled. For me the most efficient way was to take the dead lamb away from the ewe and skin it out completely, then place the fresh skin over the bummer lamb and daub its head with any urine or excrement from the dead lamb. The mother smells the hide of her dead lamb and allows the grafted lamb to nurse. After about three days, when the lamb has digested the ewe's milk, she will take the lamb as her own.

Next came castration and docking of the small lambs, which was done with a sharp knife and hot iron. Learning to castrate and dock their tales did not seem so cruel when the lambs were small, for they recovered quickly. If the task was neglected until the animals were older, castration was hard on them and could cause a setback. And if the tails were not cropped, particularly on the ewes, birth and breeding difficulties could ensue, or a concentration of urine and manure in the wool around the tail area could encourage maggots.

Our flock was growing into an operational unit, and I began to spend even more hours at the sheep shed and in the field. After lambing time was over it was important to keep the sheep where we wanted them to graze, for they were useful in controlling weeds and brush. The Cheviot and black-faced Suffolk sheep had good qualities, but neither breed had the herding instinct. I certainly got my exercise keeping them in hand.

The sheep had become my project, and the cattle John's, and we always helped each other when time permitted. John disliked the sheep as all ranchers do—it was the age-old battle between the sheep man and the cattle man. An important step along the way was learning to shear the sheep, catching and flipping each animal upon its rear end and resting its back against my legs, then thrusting the razor-sharp shears into the thick wool, making strokes as long and wide as possible without cutting the skin.

Luckily, the sheep I had when I learned shearing were the original gentle seven head. Still, it took hours to shear them, and it was a terrifying experience for the sheep as well as for me. Hard as I tried, each animal got several cuts from my sharp hand-operated shears. Shearing sheep is hot, tiring work and extremely hard on the back. Eventually I mastered it, but as the flock grew we had to hire professional help. The men who travelled shearing sheep for a living could shear 150 to 300 head per day under the right conditions, with their power shears that operated on a flexible shaft run by a gas engine. I was relieved to hire them—my back just could not stand the work, though I always managed to shear the odd one when necessary. The thick, matted, greasy wool fleece comes off the sheep in one piece, like a coat. The wool is then packed in a long burlap bag and tramped for shipment. One sack weighs about 240 pounds. Tramping the wool was another job not appealing to me. I could not stand being inside the tight enclosure of the bag.

Sheep like open areas, and while I kept watch over the ewes and their lambs, I picked roots and rocks on the rough, newly broken future hayfields, a job that seemed endless. I often thought about the pros and cons of diversified ranching, but regardless of the decisions, one thing was for sure—it took hay! Two tons to winter a cow, and you could winter eight sheep on the same amount. Sometimes there seemed to be no logic.

John and I had been talking about getting a working dog in early 1960, when he read an article in the *American Livestock Journal* by Miss Rosemary Waugh, Taloumbi Station, Maclean, New South Wales. It was about a breed of naturally bob-tailed, blue-eyed, drop-eared, long blue or merle-haired "Australian shepherd" dog, which John and

I were familiar with. She described the Australian cattle dog and the Kelpie, and the importance of both to stockmen "down under." Choosing a working dog is much like deciding what vehicle would best meet your needs. What features are you looking for? With dogs, as with automobiles, one can get a "lemon."

Penny, our Australian Kelpie, was an excellent herding dog and to our surprise she was also a fantastic hunting dog. She was my perfect companion.

In May 1961, I imported a black and tan female Kelpie. It was an eventful day when "Taloumbi Penny" arrived in Vancouver from Sydney, Australia. Photographers and journalists were there to greet the first individual of her breed known to arrive in British Columbia. Meeting the plane in Williams Lake, I felt a lump in my throat as the bewildered puppy passed by on the baggage cart, her big brown eyes seeming to search for someone familiar.

Within a few short weeks, Penny had adapted to her new home, and we were impressed by her performance. Although she was still considered a puppy, it took approximately a year for her to adjust to our climate. The first year, I made her a little coat that covered her shoulders and much of her back, and I put it on her when the outside temperature fell below zero.

Our outside dogs, with their long, thick hair and undercoat, were well prepared for Canada's extreme cold. They had good beds in the barn and plenty of choice energy-producing food. Things had to change when this very expensive puppy came along and immediately became part of the household. She had to have extra warm sleeping quarters and plenty of nourishing food to help her generate body heat. There was something about this smooth-coated puppy that stole our hearts away.

Not long after Penny arrived, we realized we had imported not only an excellent working dog but an unsurpassed hunting dog. Canada is noted for hunting, and each year substantial revenue is brought in by non-resident hunters seeking the excitement and enjoyment of hunting in the great outdoors of BC. For me, ranching and hunting had become a very big part of day-to-day life, and to have such a versatile dog as the Kelpie was the answer to my dreams. I soon imported another one, Tarion Karoo (Digger). It turned out that the Kelpies were also useful in controlling predators such as lynx, cougar and bear. These dogs provided me with countless tales of exciting and successful hunts, as well as saving many of our ranch animals from predators.

We found out the hard way that our Australian cattle dogs were too rough for the lambs, but Penny (above) was gentle and versatlie and could herd cattle, sheep and chickens.

In April 1964, I brought in two Australian cattle dogs, or "Queensland heelers," a small, sturdy breed developed exclusively for cattle work. They are silent workers, nipping at the heels of cattle with tremendous biting power. They start heeling at an early age, instinctively, working low to the ground to avoid being kicked as the animals' hooves whiz harmlessly over their heads. They were a handsome pair, and they would work, but they lacked the head-off abilities of the Kelpie, and they were definitely too rough for sheep. Once, one of them nearly stripped a young lamb of its short, curly wool coat. I had to rush the lamb home, cover the exposed area with antibiotic powder and stitch the thin skin in place.

However, the Australian cattle dogs were very useful with cattle that had never been handled with dogs. Livestock respond to the presence of dogs, making life easier for both man and beast. With their discouraging bite, they soon break the "dog fighting" cow from the habit of moving back through the herd looking for the dog to attack.

The Kelpie is extremely alert with inexhaustible energy. It is a highly intelligent animal, eager, loyal and devoted to its work and its owner. This dog employs "style" and "eye" (a fixed gaze) in moving stubborn animals. It is also shy and sensitive. The Kelpies I had were not good companions for children. They were not mean but not playful either; always at my side, ready to work at the blink of the eye and totally absorbed in the job at hand. I could not have asked for better working companions.

Sheep Camp

In late fall 1961, after careful consideration, we decided to go into the sheep business on a larger scale or get out completely. The hours I spent with the several hundred sheep we now owned kept me busy, but it wouldn't take much more effort to have band of sheep (1,400 to 2,000 head), which was considered a feasible operation. With occasional help and good working Kelpies, I could manage an increasing flock. One good working dog can take the place of several men when handling any type of livestock. The only challenge I could not meet on my own was lambing time.

Once the decision was made, there were so many things to accomplish and problems to resolve that we hardly knew where to start. Among other things, we would have to carefully cull the sheep we would winter over, getting rid of the aged and poor-producing animals and replacing them with breeds that were better wool producers with better herding instincts.

First we had to look into the availability of a suitable summer range. On the home ranch the sheep were already becoming a problem for the late spring and summer months. Sheep preferred to stay on the newly developed hay and grain fields, eating the grasses and grains that popped through the dark, fertile soil. If the fields were pastured too late in the growing season, the crops that were to be their winter feed were reduced. Although smaller open areas were accessible, they were not in valuable crop, and the sheep required herding to keep them off the farmed land. It was a common trait of sheep that they were always somewhere besides where they were supposed to be.

I knew it would not be easy to obtain a sheep range, as no cattlemen would want any "woollies" running on their cattle range. During the early days of newcomers settling the West, cattle and sheep men had fought battles over range. We would not find range near Big Lake, so we would have to find wide open land where the sheep could wander and graze reasonably close to our ranch, to avoid the high costs of trucking them to and from the range. We decided that since I had to be with the sheep anyway, I might as well drive them to the range, which would be less stressful for them. The ewes could feed on the profuse roadside vegetation on the way to and from the range, and we could make camp when or where it was convenient.

Earlier in the fall, John and two American hunters had explored the Yanks Peak, Snowshoe Plateau, in the Cariboo Mountains between Barkerville and Keithley Creek, and about sixty-five miles from the home ranch. Here was a man who loved to see any new country, as

We knew that these grazing grounds near Yanks Peak would be ideal for our new sheep business. The fields and valleys were rich with vegetation to feed our growing flock.

The view from our camp on Yanks Peak was breathtaking. From this meadow we could see the Cariboo Mountains in the distance.

long as he was on horseback. Their hunting base camp lay at the bottom of Yanks Peak, near the confluence of Little Snowshoe Creek and French Snowshoe Creek, and since they were so close to the alpine meadows they decided to go and see this vast, remote land. "Awesome beauty!" the hunters exclaimed. John, mesmerized by the breathtaking view of the Snowshoe Plateau, saw more than beauty. Through the eyes of a good livestock man he saw the economic potential of the many acres of lush alpine grass that surrounded him. Out of the blue, he emphatically suggested, "Let's apply to the Department of Lands and Forests and see if we can get range rights on the Snowshoe Plateau for sheep." He pointed out that we could not accomplish much until we had a grazing permit, and he had read and heard much about the highly nutritious grass growing above timber line, known to give a daily weight gain of as much as two pounds.

Hopeful and very excited, I immediately wrote to the District Forester, M. (Tom) Wallace, at Kamloops, British Columbia. On August 11, 1961, we received a reply stating they were pleased to hear of our plans, and at this time they knew of no reason why they could not grant the permit, providing we had the sheep and they were clear of foot rot. Unfortunately, however, they could not promise a permit on this range for the next year, not knowing the circumstances that could arise between now and then. This typical letter from a bureaucrat left us with little security. We decided to press the issue. A copy of our request went to the Grazing Department and the Fish and Game Department, and we went ahead with our plans. The permit had to be approved by the Department of Fish and Game first. After we convinced them that there was much more game in the Big Lake area than in the proposed grazing area, they sent us their approval, along with many regulations. The sheep had to be disease-free, with no foot rot and no parasitic conditions that could be passed along to the small herd of woodland caribou in the area. These rules may have made sense to an official who learned by the book rather than by experience, but to us the very idea was inconceivable. No rancher could afford to keep diseased or even unhealthy animals. Sheep have less sickness than most farm animals, but if they are not in top condition, they are less valuable for marketing and breeding. Foot rot, a common disease in both cattle and sheep, causes lameness, swelling and intense pain, which prevents the animal from moving around for food, which in turn results in lost weight and poor milk production. No rancher could afford the time and expense of treating ailing animals. The sheep would be inspected and approved by the provincial veterinarian, who would be sent from Vernon, as well as the chief veterinarian inspector, Dr. Kidd, who would travel from Victoria.

The Grazing Department also laid out strict grazing instructions, another rule we had no problem accepting. We had to move the sheep often, not allowing them to stay in one area very long, and officials would inspect the range during the summer. Here again, we had a business and we wanted it to be a profitable one. Having scraped the bottom of our savings to increase the flock, we did not need bureaucrats to tell us to practise good range management. Did they think we were imbeciles?

The next step was to locate the type of sheep that would produce the most wool and have strong herding instincts. We would need to go to the Prairies to acquire the breed and number of sheep we required. All winter we searched the advertisements in ranch and farm publications. Finally, with a hint of spring in the air, we saw an ad for a large sheep sale, listing the complete dispersal of a sizable flock near Swift Current, Saskatchewan. This sounded particularly interesting because we preferred to buy a whole flock from a single owner. We believed the sheep would be of better quality than a flock picked in small pen lots from all over, and it would be more convenient for the livestock trucks to pick them up from one area.

We were excited as we made arrangements to drive to Saskatchewan. Neither of us had ever been to the Prairies. We had travelled in the western United States, but once we had arrived in BC, we had too much work and too little money to see what else Canada had to offer.

A couple of days later, after hurried preparation, we were headed toward our destination, winding through parts of British Columbia we had never seen. The beautiful Rocky Mountains loomed ahead still dressed in heavy snow, reaching toward the azure sky—a spectacular sight. I could only imagine what these majestic mountains would look like once the snow had gone. Verdant vegetation covered the lower altitudes, and the higher altitudes offered a never-ending supply of ice-cold water. The warmer weather melted the heavy snowpacks, sending gushing white water cascading down the rocky faces of the mountainside.

We soon reached Calgary, a large city. John and I had always hoped to travel there during the famous Calgary Stampede, but what with haying and other ranch tasks at this time of year, we had never been able to do it. As we continued our journey, we encountered the immense Prairies. The snow was gone, and the vast open fields showed that winter had only recently departed. I imagined how these miles and miles of open land would look covered with bumper crops of grain. These fields were humongous, stretching as far as the eye could see in every direction. I chuckled as I thought of how proud we were with our newly developed grain field, so insignificant in comparison! There were so many differences between Prairie living and Cariboo living; never had I lived in a place where I couldn't see a mountain, and that was one thing I couldn't imagine.

It was late in the afternoon when we arrived in Swift Current, then found accommodation for the night and a place to relax and enjoy our evening meal, in surroundings very different from what we were accustomed to. I loudly declared that the reddened sun was sinking into the ground. I will never forget the expression on the waitress's face, but all my life the sun had sunk behind a range of mountains or a stand of trees. On our way back to our motel, we had our first opportunity to see the game of curling in progress. Heavy polished stones slid along on the ice as team members swept frantically with their corn brooms—we knew nothing about the game and it held little interest for us.

Next day the sale was scheduled to start early, and after a well-prepared breakfast of ham and eggs we hurriedly took off for the outlying sales yard. Close to the front of the sales ring we settled on the hard board seats and waited. The social environment was definitely that of a man's world, with only the odd woman hovering close to her partner in the chill morning air. We knew we would have to watch closely and choose carefully when the auction began.

A tall, slender, good-looking young man who stood out for his well-dressed appearance immediately stepped into the auctioneer's box. Speaking loudly into the microphone, he greeted the crowd with a warm welcome, then made a few important announcements to residents of the community.

Nearby a gate opened, and into the ring came a large pen lot of frightened sheep, followed by the ring man snapping his long black whip into the air. The jargon rolled from the auctioneer's mouth, seemingly snatching bids from the air but actually responding to the serious, sober-looking prospective buyers—the wink of an eye, quick nod of a head, short flip of the bidder's card or some other nearly indiscernible gesture.

Momentous decisions are made during this time, as the buyer mentally calculates the funds he has set aside to purchase the livestock. Everything is dependent on the current market price. The seller hopes to get top market value for his animals, which will allow him to pay his ranch operating expenses with enough left to purchase some new piece of badly needed machinery. In the ranching business, everything was contingent on proceeds from the sale of your livestock.

I wanted no part of the bidding, although during the previous ten years of attending cattle sales I was somewhat familiar with the specialized vocabulary. John, despite his dislike of sheep, was far more knowledgeable about livestock and sale procedures. Sensing the presence of a men's domain, I remained quiet, thankful they did not know these sheep were my project. After the sale ended, John stood and stretched. "I have set here too long!" he said. "Let's go to the office and pay for the sheep. We can make arrangements for the livestock trucks to haul them directly to our ranch. Hopefully we can get them loaded out first thing in the morning. These ewes will start lambing within a couple of weeks and the sooner they get settled, the better they will do."

After paying for the sheep and settling the trucking arrangements, we went back through the pens to see the sheep that now belonged to us. It was overwhelming to imagine all these sheep in my care, together with the ones I had at home. A large lump came into my throat and my skin tickled with apprehension as I thought about the challenges this would bring. I couldn't back out now, but had I overstepped my capabilities? We soon arrived back at the small restaurant where we had enjoyed our meals since arriving in Swift Current. We had become acquainted with some of the helpful and amicable Prairie people, and we bade them goodbye, extending an invitation to visit us and see our part of Canada. We did not linger over our evening meal, as it had been a long day, and we would leave early the next morning to keep ahead of the livestock trucks as they rolled toward beautiful British Columbia.

I enjoyed heading homeward through the southern part of the Prairies. We drove past sparsely populated wheat farms that lay in great blocks, and I envisioned waving grain in the summer breezes and the drifting snow of winter. In the distance rose a grain elevator, sharply outlined against the sky beside a cluster of small farm buildings and a tall windmill that seemed to have fallen onto the empty land. I loved to see the Prairies, but my heart would always be in the Cariboo.

In spring 1962, only a few short weeks after the Rambouillet and Merio cross-bred ewes had been delivered to the ranch, the ewes were dropping their new lambs and I was working around the clock. Expanding the flock had been my idea, and I knew there would be plenty of work involved, but sometimes when I could not meet the expectations I had placed on myself, I wondered if the project was overwhelming my competence.

The high, snow-capped Cariboo Mountains were still covered with drifts of snow, while in the lower elevations the creeks and rivers swollen with swirling water rushed toward the Fraser River, which drains about one-quarter of this large province. Flexing our imagination, we could see a tinge of green grass awakening in the warmth of the sun, as the fluttering blossoms of the cottonwood trees burst forth with the birth of spring. To those in the far North, where the winters are long and cold, there is no season as exciting as spring.

We were still greatly concerned, however, about getting the grazing permit for our sheep. Numerous calls and letters to various bureaucracies had not yet brought a positive decision, or any decision. We had definitely taken a chance going ahead with the project with no more assurance than we had. We were about midway through lambing when the range permit finally arrived, and we were greatly relieved.

This permit gave us range rights for the area we had applied for, high on Yanks Peak. This region was rich in history, with marks of the gold rush days still to be found. This was rugged, remote terrain, where many a gold seeker had died in the nineteenth century, perishing in churning, treacherous rivers, or dying of cold or starvation. John and I had discussed our plans for organizing this new venture on many occasions during the past few months. Since it was necessary to have someone maintain the home ranch, we decided that I would take the sheep to the summer range. John would be better able to handle the haying work, leaving me to herd the sheep and look after the boys during the summer. What respectable cowman would want to herd sheep? It was an easy decision. Many of my friends laughed, thinking I was slightly demented, and told me it couldn't be done by a woman "Just wait," they said. "You'll be back within ten days!" And, "What will you do if a grizzly bear comes along?" I had to admit secretly that I did have some qualms about this, as the range was in an area known for grizzlies. But the teasing only made me more determined. Anyway, I was no longer regarded as the dude, and I could shoot with the best of hunters.

It had been a long, cold winter with a very late spring. John and Henry were still hauling hay to the livestock, and twice a day the cows that had already calved and those still heavy with calf had to be checked. The two-year-old heifers that were having their first calf were always of great concern. They generally calved later than the older cows and were kept close to the ranch house in log corrals or small pastures, where they could be checked several times during the day and night. John said he never worried about young heifers calving in California as he did here in the Cariboo. He attributed most of the calving problems to the long feeding period, as well as hay that was of poor quality due to exceptionally icy, snowy weather conditions. Once lambing was completed, it was time to castrate and dock any lambs not previously done, and to shear the adult sheep before leaving for the mountains. Our range permit called for a turnout date of July 1 to September 15, giving us some weeks to prepare.

It was a very busy spring, filled with plenty of work and excitement about all our new ventures. The cows were calved out, the winter equipment was put away, and now there was land to clear, crops to put in, fences to repair and innumerable other tasks for the rancher to complete during the short season. The cows were taken to the government range for their turnout date of May 15. The bulls were not allowed on the range until June 15, preventing calves from coming too

Branding the calves was a big job, and now that we also had the sheep it made for a busy spring. We were never bored.

early in the spring, when inclement weather could harm many newborns. Time was fast slipping by. It was now June, and all of a sudden everything seemed to be piling up. Luck was with us—the travelling sheep shearers arrived unannounced, ready to shear the adult sheep before they were moved to their summer range, so the shearing of the sheep and the turnout of the bulls would not coincide.

It was a hectic period, the sheep to be shorn before leaving the home ranch and the bulls to be taken to the cattle range, along with the job of getting the machinery ready for haying. I had to prepare to spend the summer in the great outdoors with two small boys and a band of sheep. John had to shoe the saddle and pack horses that we would be using all summer. Before starting out we had to check the horse gear and pack boxes and tents for any necessary parts or repairs.

After nearly three days of shearing, sweat and frustration, the ewes were shorn and marked with their special paint brands. Leather straps consisting of various sounding bells were replaced around the necks of a number of sheep, helping to keep track of the flock should

The bulls were given access to as many cows as possible. Early calves brought a higher price at auction.

they stray and warning some predators. The shorn sheep were comical-looking animals, darting fearfully from the floor of the shed where they had lost their thick, lanolin-saturated wool coats. The lambs cautiously approached their newly shorn mothers somewhat uncertainly, and had to be reassured by the strong maternal instinct of the ewes. We would start our journey in a few days, after the animals had rested and settled down.

A couple of days later we prepared to take the bulls to the summer range for the breeding season. We would be joined by others, including Frank and Cherie Overton and their crew, with their bulls for turnout.

Cherie, after completing school, moved from Big Lake to Williams Lake to work at the Canadian Imperial Bank of Commerce. But her heart was not in the business world; it was in ranching. Before long, rumours of a budding romance began to circulate around the Big Lake area. Cherie had met her Prince Charming, Frank Overton, a handsome young man who had recently arrived from Keremeos, BC, to work at the Cariboo Cold Storage, a butcher shop owned by his father, Cliff Overton. On November 26, 1952, this popular young couple was married at the United Church in Williams Lake. Family and friends from near and far came to help Cherie and Frank celebrate their marriage in true Cariboo tradition.

Shortly after their wedding, Cherie and Frank moved to Keremeos, but Cherie's longing for the Cariboo soon called them back. Frank went to work for the 150 Mile Ranch, owned by Huston and Jean Dunaway, where he worked for several years, but Cherie and Frank wanted to build a ranch of their own. In 1958 her mother, Paddy, sold them the acreage known as the Lower Ranch, which was originally part of the Parker Estate. Soon they had settled in at Big Lake, the place Cherie always called home.

This energetic woman was a rancher's "dream wife." Cherie could handle almost any situation, especially when it came to livestock. Along the road of ranch life she took the bumps and made the best of any situation with a positive and determined attitude, equally comfortable in high society or with a man who was down on his luck. She fit in anywhere with her friendly smile and warm "hello."

Now the huge horned animals pawed the ground, bawling and bellowing, searching their realm as they eyed their opposition. It was time to check the cows and calves, replenish the salt blocks and look for signs of predators molesting the cattle. The black bear was the predator of greatest concern for us during the early summer months. A crafty bear rolling around on the ground will attract the curious calf or even the grown animal, and when an unsuspecting animal gets close enough to the bear, it attacks with an extremely quick swat that is nearly always fatal, or leaves the animal mortally wounded.

When the bulls were brought to the area, it was important to spread them out over a large area, giving access to as many cows as possible, as soon as possible. The earlier the contact, the earlier the calves, and the higher the prices at the fall cattle auction. The bulls were placed where the best feed and water was available and where the majority of cows preferred to graze.

On June 20, 1962, the weathered pole gate of the home ranch swung open and the recently shorn ewes and their lambs slowly moved out onto the Likely Keithley Road, headed toward Sheep Camp in the alpine range. It was a new adventure for both woman and beast, and I had to choke back tears of excitement. Michael and Gary, seven and five years old, were delighted to be going camping for the summer. We carried the basics of clothing, bedding and footwear, and only as much perishable food as we could carry. John would check on us every ten days or two weeks and bring fresh vegetables, meat and eggs, with a few treats tucked away.

Accompanying us to the range that first year was John Dean, a family friend, just fourteen years old but a good-sized young lad. He brought along his sorrel horse, Duke, a gentle-natured animal who made an exceptional camp horse—one that prefers to stay close to camp, is easily caught and never gets homesick or takes off for unknown areas. These are essential qualities for people who have no other transportation.

I had became acquainted with John Dean's mother, Mildred, quite by accident—she was the nurse on duty when Gary was born at the

Moving the lambs and ewes up the road to Keithley. We were heading for the sheep camp on Yanks Peak. Lakeside Photos.

Memorial Hospital in Redding, California. During my stay there, this wonderful nurse became fascinated with my stories of my adopted homeland. She and her husband were ranching people. They vowed they would make it to British Columbia in the not too distant future and look at the opportunities the Cariboo had to offer, and they did.

We did not take a vehicle, making us entirely dependent upon our horses, and our home for the summer would be strictly tents. The nearest telephone was at least eighteen miles from Sheep Camp, at the Creighton and Conn Ranch at Keithley Creek, which was nearly deserted. I had always been concerned about emergencies that might arise, but we had raised the boys to this age, and now I had experience.

The sheep shoved and crowded each other, grasping mouthfuls of the prolific array of fresh, varied vegetation around them, and sauntering along at their own pace. The ewes stopped to feed on the

It was quite a sight for the locals of Likely to see our herd of sheep, and a woman shepherdess passing through their town. The Hilton Hotel is on the right. Lakeside Photos.

Driving the sheep across the Quesnel River. Lakeside Photos.

grasses, or paused for a while when their lambs wanted to nurse. The lambs bumped and butted, suckling the rich, warm milk and sending their newly short tails in accelerated wiggles. It never failed to amaze me how these creatures, not the most intelligent of animals, could so quickly find their own in this mass of newly clipped ewes and lambs. The Kelpies were excited and eager to work, watching for any animal wandering too far from the gravelled roadway. Each dog had a task at which it excelled, but my treasured Penny outshone them all.

Of particular interest to the occasional people driving by was Billy, a castrated white male goat that had been given to the boys. It was common for a goat to be placed with a band of sheep as a leader, but Billy was definitely not a leader. He always stayed behind with the boys, interested in whatever they were doing, following them as they rode their horses or walking beside them as they investigated tadpoles and other inhabitants of the fascinating pools of water. With his big bright eyes and whiskered chin, he sent curious onlookers into peals of laughter when he ambled up to a car and peered in, particularly enthralled with an audience of children. Billy provided us with much pleasure and many, many laughs.

John Dean, being somewhat older than Michael and Gary, wasn't as enthusiastic about some of their plans, but they all looked forward to moving the sheep close to the Hamilton Ranch at Beaver Lake. The boys were excited about the bridge crossing the dark waters of Beaver Creek, which teemed with rainbow trout. Upon our arrival at the Hamilton Ranch, Penny, my Kelpie, was sent to block the moving sheep from going any farther, and the other Kelpies worked to bring the sheep under control. The boys busied themselves making a fish pole from a stout willow branch. Before long I heard shrills of laughter as they snaked out their flopping catch. Fish were on the menu for dinner that night, freshly caught and especially tasty if you were the lucky fisherman.

There were many camp chores to do, both morning and night. The horses had to be unsaddled and the pack saddles and boxes removed from the pack horses, giving each horse time to feed before our bedtime. We were lucky that the horses would spend their first night out in one of the Hamiltons' log corrals. This close to home, if a horse took a notion he was homesick he would soon be heading back where he came from. The Kelpies lay waiting, carefully watching the sheep, while I went about cooking dinner. The tents had to be set up as well, and after the first night or two on the trail everyone knew their evening tasks.

We had just passed the longest day of the year. This far north the days consisted of many hours of daylight, which was very convenient for me. It had been a long day for all, especially for the small boys, despite their seemingly endless energy. The rolling hills surrounding the peaceful Beaver Valley were now fading away from silhouettes to black night. Inside the tent the small boys had long since drifted off to sleep.

Shivers from the cooling night air sent me throwing more wood on the campfire, and soon it was glowing brightly. Not far away were the sheep, now settled for the night with the occasional tinkle of a bell as one or another cast its head from side to side, warding off the pesky insects of the night. The dogs lay comfortably by, always on guard and ready to work at a moment's notice.

Ray Hamilton, coming from the nearby large, two-storey ranch house, soon showed up at our camp. I enjoyed talking to the Hamiltons, who were all so knowledgeable about local flora and fauna, and the early settlers and other history of the Cariboo. Ray was a real outdoorsman who enjoyed hunting and fishing, along with working in their large ranch garden. He was a sad and lonely man after his war bride had returned to England, taking their two children with her. He was never to see them again. Ray talked about his cabin near Poquette Lake, the small, long, narrow lake just past Likely. Ray liked to prospect for gold, and when he needed to get away, he would take off for the wilderness, particularly Spanish Creek and the Spanish Lake area, and go prospecting. In late summer he would be back to pick the delicious huckleberry and high bush blueberry that grew profusely, frequented by bears but untouched by man. It was very late when Ray left our camp, the coffee pot drained and the fire fast slipping away. It had been an interesting and enjoyable evening.

The following year we were accompanied by a real city boy, Brent Curley. Brent's father, John, nicknamed Jack, moved from Vancouver to Williams Lake to take over the dealership for General Motors. Jack brought his wife, Dolly, and their children, Lynn, Donna, Randy and Brent, none of whom knew anything but city living. We became acquainted with the Curleys when we purchased our first four-wheel drive GMC pickup, and over the years we became good friends. Brent, the youngest of the family, found ranch life fascinating. He even wanted to help trail the sheep. Everything was new to this small ten-year-old boy. Brent did not stay the entire summer, but during the two weeks he was at Sheep Camp he became fully involved in rigorous ranch life, enjoying many experiences that had been unfamiliar to him.

I rose at daylight, which comes real early during June, and made sure all preparations were done before calling the boys for breakfast. It wasn't long before the camp was hopping with exuberant boys wolfing down their breakfast in hopes they would have time to catch a few trout before leaving on our day's journey. Our boys had fished since they were big enough to hold a pole. They asked Brent to join them, and he was surprised at the crooked willow pole with a short line and no reel, so different from the fancy poles and reels he had seen in magazines. Shrieks soon came from Beaver Creek as the horses were saddled and packed up and I finished the last-minute chores.

The boys were casting their fish lines with gusto and were reluctant to get on the trail—it's always hard to leave a good fishing stream. We were in no hurry, and the feeding sheep drifted slowly ahead as we departed the Hamilton Ranch. Crossing the narrow valley we wound our way up the steep, gravelled Beaver Lake Hill, noted for being one of the worst places on the Likely road, especially during the snowy, icy winter months.

This particular day was bright and clear. Having nearly reached the top of Beaver Lake Hill, I turned and looked out over the sweeping landscape from which we had come. Hovering over Beaver Valley was the heavily timbered Guy Mountain, 3,359 feet high. It was named after an early French Canadian settler named Francois "Frank" Guy, who, along with a partner, operated the well-known Beaver Lake House.

The Hamilton Ranch, always impressive to me, brought back thoughts of those early settlers and the hardships they had endured. Nestled in the vivid green valley I could see Beaver Lake, and emptying from this lake was Beaver Creek zigzagging its way through the willow-lined banks. It proceeded to Opheim, Chambers and Joan lakes, and later joined Beedy Creek. Together these two creeks emptied into the Quesnel River and finally the mighty Fraser River.

With all the animals and boys ahead of me, it wasn't long before my calm, reminiscing mood was shattered by a huge commotion. Brent, an eager and very curious, busy boy, had spied a wooden box along the road. It was the kind used during the early winter and spring months to store salt mixed with sand, to be placed on the steep icy road should anyone spin out or slip off the narrow road. Brent dashed over to the box, doubled his fist and knocked on the outside of the box. "Anyone home?" he called.

Suddenly a scene of wild confusion unfolded before my eyes. It took me a moment to figure out what was going on, but full realization hit me along with the stings of ferocious bald-faced black hornets as they swarmed from the box. The frightened sheep moved quickly, scared mostly by the saddle and pack horses that bucked and ran wildly through them. The boys ran for their lives, hollering, "It's bees! It's bees! Get out of here!" as they waved their arms furiously, trying to ward off the aggravated hornets. Everyone moved fast and got away from the hornets with only a few stings to nurse. Many years later, the boys and I still laughed when we reached this point along the Likely Keithley Road, and we exchanged memories of Brent's confrontation with the hornets.

The next day we reached the top of Beaver Lake Hill. Moving along the gravelled road, we were surrounded by the deep forest with numerous lakes and streams tucked helter-skelter in the wilderness. This area was the cattle range for the nearby Hamilton Ranch, also their guiding area for the big game hunters, mostly Americans, who they catered to during hunting season.

Our nightly camps were varied, depending on many factors, especially the weather. If it was pouring rain or too warm, the sheep were almost impossible to move. There was little traffic on the road and no power lines or fences, but fresh green feed for the animals was abundant. Some days we travelled longer than others, making it necessary to find an area where the sheep and horses could be moved off the road for the night. We needed a place close by to set up our tents, preferably a place near water, which the boys liked very much. Even if there were no fish to catch, there was always water to explore and splash in.

The road on which we travelled was the original Old Goldfield Trail, which branched off from the old Cariboo Road at 158 Mile House (Mountain House). Throughout the Cariboo there were old roads and trails, many nearly eradicated by time, leaving only the deeply scarred blazed trees that marked the trails. Many of them had been made by the gold prospectors of the late 1880s. Compared to the hardships they experienced, the adversity I had faced in my early years seemed laughably trivial.

I imagined the narrow rocky trails packed down by the plodding hooves of the pack mules, wiser, more sure-footed animals than horses and able to carry bigger loads, and teams of six and eight horses burdened with heavy loads, cutting deep ruts into the black mud. I heard the rumble of freight wagons as they bumped over the "corduroy road" (logs laid crosswise) of the muskeg, and I pictured the Dromedary Express, made up of camels imported in 1962, a failed experiment.

Next we passed Morehead Lake, a man-made lake whose water

came from nearby Bootjack and Polley lakes. The road crossed over the dam, and directly below the dam was a small outlet of water that was a favourite spot for the boys. The water from this lake was once used for mining, but now it was a popular fishing spot, surrounded by an area known for excellent hunting.

Sixteen miles from Beaver Lake was Little Lake House, where Sam and Emily Prior lived. The original building had been destroyed by fire shortly after their marriage, and replaced by the two-storey log house they now occupied. It was surrounded by numerous outbuildings, including a big log barn. I had occasion to meet this interesting couple before Mr. Prior died in January 1960, at age eighty-nine. He had various sources of income, and spent fifty years as "Hydraulic" postmaster. The Priors' two children, Joe and Bernice, lived close by.

Four miles from there, a short way from the main road, was the Bullion Mine pit, which had yielded tons of gold but was now abandoned. We spent a night nearby, with plenty of feed and water for the animals.

The next day, slowly winding our way down the hill, we could see the Quesnel River, one of the most beautiful rivers I have ever seen, with swift, clear, singing rapids. To the left above the bridge was Quesnel Lake, with a tremendous shoreline and extending arms and deep enough for record-breaking rainbow trout and char catches. The Quesnel River was a great spawning area for thousands of spring and sockeye salmon on their journey home from the sea.

Just across the river was the small community of Likely, consisting of a hotel, beer parlour, post office, general store and a few other small businesses. The village was named after John Likely, a prospector of the gold rush days. To the west of Likely lies the Quesnel Forks, a ghost town where thousands of Chinese people lived—more than any place north of San Francisco.

Not far from Likely was Poquette Lake; I had heard Ray Hamilton talk about this small, narrow lake, bouncing with fish. Below us we could see trout coming to the surface of the water to feed. The Cariboo

River Bridge area is where Spanish Creek entered the Cariboo River, which flowed from nearby Spanish Lake, another long, beautiful lake surrounded by heavily timbered mountains with an island or two in its midst. Ray claimed that fish from Spanish Creek were the best fish one could catch. Both the Cariboo and Quesnel rivers were dangerous rivers that had claimed more than one life, and under no conditions were the small boys allowed close to them. The dashing icy white water blasted over the grey rocks, roaring onward through the deep canyons. No one could ever escape should they slip and fall.

A few miles past the Cariboo River, right beside the road, was a small log cabin with a hand-hewn shake roof belonging to Gary and Mary Mitchell. Gary was a prospector, and like other miners I had met, filled with optimism that he would soon hit a windfall. I thought ranchers were gamblers, but they were nothing like miners! Gary and Mary were surprised to see dogs, boys, pack horses, saddle horses, sheep and more sheep making their way along the road.

"This is unbelievable!" Gary said. "Where's the herder?"

"I am the shepherdess," I replied, and introduced Michael, Gary and John Dean.

"Don't you know there's lots of grizzlies in the alpine country?" Gary shook his head. "You sure don't look or act like any sheep herder I've ever heard of." In no time he had wormed some information from me, and we left him to ponder my abilities.

Over the years our friendship with the Mitchells grew. Moving the sheep to and from the range, we made their place a regular stopover in the spring and again in the fall on our way home. Living in such isolation the Mitchells truly enjoyed visitors, always offering a warm welcome and a cup of tea or other goodies homemade by Mary. Gary told me many stories of the area, and showed us how to get down the steep bank to the river from their cabin to catch some Dolly Varden and rainbow trout.

By now everyone knew about the local oddity—a woman, three

boys and some working dogs moving sheep to the mountains along the road, and they drove accordingly. They were fascinated, and most of them took time to stop and visit.

The next morning, after leaving our camp near Mitchells', I spied a plant with large leaves, resembling maple leaves, that I had never seen before. We had entered the interior wet belt, with different vegetation growing than at Big Lake. Later I learned that this very spiny shrub was known as devil's club, and after my encounter with the plant I knew it had earned its name. In June their huge, exotic leaves have more than their share of thin thorns, and in late August their coarse stems sprout needle-like spines—indeed a devil's club.

Soon we came to the magnificent Cariboo Lake, 2,650 feet above sea level and several miles long. About halfway between here and Mitchells' cabin, the river dove off into the canyon, leaving waterfalls so high salmon could not enter Cariboo Lake to spawn. The semi-glacial waters of the lake abound with Dolly Varden, rainbow trout, and freshwater ling cod. Old-timer Tom Kenvig, a knowledgeable man I had great respect for, told stories of the ling cod he had caught from this lake.

Water and boys seem to go together, and at the lower end of Cariboo Lake the boys enjoyed watching the various ducks darting about with their small ducklings in the shallow water of the willow-lined cove. Nearby stood a blue heron, pretending to be part of the background as he waited for his meal to come along. Across the lake were Browntop, Goose Peak and Mount Borland, all over 6,500 feet in elevation, where snow often remained all year round. We camped on a small area of land covered with vegetation and jutting into the lake, where we and the animals had access to the lake and a sandy beach. The snow was melting in the high mountains, feeding tributaries, sending down streams of water shouting with exuberance. It was still spring here.

It always took considerable time to get the tents set up, dinner cooked, wood gathered for the campfire and horses fed and rotated, assuring us transportation for the following day. The small boys were soon ready for bed after their days filled with activity. The dark night came down quickly on the silent wilderness, our large campfire was reduced to ashes with only a few small embers smoldering. Inside my tent I could hear the soft lapping waters of Cariboo Lake, lulling me into a deep sleep, only to be broken by the staccato call of the coyote searching for its mate.

Next morning, grey clouds in the distance indicated we might have some rain before the day was over. Weather was always of great concern. Storms in the high mountains, a common occurrence, made moving and setting up camp even more difficult.

This area was rich with history. Here the seasoned miners William "Doc" Keithley, John Rose, Sandy MacDonald and George Weaver searched the surrounding area until they crossed the rich gold-bearing creek they named Keithley Creek. Gold was found here in July 1860, in pan after pan of gravel taken from the creek, with nuggets weighing up to a quarter of a pound. Word soon leaked out, and miners scrambled to the area. Before long Keithley Creek became a small community with a roadhouse and numerous other small businesses.

The next day was a short one. We spent the night at the long-deserted Keithley Creek before starting our final trek to the alpine range, eighteen or twenty miles from this point. The well-known historic ranch of Veith and Borland. George Veith and Robert Borland were well known in Cariboo history. Both tried mining with little success, and later they opened a packing and supply business. In 1869, they pre-empted 160 acres at Keithley Creek, where they ran a very popular road house, store and later a post office. They exchanged goods for gold, reported to be in tons. Later they bought the 150 Mile House Ranch. Around the turn of the century they dissolved their partnership. Borland purchased the well-known Pinchbeck Ranch at Williams Lake, now owned by John Crittenden and Bob Conn, Seattle businessmen who had bought the ranch and guiding area shortly after our arrival to British Columbia.

It was nice to have a free day to catch up with ourselves and to give the sheep with their young lambs a needed rest. The animals were content here and required little herding. It was a day to wash out a few clothes, straighten out our supplies and make ready to leave bright and early the next day. We had time to explore and gather wood for our evening campfire, something we always had in the cool evenings at the higher elevations. It was always pleasant to sit by the warmth and light of a fire, watching the sparks flare up into the darkness. The younger boys were soon snuggled in their beds, and John Dean followed shortly after, but as usual I drained the coffee pot and watched the fire slowly fade away, thinking of those rugged individuals who travelled this way over a century ago.

During the night I awoke to a noise I had never heard before. My first thought was that it must be a grizzly bear after our food supply. This was grizzly country—we had been warned of their presence many times, and I always kept my .30-30 Winchester rifle beside me with a flashlight close at hand. A cold shiver ran up my spine as I leapt from my sleeping bag and ducked from the tent, expecting to see an enormous hungry grizzly. Instead I found our favourite camp horse, Duke, who had devoured all of our dog food and was now taking huge bites from our meagre supply of potatoes. As the bright beam of my flashlight hit him, he wheeled and took off, his shod hooves smashing our most essential kettle in his flight from camp. On a pack trip one is limited to the amount of supplies one can carry, so I cooked the bitten potatoes for the dogs. At first they sniffed and turned up their noses, but before reaching base camp they realized the potatoes were nearly as good as a steak.

The next morning, the day started out cloudy but grew bright and clear, promising a warm afternoon. Shortly after setting out, we came to the Keithley Creek Cemetery, where Robert Borland was buried in 1922. Apparently the public road had been constructed over some of the graves in 1938. Few graves were marked, and in general the cemetery had been neglected.

Up the hill, as we rounded a curve of the travelled road, we could see below us a small log cabin. It belonged to Tom Payne, a prospector living alone, another man with hopes of someday fulfilling his dream. Like other old-timers, he was fascinated with the venture I was undertaking and warned me about grizzly bears. Tom was well read, and when I told him that someday I planned to write a book, he gave me an interesting book and some valuable maps.

Before long we came to another old log cabin, and quite unexpectedly, I had my first introduction to Ernie Lang, a Cariboo pioneer and long-time resident of the Keithley Creek area. He dashed from his cabin, shaking his head in bewilderment. "Thought for sure I had lost my mind!" he said. "I heard bells, and I look out and here's all these sheep and horses. Never been sheep around here before, nor horses either." Mr. Lang graciously invited us to join him in refreshments, insisting we make camp at his place for the night. There was plenty of tall grass and other vegetation around his cabin that he wanted fed off.

During these years of being a shepherdess, I met some very interesting people, and Mr. Lang was one of my favourites. He was born in Germany in 1888, and after finishing his apprenticeship as a goldsmith, he worked his passage to New York. Six months later he arrived in the Cariboo, where he had lived ever since. I had heard of him on our initial visit to the ranch, when we saw Tyee Lake for the first time. Al Weber had pointed to the deteriorating log building and property that had once belonged to Mr. Lang, and said that he had tried his luck at ranching but found his heart remained with mining.

We hadn't travelled far this day, and darkness was fast closing in as we sat around the campfire watching the brilliant tongues of flame wrapping the wood we had gathered. Mr. Lang joined us by the fire, and soon one boy, then another disappeared into the tent. I was pleased to visit with this interesting man, who told me mesmerizing stories of his experiences and of the history of this area, my new home.

The early morning sun painted the tips of the mountains with sunlight. While breaking camp and finishing last-minute chores I realized just how short our food supply was. It would likely take us three or four more days to reach the range. In packing up for the day's journey I decided the safest place for the rationed eggs would be in the end of my sleeping bag. Finally we were packed and ready. The sheep slowly moved onward as they grazed, as the dogs darted about, eager to begin their work.

We moved slowly up the mountain, and as we passed through more secluded areas near the deep forest, we became more eager to reach our destination. The vegetation was so different than at Big Lake. Here in the wet belt of the interior grew the long-lived western red cedar, thriving in the moist soil of a forest whose floor is covered with ferns, huckleberry, highbush blueberry, devil's club and carpets of moss.

We crossed the small stream known as Four Mile Creek, being four miles from Keithley Creek. After having a drink of the clear cold water, throwing a few rocks with the boys and examining some creepy-crawly insects, we moved on, hoping to make it to Weaver Creek before lunchtime—something very important to hungry boys.

The hot early July sun beat down as we reached Weaver Creek, named for the prospector George Weaver who had discovered this rich gold-bearing creek a century before. These men had feared nothing in their search for gold, venturing up creeks and mountain passes where no white man had ever gone before. I too was breaking ground. Who could know what the future held for them, or for me?

The boys had finished their lunch and were now busy climbing here and there, and playing Billy Goats Gruff under the dilapidated log bridge. I had pushed the horses across the creek from me, feeling sorry for the pack horses as well as our saddle horses, leaving them unhobbled to feed. The ewes and their lambs lay resting while the working dogs kept watch. Some time passed, and suddenly I remembered the horses I had left to graze. They were gone and nowhere in sight. I had felt sorry for them but they had not felt sorry for me, taking off with everything we owned—my gun, coats, sleeping bags, and yes, all our precious remaining food. In my mind I could hear John's voice: "Always hang on to those horses. Never let those horses loose unless they are hobbled." I definitely knew better.

One cannot imagine the feeling a woman has alone with a teenager and two small boys, in a rugged area without transportation, no gun and all these sheep dependent on her. The boys were my major concern. How could they be safe when I no longer had my gun for protection? I couldn't leave the boys or the sheep, so John Dean took off running to capture the horses. Much later he returned with them to find a very worried shepherdess. Horses are ornery critters, being most evasive when they don't want to be caught. Somewhere along the way the pack horse carrying my sleeping bag had objected to his load and tried to rub it off. Thankfully my infamous hitches had held the packs, but the eggs were well scrambled and our food supply was even shorter. We pushed the sheep along as quickly as we could with hopes of making it to French Snowshoe Creek in time to set up camp.

I knew I had a big task to do before we settled for the night. I had only the one sleeping bag so I must clean up the slippery mess of broken eggs as well as doing the usual evening camp chores. I would have to sleep in a fetal position to keep from touching the lower damp half of my sleeping bag during the night. Well, I deserved it. John had warned me many times to hang on to my horse.

I cooked the evening meal quickly, and soon after the tents were set up, the boys were sound asleep. It was so quiet, only the sound of the melting snow-fed waters of French Snowshoe Creek could be heard. I spent little time at the campfire at the end of this long and very frustrating day. During the night I was awakened by the wailing whistle of a calf moose, perhaps calling for its mother. High overhead the sky was splattered with a multitude of stars, the silence broken only by the occasional weird bird or animal sound somewhere in the vast darkness.

Next morning as the sky began to glow in the east, I rolled from my very uncomfortable sleeping bag, anxious to continue up the mountain. Today we would start working up the slopes of Yanks Peak, heavily wooded with spruce, alpine fir, jack pine, poplar and dense patches of mountain alder. The mass of fallen timber, combined

Crossing the Cariboo River on the old wooden bridge, which was significantly narrower than the new bridge at Likely.

with the undergrowth of willow, alder, sticky laurel and other luxuriant vegetation, made travel below timberline nearly impossible unless there was a road or trail. The narrow road closely followed the original trail used by the miners to reach their claims on or near the Yanks Peak and Roundtop Mountain area. The next two days we travelled in closed-in country with nothing to see but the other side of the mountain, with timber and more timber. The sheep browsed along as they moved up the mountain.

We spent one night at the old Snarlberg camp at the end of the motor road, where the boys busied themselves exploring some buildings abandoned in the 1930s. We left Snarlberg and travelled on the steep bulldozer road made during the '30s by Amparo Mining Company of Philadelphia. This road went up the mountain from Snarlberg on the north side of French Snowshoe Creek and was hardly passable for anything but a Jeep. Each year the heavy rains and melting snow gradually washed away sections of the road. It required considerable manipulation to make the eight sharp, narrow switchbacks. This road led to the headwaters of French Snowshoe Creek, the Midas and the Snowshoe

The steep canyons were covered with timber. In the distance we could see Roundtop, which was used as a directional marker.

Camp. On close observation we found an abandoned trail and wagon road leading around the southeast and south slopes of Yanks Peak.

The Depression of the hungry '30s had started a second Cariboo gold rush to this area. Men were attracted from near and far, and areas that had not known a shovel for more than fifty years were invaded by men seeking a living. They earned an average of about two dollars a day for their efforts. No one made fortunes but no one went hungry.

From 1938, Cariboo Mines Ltd. was formed by Amparo. This company had acquired the Saddle and Midas groups of claims, among others. Many of these known veins were found at the time of the first quartz staking in the 1860s. The company drove a long exploratory crosscut at the Midas along with about 35,000 feet of bulldozed stripping, then stopped work in 1940. Later, certain claims were purchased by Lieut. Col. F.H.M. Colville of Duncan, BC, who tried again at the Midas site but shut it down in 1949.

On our last day on the trail we started out early, filled with excitement. The area became more and more open as we neared the spot where we would set up our first permanent sheep camp.

Only a few short days ago we had left Keithley Creek, and now we were winding our way around the steep southeast slopes of Yanks Peak. We were reaching an altitude of about 5,000 feet, where timber was becoming smaller and patchy. Farther along toward the Snowshoe Plateau, the more open areas made travel easier—indeed a treat after the past two days of being smothered by dense forest. Here flat-topped ridges and gentle slopes above 5,500 feet connect the high points and slope downward into several valleys. These long fingers of meadowland eventually slip into the semi-alpine, then slowly vanish into the heavily timbered canyons. High in these mountains were the headwaters of Cunningham Creek, Harvey Creek, French Snowshoe Creek, Little Snowshoe Creek and numerous other tributaries fed by the remaining melting snowpack at higher elevations. These waters gained momentum as they plunged off the plateau on their way to join the Swift and Cariboo rivers.

In the canyons below us the creeks ran along narrow bottoms, and the steep sides were covered with timber and unbelievable vegetation. Most of the random outcrops were found above 5,500 feet, with resistance to erosion reflected in varying degrees among different rocks.

The Yanks Peak Roundtop Mountain area comprises approximately 36 square miles, laid in a belt of heavy precipitation where winters are long and summers cool and wet. Snow lingered in the uplands until late June, leaving drifts that remain all summer in some years. There, one could experience a summer snowstorm—all the more reason to believe, as the old-timers claimed, that there were only two seasons here: July and winter.

Having a short way to go before we reached the camp, we quickly pushed the ewes and lambs along. Here we would find the supplies John and Henry had stashed earlier, and there would be much to accomplish before darkness fell. We would find extra tarps, large white canvas-wall tents, a portable wood stove, axes, shovels and numerous other items to make a comfortable camp. Under a large canvas tarp were burlap bags and sacks of loose salt to supply the animals' needs for summer. Tucked in somewhere would be a few farrier tools, plus the handy chainsaw I had obtained during my venture with the Christmas trees. There would be an ample supply of gas, oil and tools to keep the chainsaw running so we could maintain a supply of wood for camp.

As we neared the area that was to be our first camp, the sheep fervently cropped the new growth burgeoning in the alpine meadows, spreading out after trailing the confines of the narrow rocky roadway and the dank forest. It was a relief to know that these high mountains would be our home for the next two and a half to three months, and I was instantly captivated by the beauty before me.

The area we had chosen for our first camp was above timberline near a rocky, sparsely covered spruce and fir ridge. We were surrounded by sloping meadows and still higher ridges, including Base Mountain (6,322 feet). The smaller trees showed the effects of the severe wind that whistled across this incredible wonderland God had created, while others were stunted and gnarled, bent to the ground year after year by the heavy winter snows.

Some sheep camps provided more comforts than others, mostly due to location. Now, at a more permanent camp, we set up the large white-walled tent, in which was placed the tin-type portable wood stove, which would serve for cooking as well as heating. When confined to camp by weather, we would live in this tent. Michael, Gary and John Dean shared tents, and in my tent we kept bags of grain for the horses, along with my guns should they be needed.

The next two days we spent most of our time setting up our camp. It was fun as we went about changing things from here to there, making camp as comfortable as possible, the word "convenience" having little meaning in our camp. The boys were involved in everything that was happening, contributing their ideas and efforts. After some deliberation we decided to use the large canvas tarp to cover the hard-packed earth that formed the floor of the tent. We could bring the bags of

Moving the sheep down the slope of Base Mountain.

salt inside the tent, where it would be protected from the elements of nature, and the firm salt bags would provide comfortable places to sit when they were empty. Pretty plush living quarters, we thought.

Hard as it was to believe, wood was always difficult to come by above the timberline. The prevailing atmosphere provided mostly moisture-laden wood, requiring extra persistence in getting any fire started. Whenever we went reasonably close to camp, we kept our eyes open for trees that might make good firewood. All the trees, dead or alive, were small because of their harsh growing conditions, making it possible to take our find back to camp by tying it to a rope and dragging it behind one of our horses. The wood was also hard to split. Try as one might, the blocks of wood that we sat on around the campfire displayed many axe marks from my efforts to split wood that was just unsplittable. Anyone who saw these axe-marked blocks of wood was tempted to test their skill, and I believe those flint-hard blocks are somewhere on the Plateau to this day. It was fascinating trying to count the age rings on these very old trees, a task that could only be accomplished with a magnifying glass.

Seeing the sheep grazing on this beautiful valley was a wonderful reward for the hardships of the journey.

It seemed there was always something that needed to be done. There were the sheep to check or move, wood to gather, clothes to wash and meals to prepare from the food cache of our well-filled cellar back at the home ranch. Every ten days to two weeks, John took time from his busy schedule of ranch duties to bring supplies he thought we might need and items we had asked for. The boys were always excited for the supplies to arrive, knowing there would be treats and surprises for them. It would be weeks and weeks before they would have a chance to go to a store to make their own choices. John knew if he was unable to bring the supplies before we ran short, I would be able to manage, even if it meant butchering a yearling wether (a castrated male sheep) that had been wintered over from the previous year for one reason or another.

A clean, carefully kept camp was a necessity to keep predators away. We stored perishable items near the camp, in an unnamed small rivulet that also provided ice-cold drinking water. There we kept meat, vegetables, juice, our cherished mayonnaise and other items cool in watertight glass containers. We would place these items in burlap grain bags and secure the bags with ropes tied firmly to a point along the bank. This method of storage left no enticing odours. The boys were delighted with this small creek. Although it had no fish, it provided water to splash and to sail their make-believe boats.

The mood of this rivulet and the many other waterways could change quickly with weather conditions, especially in the rocky terrain of these mountains, where the soil was very shallow. When torrential rains came, which was often, a trickle of calm water could quickly become a loud, turbulent stream. When the sun shone, we could not get enough of the alpine country and its beauty, but when angry grey storm clouds swarmed in and the rain came down in buckets, one might wonder what one was doing here. But no matter how tough things became, I knew I would never give up. Those people predicting I'd soon be back at the ranch if a grizzly bear came along—didn't they remember that I was no longer the dude?

Dude or not, there were always exciting and funny things contributing to life at Sheep Camp, and many new learning experiences. We hadn't been at camp very long before we learned a very expensive lesson. One night a fierce storm moved in, waking me up as the canvas flap of my tent door whipped and popped, giving me doubts that my small tent could withstand the storm. Not a sound came from the boys' tent, but they were sound sleepers, so perhaps the vicious storm would not disturb them. Outside, the rain poured hard and steadily. It was several hours before the rain diminished and I fell asleep again.

The next morning I went to the now-meek rivulet and found the burlap sack lying in the water, still tied but no longer bulging with our food. I opened it and found that what had not been dissolved by water was encased in millions of shreds of broken glass. During the night the furious waters of the creek had sent the burlap sack bashing against the rocks, destroying everything. We would be short some items we relished until John's next trip. Although we had no communication, I hoped John might think to bring some of these items we had lost. If not, this was life in Sheep Camp, and somehow we would make do.

The lost food was not the only surprise brought by the storm. I had left some of my personal clothing soaking in the creek a short way below where we secured our water supply, then weighted them down with a small rock or two, planning to wash them when time permitted. Now I went to see if they were still there. It was a foolish hope—I would never see those clothes again, but I had learned another lesson.

But as I stood on the bank of the small rivulet, I broke into laughter, imagining what a hermit-like prospector of this era would think should he find a woman's bra or panties clinging to the thick vegetation or lodged high in a willow shrub. Maybe he would think he had been here too long in this terrific isolation, for no one had been here for years, especially women. Little would he know that high above him, near the headwaters of French Snowshoe Creek on the Snowshoe Plateau, was an adventurous shepherdess. And before she left, she too might be doubting her sanity.

Wild Woman of Yanks Peak

I was completely enthralled with the plateau and its magnificent beauty. Thinking of my friends and family in California and their hectic lifestyle, I realized how lucky I was. Astride my mare, Black Beauty, I looked out over the boundless space from the highest point of Base Mountain. It was hard to comprehend that I'd be spending the summer here, perhaps as the only shepherdess living in such a remote, nearly inaccessible area. Behind me the three boys slowly wound their way up the mountain on horseback. As we dismounted, we watched the grazing sheep spread over the green alpine meadows below us.

The sun was bright in the azure sky and to the east, beyond the Cariboo Mountains, we could see the top of beautiful Mount Robson, Queen of the Canadian Rockies, nearly 13,000 feet at the peak. Nearby sprang the headwaters of the Fraser River, which twists its way through the Rocky Mountains, later to be joined by the swollen rivers of the Interior before sliding into the Pacific Ocean.

It wasn't long until the boys were chanting, "Time to eat, time to eat!" Boys love to eat, and every outing turned into a picnic. After lunch we would spend the rest of the day riding here and there, checking often on the sheep. We always returned to Sheep Camp in plenty of time to do camp chores before darkness. The working dogs had to be fed. The horses that had been left tied for the day were turned loose, and those that were untied during the day were tied, assuring us a horse that we could catch in the morning. Even the horses running loose would not range far from the tied horses, but during my years as the dude, I had learned many lessons the hard way. You can never guess what a horse might do, and in this unforgiving wilderness our horses could mean the difference between survival and death.

Each evening after the chores were done, weather permitting, we spent our time around the campfire. The long hours of daylight at this time of year brought beautiful long days, and after sunset the air grew cold and the colourful landscape faded slowly into darkness.

One night a cool breeze sent me shivering after some wood for the campfire while the boys made themselves a bedtime snack. Dropping the log onto the fire I watched the flames bite the darkness. The campfire was always fascinating to me; I never tired of it. The boys, full of hot chocolate, soon disappeared to their bedrolls. My attention was soon called to the shimmering veils wafting over the northern horizon, the mysterious phenomenon of nature known as the northern lights. Draperies of green, white and red light rippled across the sky, surging in brightness and then disappearing minutes later as if propelled by celestial breezes. I had seen these dramatic displays near Big Lake many times before, but here it was even more mesmerizing, and it left me with an eerie feeling. It was late and much of the wood had burned to cinders when I cast aside the remains of my coffee before retiring to my tent.

Toward the early morning I was awakened by the pattering of rain on my tent, something fairly common in the high country. We had been lucky so far, with only small showers off and on, but it didn't take long to realize this was not just a shower. The rainfall increased to a steady downpour that lasted nearly two weeks. Needless to say, I began to see another side of living in Sheep Camp with two small boys. Shortly after my arrival in the Cariboo, I had experienced cabin fever, an affliction suffered by those confined to small areas, with little or no contact with the outside world, for long periods due to extreme cold, snow, rain or some other natural reason. The remedy is simple: just get out and see something besides the four walls. But this was tent

The white tent in the front is the cook tent and the tent in behind was where the boys slept. I kept the grain and the gun with me in a seperate tent close by.

fever, stuck inside with two small boys I did not want to let outside. They would get soaking wet, and at Sheep Camp there was no way to dry their clothes.

It was difficult to remember the beautiful warm days we had spent on the trail. Once it starts raining in the alpine country, heavy fog surrounds the mountains, which left us nothing to do but stay in camp. In any weather, though, it was still important to check the sheep and move them when necessary to refresh their food supply.

The canvas tarp we had placed on the ground inside our tent had been luxurious, almost like sinking down into a plush carpet. But this comfort was short-lived, and after a few days of continued heavy downpour, puddles began spreading throughout the tent. The water seeping under the numerous bags of salt that we were using as seats was fast dissolving the salt. Not only was the salt disappearing, it was unpleasant walking around the tent on a floor covered with water. As soon as weather permitted, we would have to dig a trench around the outside of the tent, drawing the water away from our living quarters.

The cook tent was where we shared meals and had coffee if the weather was miserable. To the right is my little blue tent.

But it would be hard to do a good job of it without a pick to penetrate the rocky, shallow soil. Luckily our other tents were located where they were not plagued with this problem.

Stretched through the centre of the tent was a rope that we used for a clothesline. It was easy to be smacked in the face if we forgot to duck under the enormous pairs of wet underwear and jeans as we moved about. When the boys were in their last set of dry clothes and the line was full, only the clothes that hung directly over the small camp stove would ever dry. Confined to our tent and depending on wood for heat, we were quickly running out of wood.

Every one of us began to suffer from tent fever, and day after day I tried desperately to keep the two small boys occupied. After so many days of pouring rain, the various indoor activities I had brought along were of little interest. The flap on the tent flopped back and forth constantly, as first one boy then the other would look outside for any sign of a break in the weather. Would it ever stop? I was beginning to think of Noah and the Ark.

The next morning was the final straw. The boys had very few dry clothes left, and the wet ones were not drying. They had started to complain about their sleeping bags being cold, because although the bags were not wet, they were drawing moisture from the atmosphere and had become damp, cold and most uncomfortable. At my wits' end, I discussed the situation with the boys, and John D. suggested we could go back down to the area around Yanks Peak, where there was an old cabin. Perhaps we could use it for a few days. To the best of

We all suffered from tent fever, so when the sun came out it was a real treat to get outside. Gary loved to explore the alpine meadow.

my knowledge, this weathered, well-used cabin belonged to the Cariboo Yankee Belle Mining Company of Vancouver. "I went inside that cabin once," John said. "There's lots of split dry wood behind the door but part of the stovepipe is missing." Enthusiastically, he told the small boys more about his findings, and of course they eagerly joined in and wanted to go and have a look. Deserted cabins have a fascination for young and old, and back then cabins were left open for anyone needing shelter from the elements. "Welcome, please leave this cabin as you found it," was a rule that people respected and abided by.

John D. thought perhaps he could find the missing length of stovepipe and put it together. A fire in the cabin would enable us to dry our wet clothing. We would eat at Sheep Camp, then take our bedrolls and wet clothes to the cabin.

There was excitement in camp as we did the chores. John D. saddled his horse, Duke, for the three-mile ride from our camp back

We were fed up with the rain and suffering from tent fever, so John Dean offered to check out a cabin that we might be able to use for a few days.

to Yanks Peak, where the old cabin was situated. The rain had stopped for the moment, but the mountains were still wrapped in fog. Was this incessant rain really going to end? Slowly the fog began to lift, and finally the sun broke through the heavy clouds. We all hoped for a lasting break in the weather, which would make it easier to get our clothing and sleeping bags into the pack boxes to be carried by the horse.

John D. was suffering from tent fever as well, and needed to get away from the younger boys. He prodded his horse along eagerly and disappeared from sight.

I stepped back inside the tent, where the boys were busy gathering items to take to the cabin. I tried to explain that we would have to wait until John Dean returned to see if he was able to fix the stovepipe before packing up our wet clothes. They bombarded me with questions. What will we do if John can't fix the stove? When is John D. coming back? Why is it taking him so long? The questions continued as I tried to change the subject and keep them occupied until John returned. The books I'd brought had lost their interest with the numerous times I'd read them. We spent the time drawing pictures of what they thought the cabin might look like. Without the boys noticing, I lifted the tent flap to see if there were any signs of weather improvement. An unbelievable amount of rain had fallen, but to my surprise, there were signs that the weather was changing. It was great to see patches of blue sky breaking through the cloud cover, with promises the sun would soon be shining on a very wet Sheep Camp.

I was in the tent just before 11:00 a.m. when my attention was called to the ringing bells of the sheep. Stepping outside, I stood watching the ewes and their lambs moving quickly down the hill. It was uncommon for the sheep to move at this time of day, and I thought perhaps they were salt-hungry, or the curious mountain caribou had spooked them. But in the next moment I saw, ambling along close behind the sheep, an enormous silver-tipped grizzly bear. I was familiar with the smaller black bear so common in the Big Lake area, but this was my first encounter with the grizzly that I had been warned about so often. My first thought was to protect my two small boys who were now standing beside me. I yelled, thinking it would scare the bear away, but he threw up his shaggy head and came straight across the meadow toward us. I had read everything I could find about the grizzly in books and magazines to prepare myself for a day like this, so I knew that bear had poor vision, but an excellent sense of smell and hearing. Judging by the direction of the wind, the bear must have been responding to sound. I had also read that on average, every twenty-fifth grizzly was a very dangerous animal. How was I to know whether this was the twenty-fifth bear?

John D. had not yet returned from his excursion to the old cabin. The boys, white as sheets, desperately clung to my side. I knew I had to make some decisions but above all must remain calm. I ducked into my tent and grabbed my well-used .30-30 Winchester rifle. I did not want to shoot unless I had to, because of all the stories I had heard about near-death encounters with grizzlies by men with much larger rifles than the one I carried. John had told me that if I had to shoot, make sure it hits a vital spot.

By now the grizzly was much closer than when I had first spotted him. Loading my .30-30, I shot under him, hoping to frighten him away. Immediately the grizzly reared up on his hind legs, standing seven feet tall, with his large front paws extending from his body. Holding his head high, he looked all around, then dropped on all fours and continued after the sheep. I shot once again, hoping he would get the message he was not wanted. He stood up again, looked around and fell down on all fours, lumbering down over the hill in the direction the sheep had gone. I was more and more convinced that this was the twenty-fifth grizzly. Having nothing but a tent, not even an automobile where the boys would be safe, I had to make a decision.

Over the hill out of my view, my favourite working dog, Penny, had apparently separated the bear from the sheep and brought the bear back up the hill and beyond my sight. Perhaps he had given up, deciding this was no place for him. But no—only minutes later the grizzly appeared just 150 yards from Sheep Camp. I knew he had seen us, and now he was just too close. As I loaded my .30-30, ready to take aim, something seemed to touch my shoulder and from somewhere I heard these words in a soft, gentle voice: "Don't panic. You can do it." I am sure it was a guardian angel hovering over me.

I pulled the trigger and the crack of the rifle echoed throughout the rain-soaked mountains. The grizzly, enraged, reared up again with a loud guttural roar that we would never forget. He clutched his body with his forelegs in the spot I had aimed for, dropped on all fours and ambled into the alpine fir trees directly behind our main tent. I had expected him to fall dead in his tracks, but that did not happen.

I stood quietly for a few minutes collecting my thoughts as the boys peppered me with questions and more questions. It was only a short time before John D. returned from his excursion, filled with tales of the deserted cabin. There was excitement as the boys exchanged stories of the day's happenings. "Let's go see the bear," they all called. I had to explain that although I felt confident the shot was fatal, I could not be positive. The animal could be injured and still alive, ready to attack any prey that came along. There was no way I would venture into the area, nor allow the boys anywhere near it.

John D. reported that he had found the missing stovepipe and assured me the cabin would be a good place to spend a night. Most any place would have been better than our drenched Sheep Camp. There was much to accomplish before darkness closed in. I did not want to leave the sheep alone overnight, but the welfare of the boys was of utmost importance. I could not jeopardize their health or safety. It didn't take long to pack up, and we were soon headed to the abandoned cabin where we would be warm and dry.

The boys prodded their horses along, anxious to get there after being cooped up for two weeks and having gone through a very stressful day. It wasn't long until we were there and the old wood stove was belching smoke into the damp, foggy air. Inside we enjoyed the warmth, and the cabin was filled with wet clothes and bedrolls to be warmed up. The boys told their stories of the bear over and over again, with Michael imitating the terrifying roar the bear had made. This was too much for little Gary. "Please don't make that sound any more!" he cried. We decided we would not discuss the bear episode for the rest of the evening. It was a scary story for Gary for several years.

Unknown to the boys, I had slipped a few treats into our pack, including the makings for hot chocolate. Excitement and noise filled the candlelit cabin as I pulled out the goodies, convinced these walls had not heard so much noise since the early prospecting days had brought miners to this area. I could imagine the miners suffering from isolation, cramping their legs under the rough wood table, playing their games of chance with elation or disappointment.

When the cabin was warm and cozy, we tried to imagine who might have lived there long ago. Would he have hidden gold nuggets somewhere in the cabin? Where would they be? Why did he leave the cabin? Did he get sick and die, or did he get too old? They thought maybe someone had come and robbed the prospector of his gold, and maybe even killed him. The hot chocolate and the excitement of the day soon found the two small boys sound asleep.

John D. and I discussed the day's happenings. We decided to get up in the morning at our usual time, and John D. would ride his horse the eighteen miles to Keithley Creek to the nearest phone and ask John to come and help us find the grizzly bear. I could not be comfortable until I knew the bear was dead. While John was riding to Keithley

Creek, I would take the small boys back to our base camp to check on the sheep and do our morning chores.

A whiff of the freshly blown-out candle floated in the darkness, and minutes later, John D. was sound asleep. The excitement of the day prevented me from having a sound sleep. Although I was comfortable, I kept thinking about what might have been, over and over again. I was relieved when the sky began to lighten in the east, bringing a new day.

In the morning, everything went as planned. John D. rode to Keithley Creek, and the boys and I went back to Sheep Camp, leaving our clothes and bedrolls at the cabin. The bedding and clothes would be dry, and if necessary we could return for the night. The sheep were starting to venture out as we arrived, and were showing no sign of distress. The dogs raced about, anxious to be fed. We found our tents and supplies as we left them, which was a good sign—a grizzly or wolverine could destroy the whole outfit. We had been only a few weeks into our alpine adventure when the bear had appeared on the scene. Would this be our only experience, or would we have numerous bear encounters? The old prospectors and other residents I had talked to along the way had warned me of the many grizzlies they had seen over the years. Dogs were a very important part of my life, necessary for handling of all our livestock, but the prospectors told me they would never want dogs. A dog would not be intimidated by a grizzly, they said, and the bear might chase the dog back to your side, creating a dangerous situation.

The morning brought a few showers but nothing like the downpour we had experienced over the past two weeks. The boys darted in and out of the large tent, watching for John D. When the showers stopped we checked the sheep, keeping an eye out for any bears, dead or alive, and staying clear of timbered areas. Hours had passed by the time John D. came riding in. We were all excited when we heard the news we'd hoped to hear. Yes, John would be coming as soon as he could, and he warned us not to go near the timber until he arrived. John D. told us he had been impressed with the historic Keithley

Creek Ranch and the delicious food served to a very hungry lad by the new owners.

Several hours later John arrived. I related the details of my grizzly experience to him, and he understood how frightening it must have been for me. Giving me a smile and a hug, he said, "Let's go find him." We grabbed our guns and started out in the direction I had last seen the bear. Only yards into the timber lay the dead grizzly. As I stood there looking at the bear, the excitement, the worry and the relief overwhelmed me.

John comforted me. "Why are you crying?" he said. "He's dead! I knew before I came he would be dead, but it's pretty exciting anyway." Blubbering away, I drew my pocket knife from my pocket and proceeded to whittle a deep notch in the stock of my .30-30 Winchester, marking a very important day in my life. Back at the tent, the children were sidelined by the treats John had brought. Once the boys heard that the bear was dead, they joined us as John went about skinning the animal. John pointed out the hump located on the shoulders, which sets it apart from other bear. He called the boys' attention to the long, sharp claws made for digging and the massive mouth of teeth. Gary was not impressed when John held up the badly damaged heart. "The bullet shot from the .30-30 is what killed this bear, an excellent shot!" An impish grin came over John's face as he turned my way. "The first few years after we came to this country I thought I would never live long enough to see you reach your goal of being an accurate shot. These past few years have proven you a top-notch shot, or I would have never allowed you to take on such an obligation."

It was getting late, and now that we knew the bear was dead, we decided to move back to Sheep Camp. It wasn't a good idea to leave the sheep alone, and never again, in our years at the camp, did we have to leave them unattended. John helped us get the camp back together as I prepared the evening meal and the boys finished their chores.

John had left the home ranch on very short notice, and he had to return as soon as possible. He heaped his plate full of food, and I sensed he was troubled, hesitating in his departure, with something on his mind. Then he spoke, weighing each word with care. "I think I know the answer to my question before I open my mouth. Would you like to take the small boys back to the ranch and I will stay here with the sheep? What if there are more grizzlies around?"

Defeat was not in my dictionary. John didn't like sheep, and this was not the agreement we made when I started out on this project. I placed my hand on John's shoulder and answered him. "This bear experience was very terrifying for me," I said, "but I know with my guardian angel and the ability given me, should another bear come into camp it will get the same treatment. If one threatens the boys or the sheep, it will be killed." I told John that I felt all the problems created by the heavy rain, topped off with the appearance of the grizzly, were a test to see what I was really made of. The whole experience had only made me stronger, boosting my self-confidence to the top. Choking back tears, I threw my arms around my husband. "I'm not the dude you brought to this country," I said. "I'm keeping my gun handy and I'm staying right here!"

But I had another idea. "How about you taking the boys back with you for a few days?" I asked him. "I'm sure they would like to go home for a few days before you start haying again." Gary, who had been particularly frightened by the grizzly incident, was delighted at the thought of going home. We got everything ready, and John and the young boys left for Big Lake, leaving John D. and me to look after Sheep Camp.

The brilliant red sunset to the west promised better weather for the new day. The boys wildly waved goodbye as John slipped his vehicle into gear, and they soon disappeared from our sight. We were again alone in the real wilderness.

The next morning, after two days of excitement, I woke as the sky was breaking light. It was the beginning of another day with much to be accomplished. Dressing hastily, I thought how different things would be without the boys. They were adaptable to most situations and with their caring dad they would manage just fine. They would be able to visit the Grinder children, telling everyone else who came along about the big grizzly at Sheep Camp.

John D. was good help, and and he too was up early, ready to start his chores. He would have extra duties with the small boys away, but perhaps would not miss their incessant chatter. The wood pile needed to be replenished, a big job with the scarcity of firewood. We had to make arrangements for the livestock salt, which had been stored under the most adverse conditions. We had to either move the big white tent to a better location or trench around the tent to prevent any more flooding. We hardly knew where to start, but at least it wasn't raining.

The first thing we had to do was to have breakfast. We enjoyed the fresh milk John had brought from the home ranch and believe me, we consumed a hearty meal before starting the day's work. John D. took off to look after the horses, leaving me to finish my coffee.

Suddenly, although I was surrounded by work to do, I lacked enthusiasm. It was rare that I didn't face any domestic or farm task with eagerness. Moping around, I was hardly able to put one foot in front of the other. Finally I realized that reality hit me—the events of the past couple of days had left their mark. I would never let it be known that the bear experience had left me in this state, although I would tell anyone it had been a momentous event. This reaction was not just the reality of the bear, it was the thought of all the things that might have happened. I had lost plenty of sleep these past few days, reliving the incident over and over, never to forget the boisterous roar of the enraged grizzly.

That night I decided not to stay outside near the campfire, but to retire early. In the middle of the night, I was awakened by a *thud* against the outside of my tent. Grabbing my gun and flashlight, I flipped the tent door open, fearing the worst. I flashed my light first one way and then another, and then I found only a little mouse, shivering with fright and unable to move. The creature had only come to visit the bags of nutritious grain that we kept in my tent for the horses, and no doubt had been there many times before. The mouse must have jumped from the outside table to the side of the tent, which made enough noise to waken me. I laughed to myself; my extra senses were working overtime. When does a mouse sound like a grizzly? Only after an encounter with a real, live grizzly....

I missed the boys, but was glad they could get a break from Sheep Camp and I could secretly recoup myself. It took John and me a couple of days to get Sheep Camp back in good shape again and the livestock moved to another area.

Word has a tendency to spread and to become exaggerated, especially when the subject is interesting or unusual. It wasn't long before we began to meet curious people coming to the Yanks Peak–Snowshoe Plateau in search of the "wild woman" with the sheep. Our camp was always located close to the only so-called road, and whoever came by stopped to see what was going on. Only the most adventurous individuals and those with a certain type of vehicle could make it up the mountain, such as the occasional inspector from the Department of Lands and Forests to check that we were meeting the requirements of our range permit. Regardless of who came, for what reason, we were always glad to see someone from the outside.

Gradually we learned that many stories had been started about the "woman who has the sheep." In one of the wilder stories, I had shot and crippled the grizzly, which, according to the tale, was very dangerous and now on the search for humans to attack. Numerous other stories had spread about the type and size of gun used.

It was amusing to find out what people thought, and what they had heard. What did they expect to see? Would they wonder what had possessed some woman to come here and herd sheep in the first place? Was she a derelict or a nomad? Could or would she speak to people? I could never admit to the outsiders the experiences I had and the tears I had shed before getting to this stage in my life. I was glad to tell them I had been a schoolteacher and moved here from California; at least that statement gave me some credibility. But despite being a normal educated human being, I wondered if they thought I was really normal. Who in their right mind would take on such responsibility? At the same time, killing a grizzly was an experience rarely accomplished by a woman, and secretly I was filled with pride.

I will long remember one particular visit. A Jeep came to a jolting halt just outside the door of my tent. In front sat two men, and perched behind was another man, holding a rifle. Surely they had come to search for the wounded man-eating grizzly. The man who rode in the back had eyeballs as big as saucers, and listened intently as I answered their questions. Finally he spoke. "You mean you killed that grizzly? I sure wouldn't want to come around your tent in the night." Little did he know he hadn't better, because inside my tent beside me lay my .30-30 rifle and I could use it. It wasn't long until they bounced on their way leaving us to chuckle among ourselves.

Strange things happened after the grizzly's visit. For instance, after several days I realized that a sizable section of my hair stood straight out from my head. At first I thought it was the way I had slept, but no way could I get that hair to lay flat. I remembered hearing tales and seeing cartoons about people who were badly frightened, literally having a hair-raising experience. Even when I washed and combed my hair, it remained unmanageable for approximately three weeks before slowly returning to its normal state.

The boys came back after about a week. I had been lonesome without them, and I knew it would be hard for John to look after the boys with all the work he had to do. The setting sun was hanging above the treetops when John and the two boys arrived back at Sheep Camp. John D. was anxious to see what new food might have been brought, and the small boys told stories of their vacation from Sheep Camp. Gary was especially curious to know if there had been any more grizzlies around our camp. John said he had to return to the home ranch early next morning ready to start haying at Annie's. Smiling and glancing my way, he said, "Providing there's no more grizzlies around, we'll keep haying until we get rained out or the snow flies."

I was soon to learn first-hand that grizzly bears are not the only predator in ranchlands.

The mountain lion, or cougar, is a very competent hunter, killing deer, caribou, moose, elk and mountain sheep but often finding an easier living preying on domestic stock. The cougar can bring down a full-grown steer or horse without any difficulty, and colts seem to be a favourite prey.

Cougar are very elusive, and I had seen only two adults in the wild, other than those treed by our working dogs. On an old abandoned road on the way to Sheep Camp one day, I was fascinated to spot a large female cougar. Following close behind her in single file were three small kittens, probably less than a month old, with distinct black dots on their fawny coats. They were waving their shortish round tails as they scampered along. I knew I had been lucky to witness something very few people ever saw.

I have met people who have lived far longer than myself in the wilderness and had never seen this evasive feline. Catching even a glance of the cougar is difficult; they are almost entirely nocturnal, and their excellent sight, phenomenal hearing and large, soft feet allow them to steal away as quietly as a shadow. The female cougar must be extra wary, guarding her young from the larger male of the species—if given an opportunity, he will kill and eat the kittens.

There is controversy about whether the cougar has any vocalization or "call." Once, in the middle of the night, I heard a blood-chilling scream like a woman being murdered. It was a hair-raising, piercing sound that sent chills throughout my entire body. I have no proof, but I believed it to be a cougar, perhaps searching for a mate. There was evidence of cougar in the area at this time. Once, at Cow Camp in

California, John heard a very similar scream to the one I described. He felt sure it was a cougar, and confirmed this by finding tracks in the soft dirt the next morning not far from their cabin.

A month or so after I had seen the female cougar and her young, I had my first real experience with a cougar. One night I lay in my bedroll while the clouds steadily belched out a heavy downpour all night, pounding hard on my small tent. The uncharacteristic whinnying of my black quarter horse mare told me that somewhere out in the darkness something was not right, but there was nothing I could do. I tossed and turned anxiously, waiting for first light.

Only three days prior, Beauty had given birth to a wobbly legged, fine-looking filly. This was Beauty's first colt, and with her bloodlines, she carried possibilities of becoming a very valuable animal. I was delighted and named her "Midas," as in the Greek legend, hoping she too would turn to gold.

Daylight finally arrived. The rain had subsided, with the sky still a dull slate grey and heavy clouds still hanging overhead. The boys were still sleeping when I slipped outside the tent. A half-mile to the east the sheep were feeding on the slope, and above our camp I could see the horses, but to my surprise Beauty's colt was not visible. The mare was restless, running aimlessly and making a shrill, nasal call.

We would have to find out what was wrong, but the first thing to do was get the boys up and dressed and fed. After the morning camp chores were completed, we caught our saddle horses and went to investigate.

The day was becoming miserable, with threatening clouds promising more rain. We searched the grass-covered slopes where the horses had been grazing for several hours, and then we found the body of the missing colt. It appeared to have been killed by a cougar. The filly's fragile neck had been broken and, with a single stroke of the cougar's powerful extensible claws, it had ripped open the filly's belly. Several pounds of the loin and rib area, along with some of the small intestines, had been eaten.

Tears rolled down my cheeks; it was such a loss! The small, innocent filly would never again frolic with her mother. In the distance, the mare could be seen hopelessly continuing to search for her newborn. Had this been the handiwork of the cougar I had seen earlier in the season, searching for food for its young? Although we were several miles from the sighting, it was well within her range of travel. I was so disappointed by the colt's death. Nature can be so cruel.

My next experience with a cougar came late one fall, while I was hunting horseback on the far side of Big Lake. Several inches of new snow had already covered the ground and the sky was grey as a goose's wing, promising more snow. Suddenly I came upon a large, fresh buck track, which I began to follow, my heart vibrating with expectation. Working my way slowly along the trail, my eyes casting about in both directions, I thought I would momentarily see one of the large trophy animals that Big Lake was noted for.

Near the top of the ridge, what I did see was something I did not expect—a story written in the snow, like an open book. The cougar must have crouched on the high rocky knob, its muscles coiled like spring steel, perhaps having heard the deer coming a considerable distance away. The unsuspecting buck I had been following walked along the trail at the base of the high knoll, and the cougar, likely weighing well over a hundred pounds, had made a tremendous leap, striking the deer with immense force and knocking it to the ground.

Before me were the signs of a vicious battle—badly trampled snow, broken twigs and branches, considerable blood and hair over a sizable area. The animals had used their natural weapons to do battle, the claws and strength of the cougar against the sharp, knife-like hooves and horns of the deer.

I remounted my horse, who was badly shaken and more than anxious to leave. Horses do not like the scent of the cougar, nor do they like the smell of blood.

In December 1963, Rosemary Waugh, who had sold us our Kelpies, arrived from Australia to spend a month at our ranch. The Cariboo was deep in winter, with extreme cold and snow.

Rosemary and I had become friends, and I was glad she was coming to visit, but in a way I wished I had not invited her. Over the years she had sent pictures of her modern home, beautiful well-kept gardens dotted with shrubs and trees, with the beach not far away, and paddocks laid out to exercise the thoroughbred horses she raised and loved. Everything we had was so primitive in comparison. Our wilderness ranch house of board and batten construction, our yard now covered with snow—even in the summer we had no enhancing flowers or shrubs. I reminded myself that our home was warm, cozy, full of love, and she would not go hungry.

It turned out that Rosemary took everything in her stride, throwing herself into ranch activities despite the snow and cold. She was game for anything, including trying her luck at ice skating on Big Lake, providing many laughs for all.

She was an excellent horsewoman, and when John invited her to help him move the cattle from one feeding area to another, she was more than eager to help. When the horse John had given her to ride started to buck, she declared that he had tried to "pig root" her, an expression we never forgot.

She truly enjoyed herself, but she could not believe how hard we worked. She tried to persuade us to move to Australia, where we could live a much easier life. We said no. The Cariboo had already become an integral part of our lives, and regardless of how flighty Mother Nature could be, we could not dream of leaving!

One morning Rosemary and I saddled the horses and rode out to check the animals. All was well in the feeding areas, so we proceeded into the timber, where the cattle had chosen their bed ground used year after year. Soon we came upon the carcass of a yearling steer we had lost a few weeks earlier and had left for scavengers. Held in the grip of Nature's deep freeze, it had not deteriorated at all, but I noticed that something was different from the last time I had gone by. I rode closer and saw that the animal's body had been nearly covered with freshly scrapped dried and decaying vegetation from the forest floor, mixed with a generous amount of snow.

I could not imagine what had tried to hide the carcass, until I noticed the track of a cougar. This was a surprise. I had been told that a cougar would not feed on a sick or dead animal, other than one it had killed. Penny, now very excited, was eager to follow the trail but under command to stay.

After careful observation I gave her the signal to find the animal. Away she went, her keen nose close to the ground, followed closely by our newly imported Kelpie, Digger, who did not know about hunting predators.

What excitement for Rosemary! Imagine going along on a hunt and seeing how valuable these dogs were in controlling predators, thousands of miles away in Canada. We raced along through the thick, snow-covered trees to the sound of the barking Kelpies. At last, with adrenalin surging through our veins, we spotted the Kelpies leaping up at the base of a fir tree.

We looked up and saw a huge, sleek cougar crouching on a lower branch, eight or ten feet from the ground. Quickly dismounting, we tied the horses securely some distance from the tree. I pulled my .22 rifle from the scabbard but, after searching my pockets, found I had no shells! Rosemary, a more experienced rider than I, would get to the ranch house for ammunition more quickly than I would. I agreed to stay at the tree with the dogs, hoping the cougar would not chance an escape.

The cougar appeared in excellent condition, with a very large belly, so I assumed she was pregnant. Why had she eaten on the steer? It would have been much easier to comprehend if she showed emaciation from starvation or disease, but that was not the case.

The animal was now making repetitive low growling noises and it was frightening to stand there. Time drags by even when one is waiting under the most favourable conditions. Rather than allow myself to think about being in danger, I centred my thoughts on the safety of the dogs. It is not unusual for a dog to be killed when it tries to tree an animal or when the treed animal attempts to escape. Big cats are extremely dangerous with their strength and sharp claws. I was beginning to feel the cold as I waited for Rosemary. At last, after what seemed like an eternity, she came back with John and Henry close behind. By this time I had grown almost numb with cold, and the cougar had become more agitated, angrily lashing its long tail back and forth.

I was so excited I wanted John to shoot it immediately, but he refused, stepping back. "We have no alternative other than to shoot," he said. "It is a predator and we cannot afford to have it around. Just think how this cougar hide will look in our front room! Not many people get to see a cougar, let alone kill one. So I want you to have the privilege."

"It's not that I don't want to shoot him," I shakily replied. "I still think about my little filly colt, Midas, that some cougar destroyed! It is just that I am trembling so bad from the cold and the excitement, I am afraid I might miss my target."

John grasped my arm. "At one time I knew your bullet would miss," he smiled, "but now you're a deadly shot." Taking a deep breath I pumped the .22 shell into the rifle chamber. I took careful aim and pulled the trigger. The cougar died instantly on my first shot, falling heavily to the ground at the base of the tree.

Rosemary and I spent the rest of the day discussing the hunt and the excellent performance of the dogs. I also had to skin the cougar, which took a considerable amount of time due to its size and weight. I found that it was a female, about three years old, but not pregnant as I had first suspected. When I opened up her stomach I found gobs of fat. She was by far the fattest animal I had ever skinned.

Late in the afternoon, I picked up my cold weather attire to put it

Cougars were predators that posed a great danger to our stock. I had no choice but to shoot this one that had been hanging around our herd.

away before starting to prepare the evening meal. From somewhere in my clothes, numerous .22 shells rolled out. Where they had they been when I needed them? The anticipation and excitement of the hunt, along with the layers of outside clothing with their numerous pockets must have caused me to overlook the shells. Was I embarrassed!

Later, at dinner, we celebrated with good food, a few hot rums and lots of laughs and wisecracks. We relived the cougar hunt over and over again, each of us recounting our own version. Finally I had to admit I had had the shells with me all the time I had stood waiting for Rosemary's return. What an enjoyable evening we had, with a good deal of teasing for the mighty cougar hunter.

Penny, a great dog, lived to be sixteen years old, producing many good working dogs. She was easy to control by whistle, arm movements, eye and voice. Cowboys, who ride many horses during their life, claim that they have had only one really good horse in all those years. I believe

I could trust Penny around all the farm animals. She worked hard and was a dependable working dog and companion.

this to be true with dogs as well. I have had many good dogs, but my beloved Penny was above all others. She gave me many hours of excellent work and was a great companion. If dogs have a heaven, and I am sure they do, she will be there among the champions.

Exploring

One very early morning as I awakened at Sheep Camp, rays of light peeked furtively from behind the horizon. I slipped into my clothes quickly and left camp to check the sheep nearby. Some of them had already started to graze while others paused to lick at the salt we had placed for their needs, and which would soon need refilling. The dogs, always eager to get to work, gave no sign of distress in the herd. They raced around charging one another and awaiting their dog food.

I hurried back to base camp, started the fire and prepared our breakfast and a picnic lunch. "Let's go exploring. We need a break!" I called loudly.

Before long the boys exploded from their tent to the welcoming fire. "Are we going exploring?" they asked.

"Yes," I replied. "We've had too much rain. I've packed a big lunch. We'll have our breakfast and get our chores done and we're off to explore Yanks Peak."

At last we were on our way. The boys chattered excitedly while the dogs ran helter-skelter close by. It was a fantastic day!

Spring was long gone at home ranch, but here it was mid-July and the beginning of spring. The alpine country was beautiful. Close by our path, a rivulet ran from a thick patch of winter's snow. Standing at the very edge of the melting snow stood the purest big, bright yellow glacier lily with only two very glossy dark green leaves. Other glacier lilies grew close by—always the first flower to appear in the alpine spring. We had already seen the freckle-faced tiger lily here and there, and the Indian paintbrush with its red blooms. The growing season in this country was very short, but there were many flowers in Mother Nature's garden that I had never seen, and many others yet to open.

We rode our horses as far as we could ride, then dismounted and securely tied them to small alpine firs. We started our trek upward on a path that appeared not to have been used for many years. When we were nearly to the top, any way we looked we could see vast areas of timbered summits. This country was all new to me, with so much to learn, such great rugged beauty and vastness—certainly not like California.

For safety reasons we had to stay away from the northern slopes. There lay a deep basin gouged out by nature, known as Jews Hollow, and close by was the ominously named Breakneck Ridge.

We had many other exploring adventures during our summer in the alpine country that first year and in subsequent years. They were a refreshing break, and it was fascinating to explore this vast area where

The alpine fields were full of an amazing variety of flowers.

more than a century ago, miners with exuberant spirits had lived and worked. One of our favourite things to do was look for blazes. To blaze is simply to remove a hunk of bark from a good standing tree to indicate a path or trail, and believe it or not, blazes are fascinating. They could lead a newcomer back to their camp or their new-found mining claim, or to an area that needed more investigating.

A blaze must be made at a proper height and placement so that it can be seen easily. It must be clear of low-hanging branches and all surrounding vegetation. Visibility is difficult enough in this country, due to short daylight hours and the possibility of heavy fog, blinding snow and severe wind and rainstorms.

Whichever way we went, we played hide and seek all summer to find the next blaze. It was a game for us, since Mother Nature's handiwork had left little sign of activity. Many of the old blazes were now covered with lush vegetation and bathed in solitude and beauty.

On an August day in 1963, during an afternoon of looking for blazes, I noticed a blaze I had not seen before. I followed that blaze, then saw another, and before us stood a towering headboard. It was five feet tall, fourteen inches wide, and two and a half inches thick. I had never seen a headboard like this:

Sacred to the Memory of

William Luce—Native of Maine U.S.A.

Died 28 May 1881 Aged 60 years.

I was so excited about my find, this very distinguished tribute, and I was filled with questions that had no answers. I would have to wait until I got home to do some historical research. Right now I had to concentrate on looking after the sheep and keep moving the lambs to the best feeding areas, with the objective of top market prices later in the year.

An ear-piercing whistle shattered the silence as we approached the slopes of Base Mountain. We brought our horses to an abrupt halt. "Someone is whistling at us, Mom," the boys called.

One of our most exciting discoveries was this headboard from an old miner. William Luce came from Maine looking for gold.

Perched high on a rocky crag was the sentry—a big hoary marmot warning of danger with a shrill, high-pitched, almost human whistle, which, as I learned later, could be heard close to a mile away. These heavy, bushy-tailed rodents, too big and awkward to climb trees, lived in burrows in the ground or among rocks.

Colonies of marmots are very interesting to watch. They are definitely social and, on many occasions, I have observed what seemed like several families using the same retreats and trails.

It was a mid-August day and the remaining patches of snow were fast melting, but not gone. Winter comes early above timberline, often in late August. Thunderheads loomed in the north behind Mount Burdett and its close neighbour, Meridian Mountain. The sultry atmosphere and angry sky foretold that before the day was over we would have a thunderstorm.

The sweltering sun beat down on us, and our saddle horses tried to rid themselves of troublesome horseflies as we wound our way through one glade after another. From the steep, rocky slopes better than half a mile away came the warning of the marmot, and I realized with disappointment that they had already sensed our presence. At the bottom of the rocky slope lay an alpine meadow surrounded by the aromatic

Beside the Luce headboard we found the remains of an old stone oven, which would have been used for cooking.

alpine fir. Through the middle of the meadow zigzagged a crystal clear ice-cold rivulet, one of the many small tributaries emptying into Cunningham Creek.

What a welcome sight on such an oppressively hot, close day! We dismounted, loosened cinches, removed bridles and tied the horses to nearby trees. There they stomped and swished their long tails as the multitude of savagely hungry flies and mosquitoes encircled them. I felt bad for them. This was the peak season for the buzzing barbarous insects. The bite of the black fly is very painful, often swelling and itching. Mosquitoes are even worse. They seem especially hungry early in the morning and in the evening, but they are always around. Only the female bites, but both can drive you to the verge of hysteria with their continual buzzing. Both blackflies and mosquitoes are bloodsucking insects that are particularly voracious on sultry days and after a rain—both prevalent in the alpine country. The old-timers warned me not to wear blue or red clothing, and said that the least enticing colour was

Another exciting find was this old prospector's cabin, which we found down in the canyon.

olive drab or khaki. But with the zillions and zillions of these insects, and no shelter from them at Sheep Camp, it made little difference. How could one tell?

Leaving the boys to catch the frogs and toads that were so plentiful by the small stream, I slipped quietly toward the rocky outcropping, hoping to get some good photos of the marmots. Their two long, chisel-like incisors, both top and bottom, continue to grow all their lives, kept to proper length by use, but if one or more incisors are lost or thrown out of line, the animal starves to death.

The slate-grey boulders, striped with numerous intrusions of white quartz, were well populated with members of the marmot family. The sentinel gave his shrill call and the answer of its companion pealed from across the way. Nearby, on a large boulder, three young marmots, weighing perhaps four pounds each, sat motionless. Soon they would all be preparing to hibernate for more than six months. Another shrill whistle came from the huge sentinel marmot, sending the younger ones down into the rocks.

I stalked the sentry, coming up behind a stunted alpine fir whose roots were having a hard time clinging to the fragmented rock. Not fifty feet from me sat the grizzled, reddish brown furry animal, about thirty inches long from nose to tail. He was a comical fellow, sitting there scratching his ears and fighting the pesky flies, occasionally shrieking his whistle in marmot language.

I glanced away for just a moment, and the marmot ducked into its den at the base of the huge flat-topped boulder. A drop hole descends about two feet before branching out into several chambers with more than one exit, protecting the marmots from predators—mainly wolverine, grizzly bear, eagles and hawks.

Below, the boys were still engrossed with the frogs and water and to the west, across the valley, the sheep grazed peacefully in the wide open spaces. But in the distance I could hear a faint roll of thunder, which meant one thing—we had better get our horses and make a swift return to camp.

We had no sooner reached Sheep Camp than the wind started roaring and the black clouds came winging in, filling the evening sky in a few seconds. We were soon experiencing one of many thunderstorms so common in the high country, but this storm was one never to be forgotten. Lightning slashed the ebony sky and from overhead came huge, deafening claps of thunder that caused the tents to wobble and flap. Thunderstorms are especially hazardous to people near or on rocky peaks and ridges, and here we were!

The jagged streaks of lightning and violent thunder continued, so close we were terrorized with each discharge of atmospheric electricity. The penetrating odour of ozone gave notice that the lightning was striking very close to us. Again and again thunder rolled through the mountains and reverberated overhead. After what seemed an eternity, the lightning and thunder moved into the distance, leaving us with first-hand knowledge of a severe thunderstorm. Moments later, sheets of lashing rain came pounding down on our tent. We had lived through thunderstorms before but always had four walls or a vehicle to get into for protection. This was without a doubt the worst thunderstorm I had ever experienced.

It was now pitch dark outside. Inside our big tent, the crackling fire in the wood stove kept us warm while heating some canned milk for the hot chocolate we all needed. Before long the rain eased up. We were still shaken, but warm and dry. By the light of a flickering candle, each boy related his fears. I too had been very frightened, and knowing God was always with us, I gave thanks.

One of our favourite pastimes at Sheep Camp was to locate the small herd of woodland caribou—beautiful, curious and seemingly stupid animals—and watch them. Caribou are simply North American reindeer. Both sexes have horns, which they shed each year.

We often saw caribou near the snow patches. This is a cold country animal, well protected from winter's blast by a coat of coarse hollow hair overlapping a fine fur-like undercoat, and they are excellent swimmers. A caribou's feet are much like snowshoes, enabling it to go where small-footed animals cannot.

One warm, sunny afternoon in early July 1962, I had one of my most interesting experiences with caribou. Shortly after lunch, I saddled my black mare, Beauty, and took off under a cloudless sky with my camera, in hopes of getting a few good pictures of a caribou. I was meandering down through the alpine meadow working my way around the quagmires, when just ahead a cow caribou and her very small buff-brown calf appeared. When a caribou is disturbed, it usually stands and stares before taking off in a high-stepping trot. It is not uncommon for a caribou to trot up close to a horse, then prance away with its white tail thrown up, much like the whitetail deer. These caribou seemed never to have seen a horse, and with their springy trot they circled closer and closer to investigate.

The big greyish brown cow stood and stared while her small, alert calf stood close by, unconcerned, nursing and paying no attention to me or my horse. Suddenly the cow whirled and trotted away into a nearby thicket. The frisky calf followed right behind her, giving the appearance of a domestic kid goat—a crafty rascal! I sat quietly on my horse, and the animals soon emerged from the dwarf willow thicket to browse on the lush alpine feed. Occasionally they glanced in my direction as I rode slowly along. Then the cow got nervous, and holding her head high and her short white tail in the air, she sprang over the gentle slope into the deep forest. It was not our last encounter with this cow and her calf. We called her "the loner" and saw her often, but never with other caribou.

The last time we were to see evidence of her was when the first snow came to the plateau, not long before our journey south to the home ranch. The dogs gave warning of something unusual being around, and not far from camp we saw tracks of the loner and her calf, followed by the tracks of the carnivorous timber wolf.

In late August we came upon seventeen caribou in one herd. They had seen us many times, and we could get very close by imitating their calls or waving something white. Most of them were lying down on the gentle, wide open slope, and the rest of them browsed on the dwarf willow.

Caribou appear to have poor eyesight, much like bear. When the wind was in our favour, we could get very close before they showed any indication of knowing we were there. First one would get up, then another, then all would stand and look, unless they were frightened. Caribou stand and urinate before moving, much as domestic sheep do. They stood and watched us, apparently curious, for some time before getting jittery and moving away. They left us in a high-stepping trot, making a constant clicking noise caused by the shifting of the foot tendons and anklebones. The first time I heard this sound, I thought it was caused by the rocky terrain, but it is characteristic of all species of caribou.

Among the herd was a very large bull who carried a wonderful rack still in the velvet, a real trophy. On September 1, when I saw him again, he had stripped and polished his horns for the approaching mating season. In the late summer and early fall, prior to rutting season, the meat of the caribou is choice, very tender and full of flavour. But I found it was like eating hotcakes—it did not stay with you like other wild meat.

Hunting season opened that day, and there were far more hunters than caribou in this area. John arrived from the home ranch, bringing supplies, mail and news of the outside. John Dean agreed to stay with the boys and the sheep so John and I could hunt on opening day.

With our guns in the scabbards we rode away at dawn, leaving the boys sound asleep in their tent. My thoughts turned to the fine trophy of antlers I hoped to line in the sights of my .30-30 Winchester. We wove our way over the rocky pack trails made a century before by prospectors on their way to the goldfields. The sun climbed high in the sky as we rode toward the upper meadows. John stopped on top of a small hill, took out his binoculars and began glassing the area closely. He pointed to a dark object, small and far away, and through the glasses I saw the tremendous bull moose. His antlers were snow white, newly polished, and his sleek, fat body glistened in the sun.

Despite his enormous antlers and huge body, he disappeared as quickly and quietly as a shadow into the almost vertical canyons that dropped off into the Swift River.

It was not long before we spotted the caribou. Excitement surged through my veins. I tried to resist an attack of buck fever, because I did not want to miss the fry of liver and onions I had long anticipated. At the home ranch we never butchered lamb or mutton for our own use, but at Sheep Camp the odd yearling that had been too small to sell in the fall was better than no fresh meat at all. I dreamed of the tender steaks we'd soon have—that is, if I didn't get too excited.

"Let's tie up our horses and stalk them," said John quietly. "I caught a glimpse of several, and there's a big bull among them."

Quickly removing my .30-30 from its scabbard, I tied Beauty

securely to a nearby tree. Below me, John had tied Duke into a small thicket of firs and was wiping the scope of his 300 Savage with his bright red handkerchief. We had only gone a few hundred yards when John called, "Shoot, Doris." I stepped quietly toward him, and there, between two clumps of firs on the edge of the alpine meadow, stood a young bull. I placed the gold bead on the slate-grey target, bringing almost instant death. There was a moment's silence, and then the hills barked back with a thundering echo. Glancing over just in time, I saw John crouching and looking through his scope on the 300 Savage. There was another shot!

It was the caribou I had watched all summer. There was a sudden scurry of hooves, and the remaining herd trotted and circled in every direction before disappearing into the timbered canyons. There lay our two caribou, only a few hundred feet apart. We walked up to the bull John had killed. "Why didn't you shoot him?" John asked. "I gave you

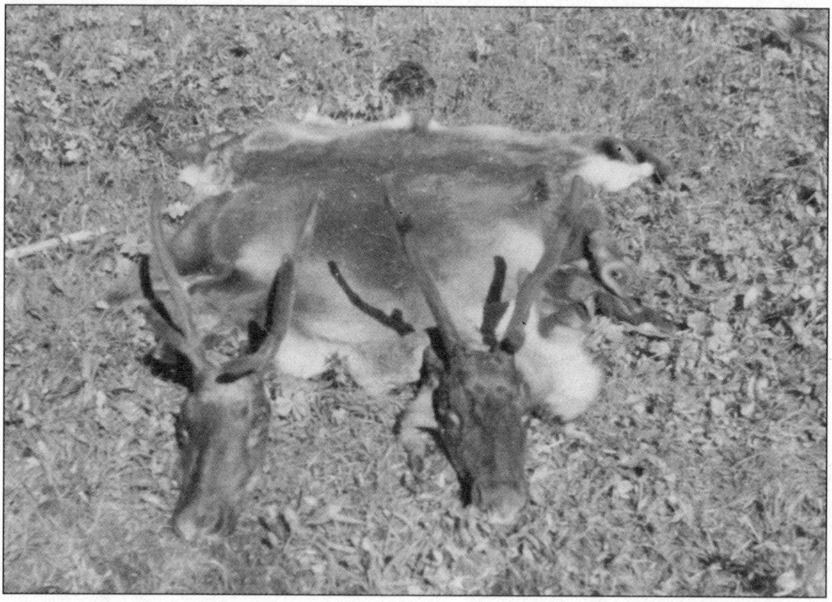

We field dressed these caribou, then skinned and hung the meat back at camp. It took us all day. Neither John nor I enjoyed killing them. I had lived with them all summer and it felt like killing a friend. We vowed never to shoot another caribou and we didn't.

first chance. Those antlers on your animal aren't much for size, and look—they're still in the velvet."

"I thought I'd let you kill him." I replied. "I was afraid I'd get buck fever and I couldn't see him from where I was standing. I bet my caribou will have the most tender steaks." We smiled at each other. We were not after antlers; we needed our winter's supply of meat.

"It's just shortly after twelve," said John. "Despite the huge breakfast I ate this morning, I'm starved. I could sure go for a big feed of those tender steaks from your caribou, but we will have to wait for those."

He took his knife and whetstone from the pocket of his Levis. The knife was sharp, but he always gave it a few licks of the stone whether or not it was needed. This is where the work began—we would field dress the animals, leaving the hide to help keep the meat clean, but immediately after reaching camp we would skin and hang them. We would never leave carcasses out overnight for fear the grizzly would devour them.

We got busy preparing the meat, and I didn't feel proud as I knelt over my stilled carcass. This caribou had seen me many times during the summer and I had never hurt him, and now he'd trot no more though the bogs or prance on the drifts of snow.

"How's your knife? Need sharpening?" John asked, pulling his animal up onto a nearby hummock.

I had no time to feel guilty now. "No, I'm almost finished," I said, "but will you help me turn him over? Warm as it is the flies will be sure to come."

We had to go back to camp and get Bucky and the pack saddle. It would take two trips, keeping us busy for the rest of the day. We washed our hands in the cool rivulet close by, walked back to our waiting horses and lost no time in getting back to camp. The closer we came to camp, the more I thought about the children. Were they all right? Soon I could hear the sound of them playing, and I felt relieved.

The minute they saw us, their game was forgotten.

"Where's the caribou, Mom? Did you get a caribou?" they asked. John Dean went to catch Bucky, while John and I had a quick lunch and told the boys about the hunt. I stayed at camp with the boys while John and John Dean packed first one caribou in and then the other.

The sun was teetering on the horizon when we finally finished skinning our caribou and caring for their hides, which we wanted to keep. It wasn't long before the smell of liver and onions filled the evening air. This was a real treat for Sheep Camp, along with the fresh vegetables John had brought with him. After our hearty dinner I did the dishes while the boys prepared for bed. Soon they were sound asleep, snug and warm in their sleeping bags.

Outside the white cook tent, the campfire snapped as the smoke disappeared into the darkness. A multitude of stars twinkled high in the heavens as John and I reclined against our saddles, consuming cups of jet black coffee by the fireside. We watched the glowing embers smouldering in their bed of ashes. It was a successful hunt and the end of a perfect day.

Homeward Bound

The end of the first week of September brought along the brilliant fall colours, and now it was time to think about moving the sheep back home to Big Lake. We were well aware of what the fall weather could bring in the alpine region, and we didn't want to experience a snowstorm in these mountains this late in the season.

We did not know exactly what day John and Henry would arrive to break camp, so we planned to be ready with our gear and packs as early as possible. As the boys stuffed in their belongings, I asked them what was the first thing they wanted to do when they got home. In unison they answered, "Just go to the store and look around. Get some ice cream and go play with the Grinder boys."

Our trip home from Sheep Camp would be much the same as when we had travelled north in the spring. We would carefully work the sheep homeward, keeping them as calm as possible to help them maintain their weight for top market prices. Our livestock buyer wanted these choice lambs sent directly to their stockyards, and the trucks would be at the ranch shortly after our arrival home. There was no time to lose.

Waking up from a sound sleep, I could see day was just breaking, and in the distance I could hear the familiar sound of our ranch vehicle. John and Henry would arrive soon, and it would be a long and demanding day for all.

We were filled with enthusiasm as we ate a quick but hearty breakfast of home-grown potatoes with bacon and eggs, topped off with lots of coffee and hot chocolate. The men were anxious to get back to the ranch and finish repairing the stackyards so no livestock could get into the winter's hay. All the gates and fences must be repaired or at least checked before the sheep were ready to be sorted and separated for shipping.

It took us some time to get packed up. We had to separate items we would need on the way home from those we would be able to send home. We would not need extra salt, gas cans or the portable stove. Everything we needed for the journey was in our packs, which the men had already lashed onto the packhorses.

Our saddle horses were ready; we started out immediately so we could make it to Snarlberg in time to make camp. "We'll see you soon," we called to the men as the farm vehicle crawled away from our last summer camp. The sheep had been held close by today, and the boys and dogs soon had them heading in the opposite direction from the way they had gone all through the summer grazing season. Didn't the sheep know it was time to go home?

It would take us several days to get there, depending what the weather might offer. Each day we would be dropping farther out of the rain forest and into a warmer climate. Getting to Snarlberg today would be a stretch of travel we wouldn't like, nor would the animals. It was steep, and dark with the dense forest close to the roadway. The road was nearly impassable now, after years of storms that had washed much of it away. We could make it down the eight rocky, rough switchbacks this time, but it was clear that it might be our last trip this way.

John Dean was anxious to get back to his home and school. We agreed to get up earlier tomorrow and keep the sheep on the road longer, but with promises not to make the sheep run or get too hot, which could affect their weight.

We moved steadily down the hills, and enjoyed the warmer climate.

The canyon at Snarlberg is so steep that driving the sheep up and down was challenging.

Each day was different from the Snowshoe Plateau, and each day took us closer to home, comfort and relaxation.

Several days after leaving Snarlberg, we stopped at Ernie Lang's property as we had promised. It was a place the boys liked, with lots of room and feed for the animals. The sheep were soon under control with help from the working dogs. They started feeding on the grass, which had grown since our visit in the spring. It wasn't long before the sheep began to settle and the pack horses, free of their packs, were let loose for the night.

The tinkling bells of the sheep and the neighing of a horse to the sauntering horses behind brought our presence to the attention of Mr. Lang, the "Old Prospector." Stepping quickly from nowhere, he smiled as he greeted us. "Glad to see you're all back! Often thought about you during the summer. No place for a woman and even more so in grizzly country. Looks like your sheep really gained weight. Did you have any

Heading home from the summer range.

predators bothering the sheep? Did you see any grizzly bears?" Questions flew so fast I had no time to answer. Turning toward his house, he called, "Come in, come in!"

He placed a match to the firewood ready in his cookstove. His callused hand ground his short cigarette into a tobacco lid, a makeshift ashtray. With this, as with most of the furnishings and supplies in his isolated cabin, he made do with what he had. "Let me make you a cup of tea," he went on. "I have some cookies that came by freight line on Tuesday. They're pretty good." The wood fire cracked away and soon the tea was prepared and served, with the cookies on a fancy plate. Mr. Lang wouldn't have many more years to probe his claims. This once tall, erect man was now stooped, and his face was furrowed with lines. Prospecting was hard work, and the inclement weather so common in this area made everything much more difficult.

It was nearly dark outside and the boys were sitting around their blazing campfire. Inside, a small glow from the kerosene lamp gave the cabin a homey atmosphere. The Old Prospector's conversation soon turned to days gone by. "Seems like you really got around over the country with those 'woolies.' Did you ever find Luce's headboard?"

"How could I forget?" I answered. "In August I found the headboard wired to a tree. Apparently it was his home site, as the area nearby showed a vague outline of a cabin and a stone outdoor oven, which had not been used for many, many years." Excitedly, I asked, "What do you know about the headboard?"

"Well, I'll tell you," said Mr. Lang. "It is the grave of William Luce. He was a tough old bastard. He was a Yank—in fact, he was known as the 'Old Yank' and that is how Yanks Peak got its name." He told me that Luce had come from Bangor, Maine, against the wishes of his well-to-do family, and had filed his first mining claim in May 1863. In May 1881, he died in a blizzard on the Snowshoe Plateau, at the age of sixty, and his family thought he should have a headboard. It was made by Johnny Knott, the old headboard maker of Barkerville, and Luce's miner friends agreed to take it to its destination.

The headboard was entrusted to the group that had offered to deliver it, but along the way they decided it was party time! Somewhere in the vicinity of Antler Creek, after consuming a few too many drinks, they sat the headboard up against a log. Later, when they were to continue, they could not find it.

The *Vancouver Province* of February 10, 1940, shows Sam Callison placing the missing headboard at the Snowshoe Plateau, at the site of Luce's Hotel in the early 1860s. The photo showed a darkened headboard that had likely been covered with leaves and moss for some years, but it showed no cracks or any sign of fire or other damage.

"When they took the headboard to the Cariboo Hudson Mine to be delivered by 'cat' freight," Mr. Lang went on, "a woman known as Mrs. Pedersen gave it a good cleaning and repainted the letters."

I laughed. I could not believe I was hearing the answers to my questions! I told him that after I had found the headboard, I had asked John to bring some paint on his next visit. He did, and I painted the letters again, thirty-three years later. No wonder the words were so legible! The headboard background had gently sloughed away over the years, leaving the letters as though they had been deeply carved—they were protected by paint.

Mr. Lang and I talked for hours, sharing stories and imagining the days of yesteryear long gone. The boys had been asleep for hours when I finally went to bed. Tomorrow we would be on the road again, and within a few days we would be home.

The green and gold leaves of the cottonwood trees quivered in the early fall air. Overhead could be heard the whistle of the mallard's wings as he flew down to join his mate and her ducklings, in a sheltered cove on Big Lake. The ducklings were now feathered out and able to fly. In a few weeks all the ducks and geese would soon be heading south for winter.

Dawn tomorrow would bring the livestock trucks to the ranch, ready to take the fat alpine-fed lambs to Vancouver for slaughter. The first thing I had to do this morning was to gather the sheep from the alfalfa field and bring them back to the home corrals. Then the sheep would have to be sorted into different pens, and repairs made to the pens and loading chute. A good supply of choice hay would have to be secured for the lambs before shipping.

There was no time to lose. The sun was climbing from behind the rolling hills as I threw my saddle on Beauty, quickly fastened the spruce pole gate behind me and slid into the saddle. Off we went, followed closely by the well-trained and experienced Kelpies, Penny and Digger.

Jogging along on Beauty, I thought about the projects I had planned for the day. When I came within view of the alfalfa field, I could hear the tinkling bells of the sheep in the distance, and I could almost smell the aroma of piping hot coffee brewing at the ranch house. I would surely need a cup or two before starting on my many tasks. Almost no one wanted to help me with the sheep, although they would willingly lend a hand with the cattle. John helped when he could, but working sheep was one thing he never enjoyed. Oftentimes I wondered whether he was finding other things he would rather do than help, but this was my project, and sheep did need more looking after than cattle and horses.

I sent Penny to gather the sheep and bring them in my direction, then I rode toward the dense mixed forest, watching Digger closely. With his exceptionally keen nose, he began to throw his head high, filling his nostrils with a particular snort, then moved slowly toward the forest. I knew something was around, but what? Down the rolling hillside, sloping toward the forest, came the flock of sheep, followed by the dependable Penny. I whistled to her and she proceeded eagerly in the same direction as Digger. Not far from where the sheep had been feeding was the answer—a nice big fat lamb lay dead.

I dismounted and went right to the limp, still warm lamb. On close examination I found a severed jugular vein, the familiar mark of the Canadian lynx.

Now the full realization of my predicament came to me. *No gun!*

Lynx posed a constant threat to our flock of sheep. I started trapping them in the '60s, and the extra cash was important income on the ranch.

Rarely, if ever, did I go without a gun, but in my haste to get started on my tasks, I had neglected to bring one.

There was only one thing to do: go back and get my .22 Remington, which I considered the best for cat hunting. Penny and Digger would not leave once an animal was treed. I really did not have time to hunt the lynx, but I could not let it run loose. It would only continue to kill the livestock. I rode back to the ranch, knowing for sure this day would not be long enough.

Upon my return I listened for the dogs, but all I could hear was the heavy breathing of my sweaty mare. One can imagine almost anything if one tries hard enough, and after listening closely, I was almost sure I heard barking. Excitement surged through me as I kicked my mare into a trot across the field. There is nothing as exhilarating as a hunt behind the sound of dogs on the trail.

Sure enough, I soon saw the shape of a Kelpie leaping up at the trunk of a large spruce tree. Standing more sedately, with her front paws against the tree trunk, was the reliable Penny. Somewhere among the heavy spruce branches was a lynx.

I tied my horse a safe distance away from the commotion, pulled my gun from the scabbard and loaded it with a number of .22 long rifle shells. I pulled special ropes with sturdy snaps from my saddle bags and snapped them into the heavy-duty collars around the dogs' necks. Both Kelpies had to be securely tied in case a bullet missed its target and only wounded the wild cat. A lynx fights on its back and its long, sharp claws can easily rip a dog's stomach wide open. I raised the gun and placed a well-aimed shot directly between the eyes of the lynx, and it fell to the ground with a thud, instantly dead. The Kelpies, who had a hatred of any cats, including house cats, went wild.

Then my full day's work on the ranch began. It was indeed a long day, much too long for my energy supply, but I worked until well after dark.

Penny, in typical herding dog style, helps us gather the sheep for market.

The next morning the livestock trucks arrived right on schedule. The fattened lambs were loaded, and away they rolled to market. I then put in another long day, and once again it was a relief to get ready for bed. Fond memories of Sheep Camp flashed through my mind, but I was very glad to be home from the mountains. By now, Yanks Peak and the surrounding area would be covered with a generous blanket of snow. And this was home—so peaceful and quiet. When the boys and I had caught sight of the home ranch on our way back, our plain board and batten home seemed like a castle. It had a big, soft, clean bed, with hot water and a tub.

Here at home, amid my small conveniences, I closed my eyes and gratification swept over me. As I fell into a deep, sound sleep, I thought, at least I'm not a dude anymore.

Leaving Big Lake

The years of ranching in the Cariboo were gratifying but difficult, and through the mid-1960s our pace began to slow. The first suggestion that we should put the ranch up for sale came after John consulted our family doctor about the chest pains he had been having. They meant one thing: a heart condition. "John, it looks like you are going to have to take life a bit easier," Dr. Atwood told him. "You will have to cut down on the strenuous ranch work." This message was hard to absorb. How could he eliminate the physically demanding work, the work he loved, and still be a rancher?

Our boys were too young to take over the ranch, and good ranch hands were nearly impossible to get. What good man wanted to work for the wages a rancher could afford to pay? Ranch work was hard, and the hours were long. Also, it was often seasonal work because most ranches were too small to hire year-round help. Many men would still give anything to be a cowboy, and some dreamed of one day having a spread of their own. But life in the Cariboo was changing. Men were searching for occupations with shorter hours, a shorter work week, better wages and benefits.

Not long after we got this news, I began having trouble with my back, with first one bout and then another. Finally, after weeks of severe pain and a lengthy stay at the hospital in Kamloops, I was told I must never lift again. The x-rays showed an arthritic condition that may have been brought on by hard work and heavy lifting, and apparently I could expect back problems for the rest of my life. This brought the inevitable to our door. We would have to put the ranch up for sale.

The thought of it was not easy. It had been our home for all these years, the best years of our lives, although they had been demanding. But now, work that had once been easy was a chore. If we did continue to ranch and to sacrifice our health and perhaps some of our remaining years for the boys, would they want to ranch when they became adults, or would they go their own ways in search of some other livelihood?

Late in the fall of 1965, we listed the ranch for sale through a local real estate agency, and it was to take nearly three years to sell it for the price and conditions we could accept. During that time, many prospective purchasers, mostly Americans, looked at the ranch. They had property to trade, everything from bean elevators to motels in the US. We had no intention of returning to our native land. We were now Canadian citizens, and the Cariboo had become a part of us, providing well for us and giving us such wonderful memories.

Progress was fast leaving its mark upon this once secluded area with its vast open spaces. Along with the influx of people came modern comforts and conveniences. Ranches rapidly began to change hands, to newcomers in search of a home away from the hustle and bustle of more populated areas, seeking all that the prosperous province of British Columbia had to offer.

On February 25, 1960, Ottawa granted a licence for CKCQ, the first licensed full-time privately owned radio station in Canada to operate in Williams Lake. The new station was a real asset to the people of the Cariboo, bringing good programming, local news and the popular "message time," broadcasting messages to and from people in the remote places without telephones or other means of communication.

We took the service seriously, but there were some funny messages, and often people seemed to send messages because they enjoyed hearing their name on the radio. For example: "We are fine. Hope you are," sent periodically to a man who was miles from his home feeding cattle in a remote valley. There was the message sent to the trapper who was way out in the backcountry: "Don't come in to appear in court until next month." The radio station was nervous about sending this message, only to find out later that the man was to appear in court to receive his citizenship, but that the ceremony had been postponed, and the message was meant to save the trapper hours of unnecessary travel. We heard many other messages, including "Your tractor parts are in, please pick them up," "I have been discharged from the hospital, please come and get me," "Your baby chicks have arrived" and "Please call the RCMP for an urgent family matter."

The most beneficial change came in the late fall of 1967, when BC Hydro brought electric power to the Big Lake area. Electricity made life better and easier in many ways. No more home lighting systems, which more often than not fail to start when they are most needed. And, even more important to me, no more temperamental gas motors or hissing gas lights. Power brought television, the deep freeze, electric blankets for extremely cold winter nights. People could have block heaters for automobiles and farm tractors—no more days spent trying to get machinery going in the penetrating cold. And there were many other appliances that were soon taken for granted.

In July the following year, telephone service was another major convenience that changed life at the off-road ranches. A school bus began running for the first time that fall, a community hall was constructed, better roads were established to accommodate the influx of tourists and new residents, along with the many logging trucks now going back and forth to the Likely–Keithley area.

In October 1968, our real estate agent found the purchaser we had been hoping for during these many months, and suddenly the sale of the ranch was completed.

The ride home from the lawyer's office that night was a quiet one, each of us alone with our thoughts. When we reached the ranch that was still home, but not legally, I slipped away, needing to be alone. The late fall wind swept raw and cold under the full moon hanging over

Big Lake. My emotions gave way and I wept as though I had never wept before. I walked and walked for hours, with my feelings as mixed up as the day I had first come to live at this ranch nearly twenty years before.

How could I face each tomorrow without seeing Big Lake, that vast, beautiful, ever-changing body of water? There was something mystic about this lake, whose moods were as changeable as the weather. The serene expanse could be mirror-like, it could be dark and murky and mysterious, or its waves could lash at the shoreline again and again as if in anger. In the winter, it was hidden beneath a layer of ice two or three feet thick, which expanded and contracted with deep, thunderous rumbling, leaving jagged lightning-like cracks across its surface.

Both John and I had mixed emotions, but we had to leave; it was something we had no control over. Once we had accepted that, the adjustment became easier. The ranch was no longer ours, and we had to think of the future. We began to pack our years' worth of goods and memories. There was much to be done, and leaving would be very difficult.

We moved from Big Lake to a small semi-residential area near Williams Lake. Neither of us liked the area, but it would do until we decided on our next step.

When we awoke on our first morning in this new world, there was no sound of the lapping water of Big Lake, no crowing of the big red rooster with his harem of cackling hens. All we could hear was the sound of traffic whizzing by on Highway 97 and other sounds of so-called civilization. I was *homesick*! We now had enough money to lead an easier life and to retire. This had sounded great at the time, but before long, we found ourselves bored with freedom from responsibility.

Having worked with horses and cattle all his life with great satisfaction, John soon received several offers of work. I had been out of the conventional working world for more than twenty years, and now I needed to find work there again—not as a teacher, but perhaps in clerical and administration work. To brush up on my skills, I registered in several night-school courses plus a three-month full-time clerical upgrade course.

Once again I was subjected to ridicule by my friends. Time and work had changed this once prim schoolteacher "dude," and people seemed to have forgotten that I was once very comfortable in the business world and the ever-changing field of education. "You'll never be able to work in an office," they said. "What are you going to do come hunting season? You will be fired for not being on time. It'll be funny to see you going to work in your Levis with a packboard on your back." The teasing and laughing only made me more determined to meet this new challenge.

In December 1970, high on a mountain rich in minerals, amid modern technology, I started to work for Gibraltar Mines, a large company

We took full advantage of living closer to town. Here we are roasting dinner in the fire pit for a group of our friends.

northeast of Williams Lake. During my years there, I held several staff positions, and finally confidential secretary to four mine managers, and available to department heads as needed. Another goal achieved!

John rode the summer cattle ranges in a much more relaxed lifestyle than when we owned the ranch. Astride his favourite saddle horse, he found contentment as he watched carefully for predators, the missing calf, the sick or lame cow, and moved the cattle onward to fresh grasses.

Each day there were rewards for John too, for pleasure comes in many varieties. For John, it came from the feel of his horse and saddle between his legs while working the livestock he knew so well, as the clouds raced helter-skelter across the sky above. To see the motionless wide-eyed mule deer with her wobbly-legged spotted fawn at her side, or the nesting mallard in her protective colouring, crouched in her hidden nest—John's trained eyes observed all of the beauties of nature that he had spent a lifetime getting to know.

John missed living on the ranch so eventually we bought a little property by the Fraser River, where we hosted "Tea Parties" for our friends and neighbours.

Memories of our days and years at Big Lake bring tears of nostalgia to my eyes as I take moments to shut out "civilization" and look into the distant mountains, still a thrilling sight. Within those mountains, there is much to be found for those who will take time for solitude, who will go in search and who are eager to accept the many challenges.

As John and I entered our twilight years and looked back, we knew that without a doubt, the mountains gave us the best years of our lives.

EPILOGUE

Mr. Luce's headboard, which I found in 1963, caught my attention again after I found an issue of the *Likely Cemetery Society Newsletter*. The editor, Dave Falconer, a schoolteacher at Likely who was interested in cemetery restoration, called to ask me if I would take him to the place where I found the headboard.

I agreed to meet with him at Likely on August 11, 1990, to take him to the site where I hoped the headboard would still be. John, our youngest son, Gary, our granddaughter Tara Lynn and I packed a picnic lunch and went to meet Dave. It was a great day. The headboard was still there, and it looked just as I had last seen it twenty-five years before, except for a lengthwise crack caused by the wire and pressure from the expansion of the tree. No one had disturbed the site or dug for artifacts in the area around it.

Today, a replica of the headboard is located at the site, and the original headboard is housed at the Cedar City Mining Museum in Likely, BC. It is well over a century old. What a thrill!

The home ranch 1963.

ACKNOWLEDGEMENTS

Thanks to my family: son, Gary Lee, his daughters Meghan and Tara Lynn, and especially my grandson, John R.B. Lee, now a grown man who enjoys and respects the great outdoors, and to my first born son, Michael G. Lee, born on November 6, 1954, who passed away December 31, 2010, after a courageous battle with cancer. We miss you, Michael!

Thank you to my friends who urged me to write this book and who joined me throughout the journey of our lives.

A special thanks to Vici Johnstone at Caitlin Press for her help and guidance. Vici, you made this book project simple and pleasurable. Thank you. And also, thanks to Sage Birchwater for his enthusiasm and for introducing me to Caitlin Press.

To this day I am fascinated by the history and vast beauty of the Cariboo, and I am grateful for the many opportunities this area has afforded me.

It's been a great journey!

Photo: Sage Birchwater.

Doris C. Lee was a twenty-four-year-old schoolteacher from Northern California in 1950 when she moved with her husband to the Cariboo in central British Columbia to become a rancher. New to the challenges of country life, Doris was at first quite overwhelmed by the remoteness of their new home, but soon came to love the Cariboo. At their ranch at Big Lake east of Williams Lake, Doris learned to ride horses, round up cattle, herd sheep, swing an axe and live without the amenities she grew up with in California. She and her husband, John, raised two sons, Michael and Gary. John passed away on November 12, 1994. Doris now lives in Williams Lake, BC.